Congressional Representation & Constituents

The Case for Increasing the
U.S. House of Representatives

Brian Frederick

Routledge
Taylor & Francis Group

NEW YORK AND LONDON

First published 2010
by Routledge
270 Madison Ave, New York, NY 10016

Simultaneously published in the UK
by Routledge
2 Park Square, Milton Park, Abingdon, Oxon OX14 4RN

*Routledge is an imprint of the Taylor & Francis Group, an informa
business*

© 2010 Taylor & Francis

Typeset in Minion by Glyph International Ltd
Printed and bound in the United States of America on acid-free
paper by Walsworth Publishing Company, Marceline, MO

Library of Congress Cataloging in Publication Data

Frederick, Brian, 1974–

Congressional representation & constituents : the case for
increasing the U.S. House of Representatives / Brian Frederick.

p. cm.

title: Congressional representation and constituents

Includes bibliographical references.

ISBN 978-0-415-87345-1 (hardback : alk. paper) –
ISBN 978-0-415-87346-8 (pbk. : alk. paper) –
ISBN 978-0-203-86461-6 (ebook) 1. United States.
Congress. House–Reform. 2. United States. Congress.
House–Membership. 3. Representative government and
representation–United States. I. Title. II. Title: Congressional
representation and constituents.

JK1319.F74 2009

ISBN10: 0-415-87345-2 (hbk)
ISBN10: 0-415-87346-0 (pbk)
ISBN10: 0-203-86461-1 (ebk)

ISBN13: 978-0-415-87345-1 (hbk)
ISBN13: 978-0-415-87346-8 (pbk)
ISBN13: 978-0-203-86461-6 (ebk)

For Lynn and Scott Frederick

Contents

List of Figures

List of Tables

Acknowledgements

There are so many people who have helped me bring this project to completion. First and foremost I wish to thank Barbara Burrell for her work. Originally this manuscript started out as my dissertation. As chair of my committee, her careful reading of the chapters and suggested changes significantly improved the quality of this manuscript. She has served as an excellent mentor for me during my brief career. Her advice and counsel have been critical in my development as a scholar. It has been an honor to work with her on the numerous projects we have collaborated on.

Special commendation is due to Matt Streb. Matt was a strong supporter of turning this study into a book. At one point the manuscript appeared destined not to get published. However, at his suggestion I submitted it to be considered for the *Controversies in Electoral Democracy and Representation Series,* something I am eternally grateful for. I am proud to be associated with this outstanding series. Beyond his friendship, Matt has served as a great professional mentor as well. Working with him has benefitted me enormously as a researcher.

I also wish to thank Mikel Wyckoff for assisting me in the process of shaping the direction of this project. His advice has always served me well as both a student and a scholar.

Completion of this project would not have been possible without the methodological training I received from Kyle Saunders. The idea for this book originated as a research design in his graduate methods class. I appreciate his thoughtful insights and encouragement on this project and on all of my other research endeavors over the years.

Irene Rubin also deserves credit for helping me learn to appreciate qualitative methods. Much of the analysis in Chapter 2 was inspired by her example. She has also served as an important mentor during my formative years as a scholar.

Michael Kerns at Routledge provided enormously helpful feedback on this project. His comments and suggestions have made this a much better book. Michael's support of this manuscript was instrumental in getting it published.

Several people gave me great feedback at various points during this project. Jennifer Lawless offered me great suggestions on how to proceed during the early phases of writing this manuscript. Brian Sala provided tremendously helpful suggestions on the data analysis in Chapter 3. Casey LaFrance offered outstanding comments on earlier versions of Chapter 4 in this book. His advice and friendship have been extremely important to me over the past few years. Several other friends offered me strong encouragement along the way, including Trent Davis, Sarah Davis, LeAnn Beaty, George Candler, Georgette Dumont, Artemus Ward and Halima Khan.

George Serra, Chair of the Political Science Department at Bridgewater State College, has been extraordinarily generous in supporting my research agenda over the past few years. I am thankful for all of his help.

A special note of thanks is required for Sergei Rodkin, Bill McCready, and the rest of the staff at Knowledge Networks for their assistance in helping to carry out the survey used for Chapter 6 of this book. Sergei Rodkin in particular made helpful suggestions in the formulation of the questions used in this survey.

A great deal of the data analysis for this book was conducted in the Sociology & Political Science Quantitative Research Laboratory at Northern Illinois University. Charles Cappell and his staff at the lab provided outstanding assistance during the many hours I spent there.

I would also like to thank Gary Jacobson for allowing me to have access to his challenger quality data base that was utilized heavily in Chapter 3. Keith Poole's decision to make his DW-NOMINATE data publicly available has not only been essential for this project but has also enhanced the research of many scholars doing research on the U.S. Congress.

Finally, I would like to thank my family, who helped to support my efforts throughout this project. My parents, Lynn and Scott Frederick, have always encouraged me to become a scholar. My sister Laurel Machen has been my biggest supporter in life. I owe them all a huge debt of gratitude.

Chapter 1

Why Study the Size
of the House?

The quality of representation the citizenry receives from its political leaders is central to evaluating the character of any democratic institution. Democratic theorists have long recognized that one of the most critical variables in determining whether citizens have access to and can influence the decisions of their representatives is the numerical size of those institutions.[1] Deciphering what constitutes the ideal number of members who should represent the people in their legislative institutions can have profound consequences for democracy.

Take the United States House of Representatives, for instance. It has been frozen at 435 members for almost a century. Notwithstanding the extraordinary durability of this alignment, in its first century of existence the U.S. House experienced a virtually uninterrupted string of decennial increases in its membership. While the House has remained constant in size for nearly 100 years, the nation's population has grown by more than 200%. Given the context of this population expansion, there are important questions that need to be answered pertaining to what the substantive impact of retaining the 435-seat figure has been on the representational capacity of this institution. The implications for legislative representation are potentially enormous, as illustrated in vivid terms by the fact that each individual House member on average now represents almost 700,000 constituents. To place this number in context, as displayed in Figure 1.1, during the chamber's formative years that figure was closer to one representative for every 30,000 people. Moreover, future population projections by the U.S. Census Bureau indicate district population size will only continue to drift higher if the House is not enlarged. By 2010 the ratio of citizens per representative is estimated to go to slightly above 710,000. In 2020 the corresponding figure is likely to be 772,000 and by 2030 the average House district population will reach 836,000.[2]

Members of the U.S. House represent far more citizens than ever before and yet there has still not been a full accounting of the consequences of this development for the U.S. political system. While several political scientists have weighed in on the present size of the House, there remain unanswered questions

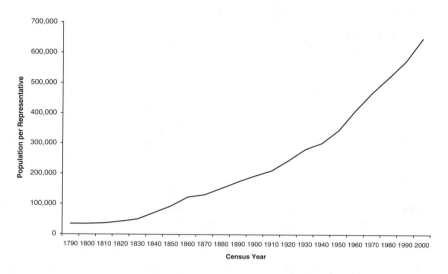

Figure 1.1 Average population per representative for the U.S. House, 1790–2000.

surrounding this issue.[3] How does the size of the nation's lower house and the average number of persons its members represent influence the character of representation in our democratic system? Can it still truly be called the people's house if its members are forced to represent an unprecedented number of constituents? Providing the answers to these questions motivates the rationale behind the dual purposes of this book. First, it will serve as the first comprehensive empirical account of the consequences of keeping the U.S. House constant in size for almost a century. It seeks to accomplish this objective through an in-depth quantitative examination of various components of representation having been identified by legislative scholars as critical in assessing the linkage between legislators and their constituents. Second, it utilizes this unprecedented volume of empirical evidence to support the normative case that many scholars have advanced in favor of increasing the size of the House.

The remainder of the chapter is organized as follows. It begins with a brief discussion of the previous literature examining the size of the House of Representatives. Second, it examines some of the previous work on legislative and constituency size in the Senate and state legislatures in order to determine what these results might suggest about how limiting the size of the House has influenced representation. Next, it previews the case for why a House of Representatives consisting of 675 members would be justified as a means to improve representation. Finally, it closes with an explanation of how the remainder of the book is organized.

The Size of the House and Representation: What Do We Know?

Generally the current body of literature on the size of the House has consisted of historical examinations of specific attempts to alter the size of the House, comparative analyses of the House's average constituency size in the context of other national legislatures and normative essays calling for an increase in the size. From a historical standpoint the size of the US House was a prominent feature of debates during the time of the nation's founding era. In the late eighteenth and early nineteenth century just what number of seats constituted the optimal size of the House was one of the key issues dividing small and large states. Representatives hailing from less populated states felt expanding the body diluted their influence in the legislative process. For representatives of the large states, boosting the membership total after each decennial census was critical to ensuring that they were afforded representation in the process commensurate with their state's true population figure.[4]

Johanna Nicol Shields systematically analyzed the debate over the 1842 Apportionment Act that mandated the first reduction in the membership of the U.S. House in the nation's history. She found that this decision was driven by the Whig reformers who wished to curtail growth in the institution for the sake of ameliorating what they believed was an unwieldy legislative environment. Detractors of this move complained it would swell district constituency size and disrupt the ability of representatives to fully interact with their constituents. Nevertheless, this downsizing was inconsistent with the norm of increasing seat levels that would reign for more than a century after the U.S. Constitution was adopted.[5]

Charles Eagles gives extensive coverage to the tumultuous transition from the norm of decennial increases to a decision by members of Congress to impose by statute a 435-seat limit on the size of the House. He points out that in 1920 rising institutional opposition to further increases beyond the 435 membership figure led to a situation where no reapportionment legislation was enacted for the decade of the 1920s. Eventually this failure led to the permanent fixture of 435 seats, and it also caused a transfer of the apportionment process from the legislative branch to the executive.[6] From 1929 on, the U.S. Commerce Department would automatically reapportion the House after each decade rather than Congress handling the matter, as it had done for more than a century.[7]

Each of these studies is a valuable contribution to the understanding of the institutional development of the U.S. House. Nonetheless, they do not capture the full dimensions of the changes in the size of the body across the full space of American history. A handful of scholars have made concerted attempts to fill this vacuum but these articles do not go into the level of depth required to accomplish this task.[8] No work has yet been able to comprehensively trace the historical changes in the size of the U.S. House and convey the central themes that have emerged from all of these debates in their entirety.

Another extensive body of research has examined the size of the House with an emphasis on how it compares with legislatures in other democratic legislatures. This research attempts to determine empirical patterns in the variation of assembly size across nations and among state legislative chambers in the U.S. The consensus findings of this research indicate that the U.S. is an outlier in terms of the diminutive size of its lower house when compared to its overall population.[9] These analysts maintain the status quo number places the U.S. outside of international legislative norms.[10] It is their contention that the actual size of the U.S. House is smaller than one would anticipate based on empirical patterns of assembly size throughout the world. The average constituency size for the U.S. House is well above the standard for the lower houses of national legislatures in most other democratic countries.[11] Figure 1.2 plots the national population and the number of seats in the lower house in each of the thirty countries in the Organization for Economic Cooperation and Development (OECD). It confirms the claim that the size of the House is far out of line with most other countries in the developed world. Many observers conclude that to bring the size of the House in line with its population growth means that the U.S. should be constituted of something close to 675 seats based on current population figures.[12]

Virtually all of the literature dealing with the size of the U.S. House consists of normative suggestions about the wisdom, or lack thereof, of augmenting the current 435-seat figure. Proponents of an upward adjustment have advanced

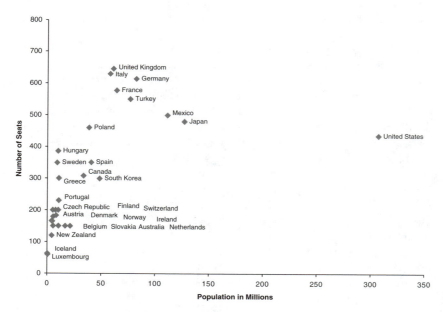

Figure 1.2 Lower House size by national population, OECD countries.

several lines of argument on behalf of taking this step. One recurring theme is that failing to do so is not in line with the original intentions of the framers of the U.S. Constitution, who wanted the size of the House to increase in order to facilitate effective representation as the population experienced robust growth.[13] According to their interpretation of the founders' intentions the House should have continued with decennial increases in its size following each census. Its failure to do so runs contrary to the idea that House members should maintain close ties to the people they represent. A variety of opinion pieces in newspapers and other media outlets have weighed in on this question in the past few years. Many editorial writers echo the charge leveled by the Anti-Federalists that the growth of House district populations resulting from preserving the 435-seat limit weakens the connection between representatives and their constituents.[14] Noted conservative commentators, including George Will and Robert Novak, have posited that a reduction in the size of government could be brought about by a substantial increase in the number of House seats.[15]

Another common complaint registered in this debate pertains to geographic representation. The concern here is that less rapidly growing states have had their House delegations slashed in spite of actual population growth in the century since the statutory cap of 435 was implemented. Supporters of increasing the size of the U.S. House have noted that since it was capped at 435 members, states losing seats in the House is a much more frequent occurrence. In the first twelve rounds of reapportionment that occurred from 1790 to 1910 an average of 4.2 states lost seats in each round over this period. The corresponding average for the eight rounds of reapportionments from 1930 to 2000 is 12 states,[16] a trend that is only expected to accelerate over the next few decades as population growth in the Northeast and Midwest lags behind the rest of the country.[17] This development is something large House proponents see as a threat to geographic representation, and want reversed, or at the very least halted.[18]

One of the most consistent arguments promoted on behalf of this cause has to do with the representational implications for members of minority groups in the U.S. A sizable contingent of scholars insists an increase will enhance descriptive representation by creating new openings every ten years for historically underrepresented groups like women and minorities to serve in the House based on the additional apportionment of seats that would occur following each census.[19] This policy would create a legislative body that more closely reflects the demographic makeup of society.

Altogether, Kromkowski and Kromkowski identify twenty-five specific reasons why the U.S. House should receive an upward adjustment in its numerical size.[20] Collectively, however, very few of these propositions have been empirically examined, an observation that skeptics of the idea are quick to play up.[21] A few recent articles have tried to address this void.[22] For instance, one study finds that a larger House would remedy interstate malapportionment of House seats by sharply reducing the difference in each state's average district size from the national average.[23] Another study documents that a larger House would allow the percentage of the national House vote for each party to better reflect the actual distribution of seats in the House.[24] However, very little is known about whether the quality of representation in the House on a number of important metrics of legislative behavior has been materially affected by the statutory limit on the institution's size.

On the other side of the debate the primary criticisms launched against enlarging the U.S. House are that it would impose increased costs on the taxpayer, lead to a diminished capacity for deliberation in the chamber, and it could undermine legislative effectiveness.[25] Some of the opponents in this debate express little reverence for members of Congress and fundamentally see more members of the U.S. House as an additional expense neither the country's taxpayers nor the federal government can afford to assume. In fact, a few observers even suggest that the U.S. House should undergo a downward adjustment in its membership. Former U.S. Senator William Proxmire relied on fiscally conservative justifications to bolster his contention that the makeup of Congress is too numerous. In his view, Congress overspends on staff and thus contributes to runaway deficit spending that has routinely plagued the federal budget. Cutting the membership of the U.S. House would provide a small yet symbolically meaningful contribution to the goal of eliminating unneeded spending. Proxmire countered the charge that such a dramatic change would weaken representation by suggesting that it would have an opposite effect. Because there would be fewer members of Congress, each representative's vote would carry more clout within the institution. In other words, U.S. House members might be less accountable, but they would carry more influence and cost less, too.[26]

Other opponents list a constricted, diminished quality of debate in the chamber, with a greater number of representatives battling for even more sought-after time for debate as grounds for continuing the status quo.[27] Another concern cited in this sphere of literature is the implications for legislative efficiency and functional effectiveness. Under this line of reasoning, if the U.S. House is enlarged any further, then an incredibly unwieldy legislative setting will ensue. Critics like Evans and Oleszek warn that if a substantial increase in the size of the membership was to occur, "delays and stalemates would multiply" in the legislative operations of the House.[28] This outcome would make legislating more difficult because coalition building would be harder to achieve and communication between members undermined.[29] This tension forms the core of the debate that occurs when institutional designers of legislatures seek to balance the need for adequate representation and legislative functionality.[30]

Analysis of Legislative and Constituency Size

The question of the number of members serving in the U.S. House cannot be divorced from the issue of legislative size more generally. This avenue of research has been more fully probed than the specific case of the U.S. House, although it too has yet to address the full dimensions of these issues.[31] A tremendous amount of the literature in this area has been produced by public choice scholars.[32] The emphasis of this work has been on the effect of assembly size on fiscal and economic policy, i.e. to what extent the level of taxation and government spending is related to the number of seats in a legislative chamber. This research has not been able to establish a firm causal connection between a jurisdiction's legislative size and fiscal policy. Furthermore, none of these authors examines this phenomenon in relation to the U.S. House of Representatives exclusively; nor do they address representation outside of the context of fiscal policy.

Legislative size has not solely been the province of public choice. Comparative politics scholars have investigated the subject as well.[33] This research attempts to determine empirical patterns in the variation of assembly size across nations and among state legislative chambers in the U.S. It has consistently substantiated the positive relationship between legislative size and population. As previously referenced, the consensus findings of this research indicate that the U.S. is an outlier in terms of the diminutive size of its lower house when compared to its overall population.[34] Other scholarship in this area has delved into whether assembly size influences rules and procedures of legislative institutions.[35] One extensive comparative analysis of legislative chambers throughout the world showed that smaller legislative bodies tend to have more decentralized operating procedures.[36]

In the U.S., the bulk of research on legislative constituency size has been undertaken on the U.S. Senate.[37] The studies carried out on this subject have produced some valuable findings that supply some insight into the consequences for representation in the House. They tend to indicate that state population may be a barrier to effective representation in some areas. According to data from the American National Election Study, senators from larger states are less likely to have had direct contact with their constituents.[38] There is conflicting evidence regarding how state population size influences the approval ratings of governors and U.S. senators, but generally they tend to be less popular as they represent larger states.[39] At the state legislative level research has shown that the approval rating of legislators is a negative function of constituency size.[40] Several studies have demonstrated that the magnitude of a state's population can introduce greater competitiveness into U.S. Senate election outcomes,[41] even as others have cast doubt upon this finding.[42] There is also tenuous evidence that U.S. senators' support for government spending is positively correlated with constituency size.[43]

While this research provides some useful insights into how legislative constituency and legislative size shape the representational dynamic between the people and their elected officials, it can only speak indirectly to the case of the U.S. House. Indeed, there is a paucity of research directly focused on the implications for this specific institution. As Squire and Hamm point out in their comprehensive examination of legislative chambers in the United States, "[t]he effect of constituency size on legislative behavior is a relatively unexplored area. Research comparing the electoral and representational effects of constituency size has been conducted using the U.S. Senate. . . . Little attention, however, appears to have been given to this variable in studies of the U.S. House."[44] The challenges posed to researchers interested in this phenomenon include the dramatic shifts in the numerical composition of congressional districts that occurs within the ten-year window between when the next census is taken. In addition, the lack of variation that exists between districts that follows the latest round of reapportionment is also problematic. These realities present obstacles to conducting comparable research for the U.S. House, but they are not insurmountable.

Main Research Questions

This study seeks to build on the prior literature by synthesizing its major elements in order to develop a set of hypotheses to empirically test the impact of maintaining the present 435-seat limit of the U.S. House while the growth of the nation's population has expanded unabated. It explains how representation was once given primacy in the debates over legislative and constituency size but was eventually supplanted over concerns from House members about retaining the institution's capacity to legislate. Did the decision to downplay representation in favor of institutional maintenance really compromise the democratic nature of the U.S. House, or have other intervening political developments offset some of the consequences feared by critics of placing a ceiling on the number of members authorized to serve? Does the present arrangement interfere with the representational linkage as Anti-Federalists contended during the debate over ratification of the Constitution and as many contemporary political scientists have argued?[45] If so, what are the consequences if indeed there is a diminished capacity for representation and how can this proposition be empirically tested?

Most of the prior research either consists of normative suggestions to increase the number of seats in the U.S. House or limits empirical inquiries of legislative size or district constituency size to fiscal outcomes. As previously referenced, while there have been efforts to study these phenomena as they apply to representation in the U.S. Senate and at the state legislative level, there has been a paucity of research about the ramifications for the U.S. House.[46] This book fills the void by conducting the first in-depth comprehensive study of this subject that employs a series of quantitative measures to analyze several dimensions of representation as they relate directly to ending the practice of allowing the House to grow in line with the U.S. population. The study seeks to empirically assess whether representation has been undermined in the aftermath of this decision. Though there have been many suppositions forwarded in the debate about the ideal size of the U.S. House and its members' constituencies, there has been a shortage of studies aimed at testing these hypotheses.

What this book does not do is explore the other side of the legislative tradeoff, the impact on operational efficiency. Instead, it focuses on the representational component of the legislative tradeoff because the key variable relevant to legislative efficiency, the institution's size, has remained constant, while the critical variable for representation, the number of citizens per district, has changed significantly over this period.

Legislative theorists have identified several conceptions of the representational linkage, including policy, service, allocation, symbolic, collective, and descriptive.[47] While this book attempts to assess how the present policy influences each one of these spheres of representation, the extent to which they can be empirically examined in this study is restricted by data limitations. Ideally there would be pre-existing survey data that actually inquired of citizens their thoughts about whether the size of the U.S. House should be increased and whether congressional districts are too heavily populated, in addition to more direct measures of the interaction of legislative size and the quality of representation. This study will address this absence of information by undertaking a survey probing the attitudes of the U.S. population on the question of whether the size of the U.S. House ought to be increased. To supplement these attitudinal data, this study will marshal evidence in other areas of representation amenable to empirical investigation, including estimating the effects on electoral competition, policy responsiveness, and citizen contact with and approval of their representatives. These areas of representation have occupied a prominent position in much of the literature on congressional studies over the past generation. Hence, they constitute domains of inquiry where rigorous empirical tests can be undertaken.

This study may not delve into all of the aspects of the debate outlined previously, but it does serve as a starting point for systematically addressing a number of fundamental questions revolving around the size of the U.S. House and the citizens represented by each of its 435 members. The main research questions explored include:

- How has the explosion of the ratio of population per representative that has occurred since the U.S. House was frozen at 435 members had an impact on electoral competition?
- Has this expansion of district constituency populations undermined the level of citizens' contact with and perceptions of their members of the U.S. House?
- How has increase in ratio of citizens per representative influenced roll-call voting behavior?
- What are American citizens' opinions about the present size of the U.S. House and the average number of citizens per congressional district?

The evidence in this study reveals that the House has become a less representative institution because of the permanent ceiling that was placed on its numerical size. It shows that as House members have taken on the burden of representing thousands of additional citizens they are less responsive, less accessible, and less popular with the people they represent. Based on these findings I argue that it is now time to increase size of in order to improve the representational capacity of the institution. This policy would involve increasing the size of the House following the 2010 census to 675 seats, which would reflect the cube root of the U.S. population called for by comparative legislative scholars. Such a law would bring the size of the House in line with international norms and help restore some balance between the competing legislative imperatives of representation and legislative efficiency. Every ten years the House would automatically increase in size to align it with the cube root of the population, preventing a further erosion of its representational character in the future. Augmenting the present size of the institution would enhance policy responsiveness, service responsiveness, descriptive representation, and improve citizens' evaluations of their representatives. In short, doing so would bring representatives closer to their constituents and make the idea of the U.S. House as the people's House more of a reality.

Outline of the Book

The rest of book is organized as follows. Chapter 2 documents the historical changes in the House's size by highlighting specific debates over how many seats should be apportioned for the nation's lower chamber at various points in U.S. history, starting with debate at the Constitutional Convention continuing in contemporary times. It begins by reviewing the deliberations of the founders at the Constitutional Convention over what constituted the optimal size of the nation's lower house and how that figure should be modified based on future population growth. Next, it concentrates on the disputes between the Federalists and the Anti-Federalists over this issue and how this exchange framed many of the future congressional debates on the matter. The chapter continues with a look at how Congress grappled with balancing the competing needs for a representative assembly and one that could carry out its legislative functions in an efficient manner, concluding with the recent move to enlarge the House to 437 seats to accommodate representation for Washington, D.C. It shows that for over a century the primary concern was for the representational imperative of not undercutting the link between House members and their constituents. However, the decision to institute a statutory limitation of 435 seats in the early twentieth century was rooted in a belief by House members that continued enlargement would make deliberation more restricted and the legislative process unmanageable. The chapter concludes with an argument about why a return to the representational imperative of increasing the size of the House in line with the growth in the population is now in order.

One of the most prominent features of scholarship in American political science has been the focus on the sharp rise in the incumbency advantage in House elections over the past generation. Chapter 3 explores whether the growth in the average population of House districts has had any impact on electoral fortunes of House incumbents. Drawing on data from the 1970, 1980, 1990, and 2000 elections, when census estimates of House district populations are most precise, empirical models are formulated predicting the margin of victory and probability of defeat for incumbent House members. The results reveal that a larger average constituency size tends to reduce the victory margins of incumbents. However, the chapter explains how this finding may not necessarily be a positive development for representation in the House.

Chapter 4 utilizes survey data from the American National Election Studies and National Annenberg Election Survey in years where accurate estimates of House district population are available to determine whether constituency size influences the level of contact citizens have with their House members. It also delves into the extent to which the House members representing more heavily populated constituencies are perceived as being any less helpful or are as successful at staying in touch. Finally, it tests whether incumbent House members' approval ratings are tied to the number of citizens they represent. The results show that House members who represent more heavily populated districts tend to be evaluated less favorably by their constituents on each of these metrics of performance.

Chapter 5 investigates whether the failure to augment the size of the U.S. House in line with population growth has had any bearing on voting patterns in the U.S. House. Using data on roll-call voting behavior, the level of divergence from constituency opinion exhibited by House members in voting records is ascertained. This evidence shows that House members who represent more heavily populated districts tend to have more extreme voting records and are generally less responsive to the median voter in their districts.

If the full representational implications of retaining the 435-seat limit on the House and permitting the ratio of persons per House district to escalate are to be evaluated there must be some understanding of how the American public feels about these issues. Do citizens believe that the size of the House of Representatives ought to be boosted to offset the growth in the number of citizens each member represents? Chapter 6 provides the results of survey questions asked of a national sample of more than 1,000 people on the size of the U.S. House and congressional district populations. These questions allow the U.S. public to answer the question of whether it is a good idea to tinker with the size of the U.S. House to improve representation. The survey includes items asking respondents whether they would support an increase in the number of House seats to offset the growth in the average district constituency size, to prevent states from losing seats in the House and to enhance descriptive representation for women and minorities. The results indicate that while there is not a majority in favor of increasing the size of the House when the responses to each of the questions are examined, about 56% of respondents expressed support for an increase based on at least one of the three justifications included in the survey.

Chapter 7 summarizes the main findings of this work and assesses their contribution to our knowledge on this subject. What does it really mean for the character of representation in the U.S. House that it has been frozen at 435 members for almost a century while the population levels in House districts have mushroomed to historic highs? This chapter will restate the findings generated by this study and discuss the implications of the representational tradeoff that has resulted from maintaining the House size status quo for such a lengthy period of time. Further, it makes the case that representation has been harmed by refusing to increase the size of the House. This chapter restates the case for why a House consisting of 675 members would better serve the interests of American democracy. Further, it addresses some of the most common objections raised by opponents of enlarging the House. In concludes by acknowledging the enormous political obstacles that any proposal to significantly lift the number of seats beyond the 435-seat figure is certain to encounter.

Chapter 2

Debating the Size
of the House

Introduction

A series of studies by historians and political scientists has added to the body of knowledge on specific periods in the nation's history when the size of the U.S. House arose as a significant issue.[1] All of this research has brought about a greater understanding of the unique features that surrounded each debate. Yet this literature has not successfully linked these individual cases to this debate over time. Moreover, there has not been much integration of some of the key theoretical questions that arise related to the numerical composition of seats in the institutional design of the legislature. Many of these themes occur repeatedly in discussions of the optimal size of the U.S. House throughout the nation's history. In order to more fully understand the contours of the present debate surrounding the permanent cap on the institution's size it is essential to figure out how the present policy was arrived at.

The purpose of this chapter is to document the historical changes in the House's size by highlighting specific debates over how many seats should be apportioned for the nation's lower chamber at various points in U.S. history, starting with debate at the Constitutional Convention until contemporary times. Textual analysis is employed to delineate many of the theoretical propositions that have been advanced in assessing what constitutes the optimal size of the nation's lower house. This chapter finds that as the House was evolving as an institution it confronted a requirement to balance the need for representation with the demands for legislative efficiency and adequate deliberation. This tradeoff has been recognized as a tension for legislative institutions struggling to allow representation of the interests of individual members and their constituencies while maintaining an organizational structure that facilitates the functional effectiveness of the body.[2] Although political self-interest has often shaped the positions individual legislators may have taken in these debates, one's stance on how many seats the nation's lower house should comprise came down to whether constituency representation or institutional maintenance ought to take precedence.

The decision to institute a statutory limitation of 435 seats in the early twentieth century was rooted in a belief by House members that continued enlargement would make deliberation more restricted and the legislative process unmanageable, thereby threatening the institution's position within the U.S. political system.[3] A systematic quantitative analysis of the House vote to maintain the 435-seat limit early reveals that this view was not exclusively held by members in positions of leadership responsible for institutional maintenance, but rather by a solid majority of members serving in the institution at the time. Since reaching this conclusion, the collective membership of the body has refused to seriously revisit the issue because there has been no perceived need to alter the present configuration. Neither internal political or organizational dynamics nor exogenous forces have dictated that representatives reverse the legislative inertia that has maintained the status quo for decades. Though the ratio of the population per representative has climbed to unprecedented levels, increasing the size of the House to offset this growth has rarely received serious consideration by the Congress. The chapter concludes with an assessment of why this decision was ill advised and an explanation of why the House should return to a policy of increases in its size to more fully reclaim its representative character.

Legislative Size: Balancing Representation and Legislative Effectiveness

Political scientists emphasize that any legislature must balance the responsibilities of governance and representation.[4] This tradeoff applies not only to the numerical size of the institution but also to what rules and procedures to establish, whether the legislature ought to have one chamber or two, the role of committees, or the length of terms, among many others.[5] In order to pass laws, a legislature must operate in an efficient manner, which often requires rules and structures that expedite the process. Representation is both a dyadic and collective concept. The former encompasses the relationship between the district constituency and the member, whereas the latter deals with the institution collectively.[6] When a legislature collectively responds to the needs of the citizenry of the nation by carrying out its governing requirements in an expeditious manner it can come into conflict with the necessity of dyadic constituency representation by the individual legislator. The former may be better served in a smaller legislative body. The latter is more likely to be fostered in a larger House with less populous districts.[7] While not always incompatible with one another in all areas of institutional maintenance,[8] legislative functionality and responsiveness inevitably clash when the issue of optimal numerical size comes to the forefront. This reality is an especially vexing conundrum in heavily populous, highly diverse societies.[9]

In order to accommodate the diversity of interests in any society, a legislature must be constituted with enough seats so that various constituencies can have their voices heard. This obligation poses a burden on the internal operations of any legislative institution. Since the legislative calendar places limits on the number of days a legislative body can be in session, not every speaker can be heard on each item that comes to the floor if the membership is so voluminous. Empirical inquiry has confirmed that the restrictive nature of legislative rules and procedures and the threshold at which debate can be terminated are negative functions of legislative size.[10] As the size of a legislature becomes progressively larger, the time for speeches allotted to individual members must decline or the consequence is that the legislative process becomes more cumbersome.[11] On the other hand, if the legislature is not enlarged in line with the population, constituency size will grow, placing a strain on the representational relationship between legislators and their constituents.[12]

In an ideal assembly everyone could represent themselves individually and full representation could be achieved, though at the cost of making legislative action and discussion of the issues virtually impossible. Conversely, in a legislature of only a handful of members the legislative process could be highly efficient, time for debate plentiful, but at the expense of severely limiting the representation for various segments of society.[13] Since both options are unrealistic, institutional designers must devise a numerical formula that reconciles the need for a representative assembly while maintaining a taxonomical legislative structure capable of enacting policy favored by the collective membership of the body.

The vexation of resolving the tension between these imperatives is exacerbated as a country's population increases. If the numerator, in this case the population, remained constant, then experimenting with the value of the denominator, the number of seats in the legislature, an evaluation of the optimal ratio of citizens per legislator required to achieve both adequate representation and organizational maintenance could be undertaken. However, because the population of the U.S. has been on a permanent upward trajectory, the numerator cannot remain fixed and thus the denominator must automatically increase just to keep the number of citizens per district constant.

An empirical pattern repeatedly observed as a determinant of legislative size is what is known as the cube root law of national assembly size.[14] According to this theory the number of seats in the lower house of a country's legislature tends to approximate the cubic root of the population, represented here by the following equation: Lower House Seats $=$ Population$^{1/3}$. Taageperra and Shugart elaborate on this model of assembly size. The model assumes that a legislator's most burdensome task is communication and "that two types of communication predominate: (1) communication with constituents, whose views are to be taken into account and to whom decisions have to be explained, and (2) communication with other representatives and monitoring communications among them, so as to have sufficient information about what is going on and to participate in decision making."[15] Legislators' time is spent trying to balance channels of communication flowing to and from their constituents and within the body itself.

The cube root law projects that the optimal assembly size is determined on the basis of a number of seats relative to the ratio of citizens per district that will accommodate these competing demands. Legislatures are not designed to expand in a limitless fashion or in direct proportion to the population because to do so would undermine the capacity of the body to legislate effectively. Hence, as Dahl and Tufte explain, "[t]he size of parliaments increases with the population of a country, but at a lower rate."[16] Conversely, if the average number of constituents in the district reaches a certain point, the legislator will be overworked and the communicative linkage mechanism will be potentially undermined. For the first century of the nation's history the U.S. House conformed rather well to this law.[17] However, in the early part of the twentieth century members of the House concluded that future increases proportional to the growth of the population were no longer compatible with a functional legislative environment.

Therein lays the quandary in endeavoring to determine the proper size of the U.S. House. How can the interest of representation be served if members of the body believe there is some limit to the absolute numerical size of the House that will stymie the effectiveness of the legislative process, while the total population expands unabated? Two focal questions were weighed extensively during the original debates over the size of the House beginning with the Constitutional Convention and throughout all of the subsequent debates on this subject. First, at what point would the U.S. House be composed of so many members that the legislative process would be undermined to an extent that threatened its independent position within the larger political system? Second, at what level would the ratio of population per representative jeopardize representational connection between the citizenry and the members of the U.S. House? The answer to the first question varied until the early twentieth century, when the House finally settled on 435 seats as a ceiling beyond which further growth was inimical to performing its tasks as a governing institution. The second question, once drawing serious attention, has now been rendered obsolete, at least by members of the House since they arrived at the 435-seat figure.

The Constitutional Convention Opts for 65

When the delegates arrived in Philadelphia in 1787 for the Constitutional Convention, there was an array of issues they would have to confront. Foremost among them was what form the new national legislature should take, including whether it ought to consist of two houses or one. George Mason of Virginia adamantly insisted upon bicameralism, as an essential feature of any proposed national legislature.[18] The delegates saw the wisdom of this argument and on June 21 approved language mandating that the Congress would consist of two separate houses by a vote of 7–3.[19] In discussing the shape of the lower chamber, determining how many members it would be composed of captured a substantial measure of attention from the delegates.[20] According to William Riker's quantitative analysis of various founding documents, the size of the House was the most frequently debated issue related to constitutional structure, accounting for almost one-third of the comments on the subject.[21] This controversy was magnified because it was so central to the quality of representation that would be afforded by the institution most closely linked to the people.

In arriving at a numerical target for the membership of the lower House, the delegates had to deal with several complicated issues, such as the ratio of population per representative and how to account for changes in population growth. There was also a collective recognition of the necessity to achieve a balance between a chamber that was representative of the people and accommodating of legislative deliberation.[22] The ratio of citizens per representative was initially set forth in language presented to the delegates at not more than one representative for every 40,000 inhabitants.[23] This threshold drew the ire of some delegates because it did not take wealth into account,[24] whereas others were concerned that fixing the ratio at this level would eventually lead to a House size that was incompatible with adequate deliberation.[25] On August 8, James Madison, who performed a delicate balancing act over the representative nature of the House during the entire Convention, proposed an amendment adopted by the delegates, stating that the number of inhabitants should not exceed one for every 40,000 because this would have the effect of "rendering the number of Representatives excessive."[26] Although Madison's motion was adopted 7-3 by the Convention, some delegates were uneasy with this ratio. During the final day of the convention, Nathaniel Gorhum of Massachusetts, cognizant of this sentiment, moved to augment the final draft of the Constitution so that the ratio would stand at not more than one representative for every 30,000 inhabitants. George Washington found the matter so compelling that he cast aside his self-imposed neutrality as presiding officer to rise in favor of the motion. Madison quotes Washington as decreeing the motion was of such great consequence that its approval was essential so that objections to the Constitution "might be made as few as possible."[27] Washington expressed sympathy with delegates uncomfortable with the ratio, observing, "The smallness of the proportion of Representatives had been considered by many members of the Convention, an insufficient security for the rights & interests of the people."[28] According to Madison's notes, Washington informed the Convention it would give him "much satisfaction to see it adopted."[29] Washington's stature and the late hour of the proceedings restrained anyone from objecting and the amendment was adopted unanimously. The figure of 30,000:1 for the ratio of population per representative was enshrined in the final document and has not changed since the ratification of the Constitution. It ought to be noted that the Constitution sets only a minimum level the ratio cannot go below and does not impose a maximum threshold the population per representative cannot exceed.

Determining how to apportion the House in response to future population increases also drew the attention of the delegates. George Mason of Virginia underscored the gravity of population growth's impact upon representation in the House, declaring "a revision from time to time according to some permanent and precise standard as essential to . . . fair representation required in the

1st branch."[30] Edmund Randolph of Virginia sought to alleviate this problem by proposing that the national legislature take a census to determine the number of inhabitants in each state. Gouverneur Morris of Pennsylvania dismissed this idea as tying the hands of future legislatures, whom he believed would readjust representation without such a measure.[31] The Convention followed the lead of Randolph by first prescribing that a census be taken every fifteen years[32] and then quickly altered the duration to once every ten years the next day, on July 12.[33] This standard was maintained until the ultimate version of the Constitution was approved.

The first apportionment of seats for the House was not based on an actual enumeration of the population, but rather on a rough approximation of the population of each state. The first census would not be taken until the first session of the new Congress convened two years later. Though it was the subject of controversy, the delegates were willing to proceed without a true head count for reasons of convenience. Madison openly conceded the first apportionment of the House was built on a foundation of conjecture, although he sought to reassure the Convention this was only a temporary measure.[34]

When the debate shifted to how many representatives should actually sit during the first session of the House itself, the delegates expressed various conceptions over what number would be optimal for legislative representation. Some wished to see a body as representative as possible, a posture which stood in contrast to those delegates who emphasized the need for the legislature to function in a reasonable manner.[35] This conflict reflected the essence of the tradeoff between representation and effectiveness identified by scholars of the legislative process.[36] The delegates first approved a total of 56 seats to be apportioned amongst the states for the first Congress on July 9.[37] The next day this figure was revised upward by the Convention to 65.[38] Several state delegations were disgruntled over the number of seats they were allotted, though attempts to change it were repeatedly rebuffed throughout the convention.

Contrary to his previous apprehensions about the future growth in House membership, Madison urged that each state's total be doubled to buttress support among the people. He discounted concerns over the costs of such a move, noting his foremost worry was that "a *majority* of a *Quorum* of 65 members, was too small a number to represent the whole inhabitants" of the United States.[39] For Madison there was a danger in a majority of twenty members being allowed to pass laws in the national legislature, an outlook endorsed by George Mason.[40] Elbridge Gerry weighed in on behalf of the Madison amendment on the grounds that enlarging the House would diminish the likelihood its members could be susceptible to corruption.[41] Some delegates made the case that an increase was advisable because a failure to increase numbers would leave some states with only one member, which in their mind was not sufficient for these states to receive adequate representation.[42] Others felt enlarging the House was ill advised, relying on the conduct of state legislatures as a reference point. Madison's motion to double the 65-seat allocation was soundly rejected by the Convention on a vote of 9–2.[43]

This debate reappeared sporadically throughout the convention once the figure was established as the benchmark, although further attempts to alter it did not materialize. Madison's position reflected both an effort to appease delegates focused on the functional effectiveness of the House and the anticipated complaints of the Anti-Federalists that representation of the people would be severely undermined with such a diminutive numerical membership. The compromise total may not have satisfied all the delegates but the assurance that this figure was only temporary managed to quell lingering doubts about the issue to resolve it for the rest of the Convention. When the Constitution was finalized the House was to consist of 65 members, and following a census in two years after the first Congress a reapportionment would occur. The action taken by the Convention far from settled the issue, as the debate over ratification would demonstrate, for the Anti-Federalists would incorporate the size of the U.S. House as one of the critical elements of their vigorous assault against the U.S. Constitution. Richard Henry Lee articulated his dissatisfaction, insisting "[t]hat in order to secure the rights of the people more effectually from violation, the power and respectability of the house of representatives be increased, by increasing the number of delegates to that house where the popular interest must chiefly depend for protection."[44]

The Anti-Federalists Attack

A centerpiece of the Anti-Federalist attack upon the size of the House revolved around the concept of "actual representation."[45] By this term they meant that the legislature should be an actual reflection of the demographic composition of society at large. This view is concomitant with descriptive representation, meaning that genuine legislative representation was only possible through the inclusion of legislators who shared the characteristics of groups that comprised society.[46] The Anti-Federalists' vision of actual representation did not encompass women and racial minorities, the parameters of the debate in modern times; their concern was rooted in class and occupation. Federal Farmer summarized this case:

> Fair representation, therefore, should be so regulated that every order of men in the community, according to the common course of elections, can have a share in it. In order to allow professional men, merchants, traders, farmers, mechanics, etc. to bring just proportion of their best informed men respectively into the legislature the representation must be considered numerous.[47]

This form of representation was the prevailing view throughout the population in many of the states, a departure from which the Anti-Federalists found untenable.[48]

Not only did the Anti-Federalists take issue with who would serve in the House, but also the ability of these representatives to reflect the will of the people.

Its membership would be isolated from the masses and would not be of sufficient numbers to grasp the wishes of the majority. Brutus lamented,

> One man or a few men cannot possibly represent the feelings, opinions, and characters of a great multitude. In this respect, the new constitution is radically defective. The house of assembly, which is intended as a representation of the people of America will not, nor cannot in the nature of things be a proper one. Sixty-five men cannot be found in the United States who hold the sentiments, possess the feelings, or are acquainted with the wants and interests of this vast country.[49]

This forceful condemnation encapsulated the fears of the Anti-Federalists that the House would become overly detached from the public, placing their liberties in severe jeopardy of being eroded.

It was not merely the absolute size of the chamber that drew their scorn but also the ratio of population per representative. A small legislative constituency size was a vital linkage mechanism in maintaining the representative character of the House. According to Federal Farmer:

> A small representation can never be well informed as to the circumstances of the people; the members must be too far removed from the people in general to sympathize with them, and too few to communicate with them. A representation must be extremely imperfect where the representatives are not circumstanced to make the proper communications to their constituents, and where the constituents in turn can not, with tolerable convenience make known their wants, circumstances and opinions, to their representatives. Where there is but one representative to 30,000 or 40,000 inhabitants it appears to me he can only mix and be acquainted with a few researchable characters among his constituents; even double the federal representation, and then there must be a great distance between the representatives and the people in general represented.[50]

The Anti-Federalists' vision of effective representation held that it could only occur within a limited sphere of population. Brutus cited representation in Great Britain as an example where the district constituency size was half that of the United States. With an even more widely dispersed population, the United States necessitated an even smaller ratio than Great Britain "because this country is much more extensive, and differs more in productions, interests, manners and habits."[51] Being accountable to a relatively diminutive constituency would mitigate the effects of geographic distance from the nation's center of government but also be amenable to serving the heterogeneous population in the extended republic. Patrick Henry honed in on the language of the Constitution, noting it simply placed a floor on the ratio and not a ceiling. He invoked the specter that Congress could impose a limit of one House member per state.[52]

A third component of the Anti-Federalists' indictment against the size of the House was the prospect that its membership could be too easily corrupted. A voluminous number of representatives would create a buffer against a national legislature captured by nefarious influences. Federal Farmer maintained,

> Where there is a small representation a sufficient number to carry any measure may with ease be influenced by bribes, offices and civilities; they may easily form private juntos and outdoor meetings, agree on measures, and carry them by silent votes.[53]

In the spirit of preserving an honest government paying heed to its citizens' liberties, a larger house was essential to this cause. Federal Farmer continued, "I mean the constant liability of a small number of representatives to private combinations; the tyranny of the one, or the licentiousness of the multitudes, are, in my mind, but small evils, compared with factions of the few."[54] Frightened by a government overtaken by tyrannical forces that could eviscerate their liberties, the Anti-Federalists were convinced an enlarged House was an insurance policy against such an outcome. Brutus scoffed at the size of the House, charging, "No free people on earth, who have elected persons to legislate for them, ever reposed that confidence in so small a number."[55] The Anti-Federalists dismissed the argument that larger legislative bodies could not effectively function by highlighting images of a treacherous band of legislators subverting the democratic process.[56] What could be more dangerous to the functionality of the legislative process than one overridden by corruption, they asked? This potential outcome outweighed the possible gridlock and unwieldy legislative atmosphere that might emerge in a more expansive House of Representatives.

The Federalists Respond

The Federalists were well aware of the need to engage in a systematic response to the attacks leveled against the Constitution more generally and the size of the House more specifically. It was James Madison who was designated with the responsibility of defending the size of the U.S. House of Representatives in *Federalist* Nos. 55–58 against the onslaught of the Anti-Federalist crusade. In *Federalist* No. 55 he acknowledged the immense burden associated with determining the ideal size of the national legislature, observing, "It may be remarked on this subject, that no political problem is less susceptible of a precise solution, than that which relates to the number most convenient for a representative legislature."[57] Madison conceded there was merit in a national legislature with enough members to guard against corruption, noting, "Sixty or seventy men may be more properly trusted with a given degree of power than six or seven."[58] Although he had supported doubling the size of the House at the Constitutional Convention, he was unwilling to extend this logic to a legislative body consisting of six or seven hundred members. Madison saw the need to place a limit on the membership of the House "to avoid the confusion and intemperance of a multitude."[59] For Madison a larger assembly was no panacea and could lead to negative consequences for representative government. He sought to allay fears of corruption by expressing his confidence in the people's judgment. They were fully capable of rejecting anyone unfit for public office every two years at election time. Madison was "unable to conceive that the people of America" would consistently re-elect 65 members of the House who were corrupt or who would endanger liberty.[60]

In *Federalist* No. 56 Madison trained his focus on the Anti-Federalists' accusation that the size of the House would be inconsistent with allowing its members to be responsive to the desires of their constituents. He accepted the premise that "it is a sound and important principle that the representative ought to be acquainted with the interests and circumstances of his constituents."[61] Nevertheless, this concession did not imply that the representatives of the House would be incapable of being so. The legislator need not be versed in every aspect of the district constituency but only issues of relevance to legislative process. Madison articulated a picture of members of the House who would "bring with them a considerable knowledge of its laws, and a local knowledge of their respective districts," since they most likely would have served in the capacity of state legislator prior to coming to the House, diminishing the fear that they would be oblivious to the concerns of the people.[62] He claimed that a fair comparison to the British House of Commons indicated the ratio of population per representative called for in the Constitution was adequate to safeguard the interests of liberty.[63]

In *Federalist* No. 57 Madison addressed the issue of actual representation, defending the proposition that elite citizens were best suited to serve in the national legislature. He stressed that it was "distinguished" members of the district constituency who would be selected to serve in the House of Representatives.[64] The Federalists were generally unified in their belief that descriptive representation was not an ideal basis for legislative representation.[65] In *Federalist* No. 35, Hamilton also discounted the need for a true demographic reflection of the constituency, describing "the idea of an actual representation of all classes of the people by persons of each class" as an extremely unlikely prospect.[66] Responding to the allegation that representatives would not be sufficiently responsive because of district population size, Madison alleged that in several states legislative districts contained approximately the same number of citizens as House districts would encompass under the first apportionment.[67]

On the question of adjusting the membership of the House in accordance with population growth, Madison made it clear in *Federalist* No. 58 that the initial figure of 65 representatives was only temporary and that, as it had been for state legislatures, the requirement for the taking of decennial census would permit the ratio of population per representative from escalating too dramatically. He highlighted the experience of the state legislatures as evidence that "a gradual increase of representatives under the state constitutions has kept pace with that of the constituents."[68] While Madison's defense of the original size of the House explicitly rejected many of the assertions of the Anti-Federalists, his willingness to accentuate the virtual certainty that the House would need to be enlarged along with population growth indicated that he believed legislative size was a crucial variable in ensuring that representation of the people was not seriously undermined.[69]

Apportionment of the House: The Early Years

Following the ratification of the Constitution the first session of the House of Representatives would convene with a membership total of 65 until the inaugural census could be taken. After the results of the first census were revealed, the question of how to apportion the seats among the states moved to the forefront. As Balinski and Young point out in their comprehensive study of apportionment methods

> The habit of thought in those days was not first to determine the total number of seats or *house size* and then to distribute them, but rather to fix upon some "ratio of representation," that is to declare that there shall be "one representative for every x persons," and then allow for the house size to fall where it may.[70]

Nevertheless, there was a near consensus that the amount of seats allocated to the states would have to be adjusted upwards.[71] At this stage of the House's institutional development the issue of securing representation outweighed concerns over whether additional members might hinder the legislative process.

The principal disputes over the first apportionment bill revolved around whether the House should consist of 120 members, as called for by representatives of the large states, or 105 members, as urged by advocates of the small states, and what to do with the fractional remainders that existed after dividing the apportionment population by the total number of seats.[72] On the first issue, members from small states preferred the lower number to maintain maximum influence in the House, while the large-state congressmen viewed the additional seats as more representative of their interests.[73] The disagreement over apportionment divided not only small-state and large-state factions but followers of Jefferson and Madison as well.[74] Jeffersonians felt a larger House "would be more democratic."[75] In regard to the second question, supporters of the Hamiltonian position insisted that states be ranked by the size of their fractional remainders. Jefferson and defenders of the small-state interests proposed a method that would apportion seats on the basis of the percentage of unrepresented population rather than absolute number of the remainder.[76] After passing legislation that contained the outlines of the Hamilton proposal, President Washington vetoed the measure at the prompting of Thomas Jefferson.[77]

He objected to the bill on the grounds that it did not include a single divisor that could be applied to the states to produce 120 representatives and that for several of the individual states the ratio of population per representative had exceeded the Constitution's limitation on one seat for every 30,000 inhabitants.[78] Eventually Washington signed legislation on April 14, 1792, that settled on Jefferson's equal proportions method and set the size of the size of the House at 105 members, with a ratio of persons per representative of 33,000.[79] The first amendment to the Constitution proposed in Congress aimed to standardize the process of apportioning House seats to avoid future controversies of this sort, but it was never ratified.[80]

The First Reduction in the Size of the House

Over the next four decades the fault lines between the small and large states was the pivot point in the decennial battle over reapportionment rather than a fear that the House was expanding to an unmanageable level.[81] From the period of 1790-1830 the House jumped from 105 to 240 seats and the ratio of population per representative had only gone up to one per 47,700.[82] However, the consequences of legislative size would return to the forefront in the debate over the 1842 Apportionment Act. During the course of deliberation over the Act, many Whig members of Congress sought to ameliorate the condition of what they believed was an unwieldy legislative body by scaling back the number of members in the US House.[83] Rep. Joseph Underwood of Kentucky called large legislative bodies "mob government by confusion,"[84] while Rep. John Thompson of Kentucky warned that a reduction was essential to prevent the House from becoming "emasculated" in its dealings with the Senate and the executive branch.[85]

Several members suggested that a smaller House would bring about a larger constituency size for each representative, lessening the importance of catering to voters' immediate passions. Large House proponents denounced such sentiments and claimed that downsizing the House would mean enlarged district populations, severely jeopardizing representative government. Rep. John Pope of Kentucky averred, "as you increased the number of the people's Representatives in the Legislature you increased the actual power of the people." He "advocated a comparatively small Congressional district as better enabling the Representative to have a personal acquaintance with his constituents."[86] Other members downplayed complaints that the legislative process would be less efficient by stressing the interests of the lessening of corruption and the ability of members to serve as responsive agents of the people that were afforded by sparely populated congressional districts.[87] Maryland Rep. John Mason countered the Whigs' assertion that the "independence" of the body from other branches was at stake without a cutback in membership, contending it was "much easier for the executive to corrupt a small majority of the house floor than a large one."[88] Former Speaker Henry Clay, in opposing his party on this matter, objected to the proposed reduction, maintaining that a large House could function as well as a smaller body if the rules were fashioned properly.[89] This view would not ultimately prevail and for the first time in the nation's history the U.S. House of Representatives would experience a drop in its total membership when President John Tyler signed the Apportionment Act into law in June of 1842.[90] The Act trimmed the House to 223 members, required single-member districts, and expanded the ratio of population per representative from about one per 50,000 to around one per 71,000. This development marked the end of holding the average House district constituency size at a level hovering around what it had been in the first couple of decades after the ratification of the Constitution.[91]

435 is the Limit

Despite this temporary deviation, the second half of the nineteenth century would witness a return to the regular order of increasing the size of the chamber to accommodate a rapidly escalating population.[92] From 1850 to 1910 the U.S. population grew more than fourfold, going from almost 22 million to just above 91 million. The size of the House did not match that pace, but, it did nearly double during this period, while the average number of persons per representative crept up from approximately 93,000 to slightly above the 200,000 mark. While controlling the soaring growth of constituency size was still of concern to House members, the foremost reason behind apportioning additional seats following each census was to prevent any state delegation from suffering a loss of seats due to shifting population patterns.[93] This trend continued when Congress approved the 1911 Apportionment Act that allocated 433 seats plus two more when New Mexico and Arizona entered the union later in the decade.[94]

Yet, as the Congress geared up for the apportionment process in 1920, projections indicated that more than 60 seats would be required to adhere to this precedent. This imperative to accommodate colleagues from slower growing states now ran up against a powerful segment of elite opinion that believed that it was time to curtail the growth of the chamber. Several prominent publications, including the *New York Times*, *Washington Post*, and *The New Republic*, opposed going beyond 435 members on the grounds the House floor had become exceedingly crowded and inefficient.[95] In an editorial published October 9, 1920, the *New York Times* complained that the House was "too unwieldy to enact legislation effectively and even committees say they are too big to permit . . . proper and deliberate consideration of measures."[96] This perspective was also shared by former leaders of the institution as well. Ex-speakers Joe Cannon and James Clark announced their support for a diminution in the size of the House, with Clark going as far as endorsing a constitutional amendment to cap the membership of the body at 300.[97] The views of these former leaders indicate support for the notion that managing orderly legislative business became progressively more difficult as the House grew in size, necessitating action to reverse or at least counter this trend. This position stands in stark contrast to Henry Clay's feeling that rules and procedures were sufficient to maintain a reasonable environment in which to legislate as the House expanded during the course of the 1842 debate over reduction.

These sentiments expressed by the press and ex-speakers were not persuasive enough to win over the House Census Committee responsible for drafting reapportionment legislation. On January 6, 1921, the committee approved the bill HR 14498 to increase the House to 483 members despite the objections of a vocal minority that bitterly complained about the negative implications this decision would have for the institution.[98] Once the bill reached the House floor, proponents of enlargement were put on the defensive by critics who felt 435 members was already dysfunctional and that the underlying legislation would make matters worse by prolonging legislative action needlessly, in addition to the extra fiscal burden of more members.[99] Rep. Andrew Montague of Virginia groused that the additional members would exacerbate the "top-heavy and inefficient legislative operation" the House had become.[100] House Census Committee Chairman Isaac Siegel of New York promised his colleagues that he would sponsor a constitutional amendment to limit the membership in the House to 500 but urged that the underlying bill be approved nonetheless.[101] The fundamental logic presented by large House supporters was that to ensure adequate representation congressional districts had to be of such a magnitude that members could keep in close contact with their constituents' wishes. The only way to keep the nation's population growth from creating House constituencies that were too enormous was for the number of seats apportioned to rise. Tennessee's Thetus Sims asserted that an increase was essential so "that the individual citizen should have the greatest opportunity to present his views to his immediate representative."[102] Despite such appeals on behalf of representation, the House approved an amendment offered by Rep. Henry Barbour of California that kept the membership at 435 by an overwhelmingly bipartisan vote of 279–76 and went on to pass the final version of the bill.[103]

While some past and present House leaders were adamantly in favor of preventing another expansion of the membership total, there was also broad support in the House for this action, as exhibited by the lopsided vote in favor of the Barbour Amendment. Some members assailed further enlargement of the House as an inevitable transfer of power to the leaders of the institution. Rep. Clifton McArthur of Oregon summed up the feelings of members who opposed an increase on the grounds that it would "centralize power in the hands of a few leaders. The larger the lawmaking body the less the individual Member feels his responsibility and the more he is tempted to pass it along to the leaders."[104] This outlook reflected the desire for greater decentralization in the legislative process that prevailed in this era.[105]

Was the position that the House had become too large for efficient operation more likely to be taken by members charged with the responsibility of directing legislative operations in the chamber or was this view not significantly different from the average membership of the House? To more systematically analyze the factors that led members to support retention of the 435-seat limit, a pair of logistic regression models were formulated predicting how members voted on the Barbour Amendment. These models include an independent variable that codes whether a member was an elected party leader, a committee chair, or a ranking member. They also incorporate other variables that might influence how members may have voted on this issue, including whether the representative's state would gain or lose a seat if the House remained at 435 members, ideology, partisan affiliation, and whether they were members of the Census Committee which had jurisdiction over this matter.[106]

The results depicted in Table 2.1 indicate that those individuals charged with institutional maintenance were not significantly more likely to back retaining the 435-seat limit. Though many leaders may have believed the House was becoming unmanageable, their view was not distinct from other members of the body. The negative sign of the coefficient for the first dimension

Table 2.1 Logistic regression analysis of roll-call vote on amendment in the 66th Congress to keep the House at 435 members

Independent variable	Model 1	Model 2
Committee leader	−.516	−.525
	(.399)	.397
Democrat		−.664
		(.789)
First dimension	−1.002*	−1.681#
DW-NOMINATE	(.433)	(.923)
Second dimension	−.039	−.067
DW-NOMINATE	(.366)	(.367)
Member of the Census	−1.257	−1.283
Committee	(.787)	(.797)
Member's state gained seats	.537	.511
	(.570)	(.571)
Member's state lost seats	−3.448***	−3.441***
	(.406)	(.407)
Party leader	−.355	−.361
	(1.421)	(1.426)
Constant	2.513***	2.878***
	(.285)	(.525)
Pseudo R²	.352	.354
Log-likelihood	−117.796	−117.430
N	344	344

#p < .1 *p < .05 ***p < .001.

Notes
Standard errors in parentheses.

Dependent variable is coded 1 for a yes vote and 0 for a no vote on the Barbour Amendment to HR 14498, January 19, 1921.

DW-NOMINATE variable signifies that more conservative members were less likely to support the Barbour Amendment but that partisanship was not a factor as evidenced in Model 2, with Democrats not significantly more likely to support it than Republicans. The other variable yielding significant leverage in both models was whether a member's state was projected to lose a seat if the 435-seat figure was not increased. For these members political self-preservation and retention of the state's present level of representation seemed to trump the concern that the House was growing too large in membership. In fact, although Minority Leader Clark had been open to the idea of cutting back on the seats apportioned to the states, when it became clear Missouri would lose two seats if the House was not increased as called for in the underlying bill, he cast his vote against the Barbour Amendment. Rep. Clark was not alone in protecting his own political interests or the interests of his state.

Figure 2.1 displays the predicted probabilities of how representatives voted on this amendment, comparing members for states losing and not losing states under a continuance of the 435-seat allocation, holding all the other variables in Model 1 at their appropriate means and modes.[107] Representatives in states not facing a loss of a seat if the amendment passed had a predicted probability of .914 of voting for it versus a .264 predicted probability for members from states who would lose a seat if it were adopted. Therefore, very few members of the House, regardless of their position within the institution, were willing to assent to another enlargement of the House unless their state or potentially their own career would suffer. As one scholar observed, this decision by most members of "the House was actuated solely by the desire to keep down its size."[108]

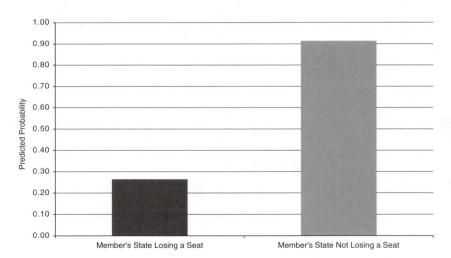

Figure 2.1 Predicted probability of voting to keep the House at 435 members in the 66th Congress.

Once the amended version of HR 14498 reached the Senate no action was taken prior to the final adjournment of the 66th Congress. Senators from the 11 states that would have lost seats were instrumental in obstructing the passage of the apportionment bill.[109] This inaction was critical because in this era the House was not automatically reapportioned after every ten years, as new legislation had to be adopted before seats could be reallocated based on the new population estimate. If no legislation was passed, then the House would continue as currently constituted regardless of whether changes in the population skewed representation. This scenario did unfold despite several ill-fated attempts to salvage a compromise during the 1920s. For the first time in the nation's history the Congress failed to reapportion House seats among the states.[110]

Members of the House tried again to pass an apportionment bill in 1921 that would have only increased the body to 460 members; however, this measure met stiff resistance from opponents who criticized it as a political move to spare certain states from losing seats. Yet before the bill could reach final passage a motion to recommit the bill was approved narrowly, 146–142, dooming its prospects for enactment.[111] During much of the 1920s the Congress neglected to deal with the issue at all.[112] By the end of the decade, however, pressure began to mount for action on reapportionment as it became apparent that inequities in the distribution of seats based on the 1910 population were extremely pronounced. In March of 1928 the House Census Committee approved a bill to retain the 435-seat limit that garnered critical support from Speaker Nicholas Longworth and Majority Leader John Q. Tilson, but it was once again thwarted by a motion to recommit.[113] In the waning days of the 70th Congress in 1929 the House leadership intensified its support for reapportionment legislation sponsored by House Census Committee Chairman E. Hart Fenn of Connecticut that would have permanently frozen the House at 435 members and provided for an automatic apportioning of seats to be determined by the Secretary of Commerce as an administrative action.[114]

Allies of a permanent ceiling on the House membership gained valuable assistance when Senator Arthur Vandenburg of Michigan began a crusade for apportionment legislation citing the gross negligence of the House in its inability to act.[115] By this time, the obligation of enacting an apportionment bill eclipsed the debate over the proper size of the House. During the first session of the 71st Congress each chamber passed slightly different versions of legislation that permanently fixed the House at 435 members by substantial margins.[116] The emphasis of the floor proceedings over these debates was devoted largely to the merits of transferring the task of apportioning the House to the executive branch, whether the alien population should be counted in the process, and the date for taking the census. Given their earlier failure, House enlargement advocates seemed consigned to the reality that a majority in Congress felt it was ill advised to take such a step. After the 1929 Apportionment Act was agreed to in Conference Committee the House gave it a truncated debate and passed it without a roll-call vote, while it was only approved by a vote of 48–37 in the Senate. Finally, President Hoover signed it into law on June 19, 1929.[117] The Act mandated that the Secretary of Commerce automatically apportion 435 seats for the House following the completion of the decennial census.[118]

According to legislative scholar Nelson Polsby, one of the hallmarks of an institutionalized organization is that an "organization tends to use universalistic rather than particularistic criteria, and automatic rather than discretionary methods for its internal business."[119] It can be argued that by relinquishing this responsibility to the executive branch the House set up an automatic process of reapportionment rather than having to carry out this exercise every ten years. To a certain extent, this development was another measure of how the House was becoming institutionalized in a variety of ways during the early twentieth century.[120] The view of most members was that the House needed a degree of stability in its size for an efficient legislative process to remain viable and adopting this policy facilitated that objective.[121] This action relieved the House membership of having to deal with not only the question of legislative size but also the ratio of citizens per House district. Additionally, it freed members from having to placate colleagues from states with population growth less than the national rate. Since the number of seats apportioned would not have to be renewed by passing a statute, the House would be spared from having the painful debate over which states would lose seats. According to one analysis, "the 1929 Act placed the House's reapportionment on automatic pilot; and in so doing, provided an administrative answer to what had been considered a political question."[122] Furthermore, by transferring this power over to the executive branch there would not be an embarrassing repeat of what occurred during the 1920s; when failing to pass legislation to reapportion the House turned out to be a stain on the institution's reputation.

No Turning Back

Delegating the authority of apportionment to the executive branch relieved the House of the responsibility of dealing with decennial battles over the size of the chamber and the political fallout for states that would lose seats due to lagging population growth. With this precedent firmly established, the House members resolved the tension between legislative efficiency and representation, opting for the former. If members felt that their ability to effectively represent their constituents had been undermined, they did not feel compelled to take action to augment the status quo number.

Table 2.2 displays the apportionment population, the size of the House, and the ratio of persons per representative from the nation's founding to the present. It shows the House has remained at 435 seats for almost a century. It reveals that each member of the House represents on average 646,000 people following the 2000 census, as compared with approximately 210,000 in 1910, the decade when 435 seats were first apportioned. Rarely has the membership of the House decided to seriously debate changing the institution's numerical size.

Table 2.2 Average U.S. House district population size, 1789–2000

Year	Apportionment population	Number of districts	Persons per representative
2000	281,422,177	435	646,498
1990	249,022,783	435	572,466
1980	225,867,174	435	519,235
1970	204,053,025	435	469,087
1960	178,559,217	435	410,481
1950	149,895,183	435	344,587
1940	131,006,184	435	301,164
1930	122,093,455	435	280,675
1920	106,021,537*	435	243,728
1910	91,603,772	435	210,583
1900	74,562,608	386	193,167
1890	61,908,906	356	173,901
1880	49,371,340	325	151,912
1870	38,115,641	292	130,533
1860	29,550,038	241	122,614
1850	21,766,691	234	93,020
1840	15,908,376	223	71,338
1830	11,930,987	240	49,712
1820	8,972,396	213	42,124
1810	6,854,231	181	37,689
1800	4,879,820	141	34,609
1790	3,615,823	105	34,436
1789		65	

Source: US Census Bureau.
*No reapportionment legislation was passed by Congress for the 1920s.

For the first time since the enactment of the 1929 Apportionment Act the Congress seriously entertained a proposal to augment the statutory limit of 435 House seats following the admission of Hawaii and Alaska as the nation's 49th and 50th states.[123] With the addition of the two new states in 1958 and 1959 Congress temporarily increased the House to 437 members until the next census.[124] With more states increasing the denominator in future rounds of apportionment, some states would lose representation, with Alaska and Hawaii entitled to three combined seats after the next census was taken. This scenario created an opening for representatives who wanted to push for a more significant enlargement of the House. *Congressional Quarterly* noted,

> In 1961 various proposals were made to increase the permanent size of the House, ranging from additions of three members to 34 members.

Speaker Sam Rayburn, however, opposed any increases, contending that the House was already too large for efficient operation.[125]

Once again leadership resistance to a larger House resurfaced as even a relatively deferential Speaker like Rayburn thought his task to build coalitions for successful governance was hindered by the scale of the membership that was already in place.

During the hearings on these various proposals the impulse for enhancing representation by increasing the House was voiced as well. Members from states that were going to lose seats in the latest reapportionment unless the House was enlarged dominated the roster of witnesses. The testimony concentrated on the historical precedent of adding more seats to the House any time a new state was admitted and the fact that failing to so in this case would be unfair to states that were losing representation in the body. Rep. Frank Chelf of Kentucky protested the impact of the 435-seat limit on representation, remarking, "With our population explosion, if we keep adding tens of thousands of constituents to . . . an individual Member of Congress . . . will have . . . practically no time in which to visit or mingle with his people, which is most important. Through no fault of his own a Member would become unavailable and inaccessible, which is just the reverse of what the Founding Fathers envisioned when they drafted our Constitution."[126] Rep. Jamie Whitten of Mississippi insisted that enlarged congressional districts had forced a colossal increase in staff to compensate for the additional workload that had accompanied the massive expansion of the federal government. Trying to spin the workload argument in favor of increasing the House, Whitten testified,

Any check of the matter will show there are at least 1000 times as many Federal questions today as there were in 1910. . . . With the workload of Congress the Federal questions that come through your office, the way the Federal Government touches the people in your district and mine, it has gotten to where an additional number of Members to help spread the load would be sound.[127]

Rep. Chelf responded to the detractors of an increase, asking, "If the House is too large and too unwieldy, as our opponents argue, why is it that we 435 Members of the House are always through with our work, difficult as it may be, at the end of a given session, and often have to wait on the other body to finish their work?" He also noted that "the British House of Commons has 612 members, but it also has a distinguished record of achievement, despite its size."[128]

However, in spite of these sentiments and others in favor of boosting membership levels in the chamber, House Judiciary Committee Chairman Emmanuel Cellar of New York acquiesced to leadership pressure and worked strenuously to defeat any of these measures.[129] Rayburn would pass away late in 1961 and Rep. John McCormack would replace him as Speaker. This transition altered the landscape for the legislative process as McCormack's home state of Massachusetts was slated to lose a seat if the House was not increased. So early in 1962 he lent his support to a proposal to permanently lift the membership to 438, to offset the number of seats that Alaska and Hawaii would now be entitled to have.[130] Thus, this movement for an extremely modest increase was driven by political expediency rather than by any change in outlook on the legislative operation or the quality of representation of the institution. The bill came to the House floor via an open rule allowing all germane amendments. Rep. James Trimble of Arkansas seized this opportunity and offered an amendment to permanently increase the House to 467 members so that no state would lose seats during the latest round of reapportionment.[131] This move triggered the recurring tradeoff questions of legislative size during the debate over the amendment. Rep. Stan Tupper of Maine issued an impassioned plea for an increase:

> In short the basic question today is this: To what extent shall we against the background of reapportionment, permit the voice of each and every one of our American citizens to be heard? The problem for us to resolve here today becomes eminently clear when it is realized that as our American population increases, the influence of each element of the population decreases or increases in proportion to the size of the US Congress. As the size of Congress increases, so does the representation of each individual in the American society. Conversely as the size decreases, so diminishes the individual's control over the affairs of his government.[132]

Rep. Charles Hoeven of Iowa summed up the feeling of the majority, however, when he asserted that any movement toward expansion of the House would lead to "an unwieldy body that cannot operate properly." Rep. Perkins Bass of New Hampshire elaborated on this theme, noting, "Students of good government argue that the present membership of the House is too large for efficient government." It was his contention that "every enlargement tends to make legislative procedures more unwieldy. We are faced with the prospect that the House of Representatives will become a formless mass of people, hampered in its constitutional role to enact laws for this Nation."[133]

The House rejected the Trimble Amendment 51–142. The underlying bill also collapsed when another amendment passed to require statewide, at-large elections for states awarded new seats who did not redistrict before the 1962 elections. Once the members of the House got word of this provision the bill was removed from consideration and no further action on the matter was taken.[134] According to *Congressional Quarterly*, "[t]he failure of House expansion bills in 1961 and 1962 . . . actually created a new precedent for not increasing the House, even when new states join the Union."[135] If members could not even agree to a modest increase in the House under these circumstances, what conditions could foster an environment hospitable to change?

In recent years the renewed efforts to secure a voting member of the U.S. House for the District of Columbia further illustrates the collective institutional will to avoid tinkering with the size of the institution. Rep. Tom Davis of Virginia pushed for legislation in the 108th Congress and again in the 109th Congress to temporarily increase the House by two seats, awarding one to Washington, D.C., and the other to Utah, which just lost out on a fourth seat in the 2000 reapportionment process.[136] Originally, the Davis proposal specifically called for the House to return to 435 members after the next census is taken.[137] Rep. Davis intentionally drafted the legislation to adhere to the precedent established by the House when Hawaii and Alaska were admitted to the Union, that any increase in the membership be only a temporary measure. Later in the 109th Congress Rep. Davis reversed his position and augmented his proposal to permanently increase the House to 437 members after representatives from slow growing states expressed concern that the new House seat for Washington, D.C., would come at their expense.[138] With Democratic victories in the 2006 congressional elections new life was breathed into the proposal. House Speaker Nancy Pelosi promised to bring the bill to the floor in the early part of the 110th Congress. After procedural maneuvers by the Republican minority delayed final passage, on April 19, 2007, members of the House approved the bill largely along party lines by a vote of 241–171. However, on September 18, 2007, the bill died in the 110th Congress at the hands of a Senate filibuster.[139] The bill was revived in the 111th Congress and seemed on its way to being enacted with the support of President Obama. It passed the Senate on February 27, 2009, but as of this writing the bill is stalled in the House over an unrelated amendment repealing the District's gun laws.[140] Considering the modest nature of this increase, even if it is eventually enacted, this proposal does not constitute a fundamental shift away from institutional maintenance toward greater representation on a broader scale by dramatically reducing the ratio of citizens per representative.

One member who has shown an interest in re-evaluating the size of the House in a comprehensive manner is Rep. Alcee Hastings of Florida. In recent years he has repeatedly introduced legislation that would "establish a commission to make recommendations on the appropriate size of membership of the House of Representatives."[141] This commission would be comprised of members appointed by the president and House leadership but would only be advisory in nature. Any recommendation it would put forward would require statutory approval by the Congress. Rep. Hastings annunciated similar themes heard in previous debates over the consequences of not increasing the size of the House commensurate with the population:

> When I was first elected in 1992, I represented roughly 589,000 South Floridians. Today, each of us now represents nearly 663,000 or 12.5 percent more people than 10 years ago. In 1982, each Member of the House represented about 534,000 and in 1972, the number was a mere 482,000 or

38 percent fewer people than today. This means that we represent well over 100,000 more people today than did our predecessors—and some Members still serving today—20 years ago. Frankly, at some point Members in this body are going to have to accept reality and begin asking, "As Representatives, are we as effective today as the Representatives of the 1970s when they had fewer people to represent?"[142]

Despite this passionate appeal, apparently very few of his House colleagues openly share the concern expressed by Rep. Hastings that the quality of representation afforded constituents may have suffered as House districts encompass thousands of additional citizens compared to just a few decades ago. During the 109th Congress, only one other member signed on as a cosponsor of this legislation. Considering the bill merely created a commission to study House enlargement, the lack of interest exhibited by his colleagues suggests bleak prospects for any proposal to adjust the size of the House to make it more representative any time in the foreseeable future. The interest expressed by Hastings in halting the growth of constituency size may also be linked to fears among some African-American representatives that in the future it will become progressively more challenging to create minority-majority districts that facilitate the descriptive representation of the nation's minority population in Congress.[143]

Some Perspective on this Debate

As this historical review has shown, the appropriate size of the U.S. House once provoked spirited debate among legislators at various temporal reference points in the nation's history. In the context of a growing population, what number will achieve optimal representation and legislative efficiency? This conundrum perplexed the delegates at the Constitutional Convention through the early 1900s. For the most part, greater deference was given to the need to check the growth in average constituency size rather than the size of the House itself. When the House reached the 435-seat threshold the membership felt further increases would hinder its legislative operations, and concern over the ratio of citizens per representative was put aside. If the House could not fulfill its obligation to enact legislation in a timely manner while still providing opportunity for reasoned debate, then collective representation would suffer impairment. By capping the House at 435 seats, members of the House were aiming to protect the ability of the House to collectively represent the citizenry even as representation on the district level became less of a concern. Continuing with decennial increases in the House was perceived by representatives as inimical to the body's capacity to legislate even if an enlarged constituency ratio made representation at the district level a steeper challenge.

So based on this review of the debates, which side has the better case? It is my position that Rep. Hastings and other enlargement advocates have the best of this argument. When members of the House decided to place a permanent cap on its size they failed to seriously consider the full implications for representation. Preserving legislative efficiency is important but if representation is sacrificed in the process to do so betrays the intent of the institution in the national government the founders sought to keep closest to the people. The House is first and foremost a representative institution. House members were too cavalier in dismissing the representational implications of permanently limiting the size of the House in the face of the population explosion of the twentieth century, especially considering they had very little evidence the House could function less effectively or efficiently if the number of members in the House kept pace with the growth of the population. It is hard to believe that members of the House would have approved a permanent limit on the allocation of seats had they foreseen the prospect that the nation's population would one day pass the 300 million mark. With this background mind, in order to maintain its representative character the institution is long overdue for upward adjustment in its numerical size. Whether it is making it easier for House members to stay in touch with their constituents, improving the policy responsiveness of House members, or providing better representation for demographic and geographic interests in society, the supporters of increasing the size of the House commensurate with the growth of the population have made a fairly persuasive case.

So what principles should guide altering the present size of the institution? The decision to impose a limit of 435 seats was an arbitrary accident of history arrived at based on no empirical formula. In contrast, there are more systematic ways to calculate what the present size of the House should be. The cube root law of national assembly size discussed in the opening of this chapter seems like the obvious way to go. The cube root law provides the optimal means to resolve the tradeoff dilemma involved with determining the size of any legislative body. Not only would it bring the House in line with international legislative norms, it would also help restore some balance to the representative side of the ledger in the competing legislative imperatives of representation and legislative efficiency. The House would be well served to return to the policy of increases every ten years linked to the cube root of the nation's population. Enacting such a law would mean that following the 2010 census the House should be increased to approximately 675 members, which would be the projected cube root of the population in that year. This policy should improve the capacity of representatives to communicate with their constituents but also prevent the House from becoming so large it could not operate efficiently. After all, even if the US population reached one billion people, a remote possibility for the foreseeable future, it would still only be constituted of 1,000 members.

To prevent a debacle like the failure to apportion the House in the 1920s these increases would occur on an automatic basis after each census is taken. The process would remain similar to how it works now, with the only exception being that once the census was completed the number of House seats would be apportioned by the Commerce Department based on whatever the cube root of the population happened to be, rather than the total of 435 seats that has been the standard in the past century. Therefore the House would avoid the contentious apportionment battles detailed in this chapter. After all, previous research has established that the size of the House was closely tied to the cube root during most of the nineteenth and early twentieth centuries.[144] There is every reason to believe the House could successfully return to that tradition once again.

In order to bolster the case for House enlargement it would be helpful to better understand to what extent it would actually achieve the objective of better representation. Therefore the research question explored in the remaining chapters of this book is not how legislative size influences efficiency. Rather, it is the representational component of the legislative tradeoff that will be scrutinized. The size of the House has not varied over the past century but the number of constituents per House district has. Although critics of the cap on the number of seats in the House complain that the growth in constituency size it has created has undermined the representational relationship between members of the House and their constituents, there is scant empirical verification of this premise. From a normative perspective the opponents of the permanent ceiling on the size of the House may have a plausible argument that the House has become less representative. The arguments of House enlargement advocates throughout history have stressed that constituency population matters in what type of representation citizens receive. On its face this claim would not seem controversial. Still, even if there is some impact, the dynamics of the relationship require greater clarity. Just how has representation at the district level been destabilized, if at all? Are legislators from larger constituencies less able to communicate with their constituents? Has the representational linkage between U.S. House members and their constituents been damaged by not moving away from abandoning decennial increases? Have constituents had access to their representatives restricted by House districts composed of 600,000 going on 700,000 people? Are representatives less responsive in the area of policy desires? These criticisms and others are persistently levied against failing to elevate the size of the House congruent with the growth in the population, from the Anti-Federalists to the present. However, there is not much available evidence to buttress this claim. The cube root law of national assembly size has not been subjected to rigorous empirical testing. The objective of the remaining chapters of the book is to attempt to provide empirical insight into the extent to which these claims are indeed valid. Are there solid evidentiary grounds to abandon the status quo or is there insufficient evidence to tinker with the institution's current size? If so, then re-evaluating the present cap on the size of the House, as called for in this chapter, would certainly be in order.

Chapter 3

The Growth of House District Populations and Electoral Competition

Introduction

The subject of U.S. House elections has not lacked for attention among American political scientists. Scholars of congressional elections have intently studied the enormous success of incumbents in the post-World War II era and the reasons behind it. Elections matter because they provide the means by which constituents can hold politicians accountable for their actions in government. Many critics castigate members of the U.S. House of Representatives for being insulated from electoral sanction because of uncompetitive districts and being out of touch with their constituents.[1] So any attempt to understand how the dimensions of representation have been altered by the rapid growth of the U.S. population as the size of House has remained constant must include an investigation of the implications for the electoral process.

The impact of constituency size on electoral outcomes has captured a great deal of interest from students of elections at all levels of government in the United States. Nevertheless, in spite of the steep rise in the average number of citizens in House districts over the past century, for various reasons no comprehensive systematic analysis has been undertaken on whether district population size makes a difference in House elections. This chapter fills this vacuum by formulating and testing empirical models of whether constituency size has any bearing on the margin of victory for House incumbents and their probability of defeat. It begins this book's empirical examination of how the growth in constituency size has influenced representation in the U.S. House. The analyses presented in this chapter help to illuminate the extent, if any, to which the escalation of House district populations has affected the minimal level of competition that has become a signature feature of the electoral process in the House. The results reveal that a larger average constituency size tends to reduce the victory margins of incumbents. At first glance it may appear that more competition is a positive development and might work against the case to increase the size of the House because it would serve to create less competitive constituencies. However, the concluding section of the chapter offers up an interpretation of this finding that explains how it may not necessarily be a positive development for representation in the House.

The Dominance of House Incumbents and its Causes

One of the most prominent trends documented in the scholarship of American political science is the dominance of incumbents in U.S. House elections during the post-World War II era. Over this period better than 90% of incumbent House members have sought re-election and greater than 90% of them have emerged victorious.[2] In the early 1970s, political scientists took notice not only of these increasing success rates but also of the fact that incumbents were expanding the margins by which they defeated the opposition.[3] Though some scholars remained skeptical that incumbents were as safe as conventional wisdom suggested,[4] in the past few cycles there are very few House campaigns that have not been lopsided affairs.

Several explanations were posited as to why the advantage of incumbents jumped so dramatically in the second half of the twentieth century and has persisted in successive years. One proposition was that representatives were engaging in strategic abandonment of their House seat with greater frequency than in the past, retiring before they would suffer certain defeat in the next election.[5] Many studies identified redistricting that occurred in the wake of the reapportionment revolution of the 1960s as the principal culprit.[6] Observers of contemporary elections have also blamed gerrymandering as a primary contributor to the lock House incumbents have on re-election.[7] The allegation that redistricting was responsible for the rise of victory margins in the late 1960s was sharply questioned by some scholars.[8] Additional studies suggest the lack of turnover of more recent vintage is attributable to the migrations of like-minded partisans that have made congressional districts more politically homogeneous.[9] Other scholars pointed to the de-alignment of the electorate in the 1970s as a factor, since voters were beginning to substitute the cue of incumbency for that of partisanship.[10] However, this phenomenon may have been temporary, as partisan voting in congressional elections is in the process of a noticeable resurgence in the past two decades.[11]

Another explanation rested on the growth in resources available for incumbents, such as the franking privilege, to advertise themselves to voters at unprecedented levels,[12] although there was not much empirical evidence to validate this theory.[13] Morris Fiorina picked up on the resources argument and claimed that due to the increase in the size of government in the 1960s members of Congress assumed the role of ombudsmen who won re-election by helping their constituents navigate the bureaucracy and securing distributive benefits that they could emphasize to voters rather than focusing on more controversial policy issues.[14] Subsequent tests of the resources explanation have been inconclusive at best, with studies showing additional time spent in the district has negligible benefits for incumbents.[15] Some research has found that citizens' perceptions of constituency service by their member of Congress had little impact on voting decisions,[16] but other scholars conclude that they do.[17] As far as distributions of spending programs to district constituencies are concerned, the link to improved electoral success there is mixed too, with some studies only finding support for this relationship at the aggregate level,[18] and others failing to substantiate it for individual vote choice.[19] Even so, the growth in the disparity of campaign spending between incumbents and their challengers does appear to have played a role in fortifying the position of U.S. House members.[20]

Constituency Size and the Advantage of Incumbents

All of these factors may have contributed to the virtually invulnerable position most incumbent U.S. representatives now experience, although the partisan slant of most districts now predominates more than in the 1970s and 1980s.[21] This trend toward greater incumbent electoral security in the House has coincided with the growth in the ratio of population per district.[22] Yet, only one study to date has investigated whether these two phenomena are related. Historian Lex Renda asserts that incumbents have benefited from the increase in the mean population size of House districts. In his study of the last 37 midterm elections since 1854 Renda finds a correlation of .730 between the success rate of incumbents seeking re-election and the population ratio of House districts. He speculates that enlarged district constituencies have made dislodging incumbents more difficult for their challengers.[23] However, he does not test a multivariate model that controls for other variables that are influential in House outcomes to substantiate this claim, which means the jury is still out on whether constituency size has been a boon to incumbent House members and a burden for the candidates challenging them.

Renda's assertion runs counter to what other research has found on the magnitude of population and competition in Senate elections. Overall, incumbent senators, who in most cases represent more citizens than their House counterparts, have been re-elected at lower rates in the post-World War II era.[24] Furthermore, a collection of studies on the performance of senators has uncovered a negative relationship between state population and incumbent vote shares.[25] The consensus view emanating from this scholarship is that the heavily populated states tend to be the most diverse and create less favorable conditions for incumbents seeking re-election as compared to senators in the least populated states in the country. Hibbing and Brandes estimated the vote shares of incumbent senators seeking re-election as a function of the number of House districts within a state after controlling for party competition within the state. Their results revealed a difference of approximately nine points between senators running in the largest and smallest states in terms of population.[26]

Abramowitz and Segal produced similar findings in their model predicting incumbent senators' vote shares in the 48 contiguous states from 1974 to 1986. It showed that senators in states with the population of Wyoming would win by about three percentage points more than a Senator in states the size of California, all else equal.[27] The most comprehensive study of this relationship looked at all contested Senate races from 1914 and 1996 and found that margins of victory were highest in the states with the smallest populations.[28]

In spite of this evidence, not all political scientists are convinced that state constituency size is negatively associated with senators' electoral security. While conceding that regression analysis does demonstrate that higher population levels lead to closer races for incumbent senators, other studies lend scant empirical support to the proposition that this variable actually has a discernable effect on senators' probability of defeat. Hence, even if a larger constituency costs senators a few points in their margin of victory, overall, variance in population levels has limited predictive power in estimating which incumbents are the most likely not to win re-election.[29]

For state and municipal elections the verdict is mixed on whether constituency size and incumbent security are related. In races for the state legislature in 49 states for 1992 and 1994, one study found that the probability of victory for incumbents was a negative function of district constituency population, controlling for other relevant factors.[30] Another evaluation of state legislative races in 14 states for 1996 and 1998 reported that incumbents received a higher percentage of the votes in smaller districts.[31] In contrast, research on county and city elections has revealed a weak or nonexistent association between population and electoral competitiveness.[32] An analysis of races for the Board of Supervisors in counties in California from 1996 to 2002 uncovered evidence that the number of citizens in the district increased both the percentage of votes received by incumbents as well as their probability of victory.[33]

Despite an ample amount of research on this topic for U.S. Senate races and the less voluminous collection of studies at the state and local levels, there has been no multivariate analysis of how district constituency size influences races for the U.S. House of Representatives. Drawing reasonable inferences on the nature of this relationship for House contests based on the contradictory evidence produced in the studies just referenced is a questionable proposition. One of the problems of extrapolating from some of the previous studies is that they rely on population estimates that can be outdated in the ten-year intervals between censuses. This concern is of particular relevance to House races because, even though the population deviations between congressional districts must be minimized when a new round of reapportionment takes place, massive shifts in the size of congressional districts can occur within this ten-year time frame. For instance, in Nevada's 2nd Congressional District, the population grew an astounding 76.8% from 1990 to 2000, going from 600,791 persons in 1990 to 1,062,153 in 2000. Conversely, over the same time frame in Maryland's 7th Congressional District the population dropped 9.7%, going from 597,660 in 1990 to 539,439 in 2000.[34] These cases are illustrative of the increasing peril of utilizing census estimates of House district constituency size the further in time the election cycle is from the year the census was taken. This obstacle may be overcome in state or county-wide races because the U.S. Census Bureau provides estimates on an annual basis for these jurisdictions, but these estimates are not supplied for House districts in the same fashion. However, there are elections when the most accurate estimates of House district population are known, and that occurs in the year the census was taken. Therefore, this chapter will conduct the first multivariate test of how district population impacts electoral outcomes in U.S. House races utilizing district population figures from the years 1970, 1980, 1990, and 2000. This strategy permits an evaluation of how these variables interact with the greatest level of precision that can be achieved given the limitations of the data.

There are three hypotheses that will be tested in the remainder of this chapter: (1) *the competition hypothesis*—as district population *increases,* an incumbent's margin of victory *decreases;* (2) the *safety hypothesis*—as district population *increases,* the margin of victory for an incumbent *increases;* or (3) there is no relation relationship between the two variables. The same set of hypotheses will be tested for the probability of victory for the incumbent House member: (1) as district population *increases,* the probability an incumbent will win re-election *decreases* (2) as district population *increases,* the probability an incumbent will win *increases;* or (3) there is no relationship between these variables. While the design executed in this study cannot definitively answer the question of whether allowing the House to remain fixed at 435 members and the resultant expansion of House district populations has made elections more or less competitive, it will shed some light on it. Examining this relationship over four election years with accurate population figures will allow for the most reliable empirical test that has been undertaken to date.

The Relationship between District Population and Electoral Competition

In order to estimate the relationship between district population size and electoral competitiveness in House elections, a multivariate model must be formulated that controls for the other factors that shape outcomes in these races. As was previously noted, what makes studying this question for House elections a thorny issue is that accurate estimates of district populations are only available once a decade from the U.S. Census Bureau. As the decade unfolds, shifting migration patterns cause House district population figures to fluctuate rather dramatically. However, in the first year of the decade there are precise estimates of population levels within congressional districts. The present analysis looks at this relationship at four points in time, the election years 1970, 1980, 1990, and 2000. If either of the competing hypotheses regarding electoral outcomes is to be strongly confirmed, the relationship should hold in each cycle individually and when data for each of these cycles is pooled in a comprehensive model controlling for other variables. Dummy variables for specific election years are added into these models as well. For ease of substantive interpretation, district population throughout this chapter is coded in hundreds of thousands.

Since the incumbency advantage has drawn the bulk of attention in congressional elections scholarship over the past generation, and because races involving incumbent House members supply a wealth of information to rule out the possibility that any linkage between constituency size and electoral competition is spurious, this analysis excludes open-seat races. Two dependent variables are utilized: (1) the incumbent's margin of victory measured by subtracting the challenger's percentage of the two-party vote from the incumbent's percentage of the two-party vote; and (2) a dichotomous measure of whether the incumbent won re-election or was defeated.

A member of the House can win re-election with a substantial margin based on the personal and institutional benefits of being an incumbent, but some members win re-election simply because of the favorable distribution of partisanship within the district.[35] Districts heavily concentrated with individuals of the same party affiliation as the incumbent member of Congress ensure a higher degree of electoral safety. In contrast, when partisan loyalties are more evenly split within a district or slanted against the incumbent, a more hotly contested race is likely. District partisanship can be measured by the presidential vote received by the candidate of the incumbent's party in the election, although short-term forces such as an incumbent president's popularity or the challenger's weakness as a candidate in a particular election may not accurately reflect the normal partisan distribution. To control for any short-term bias, the measure of district partisanship used here is calculated by subtracting the percentage of the two-party vote received by the presidential candidate of the incumbent's party in the entire nation from the margin in the district. A similar measure of the normal partisan vote has been employed in other studies of U.S. House elections.[36]

The number of incumbents for whom the partisan landscape in their district is unfavorable has been on the decline over the past two decades, meaning the personal value of incumbency may be less influential than in years past.[37] Nevertheless, incumbents still gain some electoral edge simply by virtue of the fact that they are a sitting member of the U.S. House.[38] Moreover, since part of the study covers elections when congressional districts were routinely won by a House candidate of one party and a presidential candidate of the other party, it is essential to measure the incumbent's personal incumbency advantage. The personal vote is the previous margin of victory achieved by the House incumbent in the last election. Incumbents who did not face a major-party opponent in the previous election were not included in the analysis. This formulation of the personal vote has been used in previous studies of the incumbency advantage.[39]

Another facet of the incumbent's record that has been shown to affect the number of votes received is the level of extremism in their roll-call voting. Members with more extreme voting records tend to lose support within their district.[40] The policy extremism exhibited by the representative will be estimated by the absolute value of that member's first-dimension DW-NOMINATE score in the previous Congress.[41] A representative's seniority in the House may also matter, but the direction is less certain. It could be that the enhanced power and prestige that come along with extended House service improve the odds for re-election or they might lead to the perception that the incumbent is devoting too much time to responsibilities in Washington D.C. and is losing touch with the constituency. One empirical investigation of this question found that tenure was once associated with higher re-election rates and margins of victory, while observing that seniority has diminished power as a predictor of electoral performance as compared to the mid-twentieth century.[42] To control for whatever seniority effects may be operating in U.S. House elections, the number of terms served by the representative will be included as an explanatory variable in each of the models. One aspect of tenure that is not a mystery is that a member in his or her initial attempt to win re-election benefits from a sophomore surge.[43] The sophomore surge is measured by a dummy variable coded 1 for an incumbent running for re-election for the first time and 0 otherwise.

National political forces can also shape the electoral environment to the advantage or detriment of the House member seeking re-election.[44] Most of the elections covered in this cycle produced a political climate unfavorable to incumbents of one of the two major parties. In the midst of Ronald Reagan's decisive victory over President Jimmy Carter in 1980, several Democratic incumbents in this cycle suffered from their ties to a deeply unpopular president. To account for this development, both the pooled and separate 1980 models include a dummy variable coded 1 for Democratic incumbents in 1980 and 0 otherwise to capture the effects of the pronounced anti-Democratic trend of this election. Despite recent exceptions in 1998 and 2002, the president's party typically loses seats in the U.S. House in a midterm election as occurred in 1970 and 1990.[45] To control for the effects of midterm loss, Republican incumbents running in 1970 and 1990 will be coded 1 and 0 otherwise in these models. There was no discernible edge for incumbents of either party in 2000 as very few seats changed hands, so incumbent party effects are not modeled for this year in the pooled or separate analyses.

Other district-level forces also dictate how the incumbent will do come election time. One of the most pivotal is the quality of the candidate challenging the incumbent. Politically experienced challengers pose a more formidable obstacle to re-election than do political neophytes.[46] Although challenger quality can be operationalized in a multitude of ways,[47] the most frequently used is a dichotomous measure of whether the challenger has held any previous elected office. Thus, congressional elections scholar Gary Jacobson's post-World War II

House election database was relied on to estimate the effect of the candidate challenging the incumbent where challengers with a prior elected office are coded 1 and 0 otherwise.[48]

A further controversy raised in the literature on congressional elections is the nature of the relationship between campaign spending and an incumbent's share of the vote. There is broad agreement that the amount spent by a challenger is negatively related to an incumbent's vote share and probability of victory.[49] However, whether incumbents' spending enhances their electoral performance evokes a contentious debate. Some scholars suggest that House incumbents' vote shares are not affected or in some cases are actually negatively associated with their level of spending.[50] Other research using an instrumental variables approach finds that additional spending does increase the percentage of the vote a sitting officeholder receives.[51]

Of course any time incumbent and challenger spending is analyzed there is a problem of reciprocal causation. The most endangered incumbents are forced to spend the most money, and thus it is a complex exercise to decipher just how much they benefit from extra campaign spending. In addition, challengers expected to perform the best tend to raise the most money, which may inflate the importance of this variable. The models presented in this chapter do not attempt to resolve this dispute around how to properly estimate the effects of campaign spending in House elections, since that variable is not of central interest in this study. To account for the likelihood that spending by both a challenger and an incumbent is likely to be subject to diminishing returns, squared transformations of these variables are incorporated into the various models presented in this chapter.[52] Spending effects can only be evaluated for the 1980, 1990, and 2000 elections because the campaign finance disclosure laws in operation today did not exist in 1970. To control for inflation and the extra cost associated with running in a more populous district, campaign spending is measured on a per capita basis in year 2000 dollars. While this list may not exhaust the potential variables that help predict the outcomes of elections involving incumbents, it does provide a powerful set of multivariate controls to test whether House district constituency size is a contributor to incumbent security, is a hindrance, or merely has a negligible impact.

Before presenting the multivariate analysis it might be instructive to look at the performance of incumbents across the range of district population on the two dependent variables of interest in this chapter (Table 3.1). From these data it does appear that smaller House districts aid incumbents. In districts below 400,000 in population the average margin of victory is 41.5 points compared to 30.3 points in districts comprised of 600,000-699,999 citizens and 25.2 in districts with more than 700,000 people. The same is not the case for the percentage of incumbents defeated across this range. Table 3.1 shows minuscule variation in the probability an incumbent will be defeated at different levels of district population. Based on these preliminary numbers, incumbents win by

Table 3.1 Average margin of victory and percentage of incumbents defeated by level of district population

District population	Average margin of victory	Percentage defeated
400,000 or fewer	41.5	3.1
400,000–499,999	31.3	6.1
500,000–599,999	30.5	5.0
600,000–699,999	30.3	4.3
700,000 or greater	25.2	4.2

Notes
This analysis excludes incumbent candidates without major opposition.
Results include the 1970, 1980, 1990, and 2000 U.S. House Elections.

reduced margins in larger House districts, but district population size does not appear to influence the re-election rate of incumbents.

Models Testing the Relationship between District Population and Margin of Victory

Table 3.2 displays the results for the pooled regression models predicting incumbent victory margins. Model 1 includes the results for the 1970, 1980, 1990, and 2000 elections. Several of the traditional independent variables have the anticipated effects in predicting the performance of an incumbent U.S. House member against a respective challenger. Those incumbents receiving strong support in previous elections tend to retain that support in the subsequent election. Members in districts packed with their fellow partisans also tend to outperform their colleagues where the partisan complexion of the district is more balanced. Freshmen running in their first re-election experience the sophomore surge that has been previously documented.

More ideologically extreme members have their margins of victory reduced. Democratic incumbents running in 1980 suffered at the hands of a national tide running against their party's fortunes, while Republican incumbents in the off-year elections of 1970 and 1990 saw their margins of victory trimmed. Quality challengers also inject additional competition into a race involving a sitting incumbent. Seniority has a significant negative impact on how an incumbent fares in this sample.

Turning to the variable of most interest to this study, the results signify that population is negatively linked to margin of victory by incumbents. Controlling for all the other variables in Model 1, incumbents lose about 1.4 points off their margin of victory for each additional 100,000 constituents in their district ($p < .004$). So the typical incumbent in a district of 500,000 people would see his or her margin of victory cut by 7 points, while an average incumbent in a district of a million people would lose about 14 points. This number is not

Table 3.2 Impact of district population size on the victory margins of incumbent House members: pooled analysis

Independent variable	Model 1	Model 2	Model 3
Challenger quality	−5.086***	−2.434*	−2.347*
	(.940)	(1.002)	(1.181)
Challenger spending		−18.029***	−14.284***
(per capita)		(1.895)	(1.767)
Challenger spending squared		2.757***	1.999***
(per capita)		(.303)	(.453)
Democratic incumbent	−10.303***	−7.167***	
in 1980	(1.719)	(1.432)	
District partisanship	.401***	.473***	.409***
	(.055)	(.059)	(.077)
District population	−1.430**	−1.642***	−2.685***
(in 100,000s)	(.493)	(.513)	(.614)
Freshman	7.127***	7.483***	7.207***
	(1.307)	(1.276)	(1.591)
Ideological extremism	−9.844***	−11.026***	−10.076*
	(2.731)	(2.971)	(3.988)
Incumbent spending		1.017	1.088
(per capita)		(.930)	(1.052)
Incumbent spending		−.152#	−.157#
squared (per capita)		(.084)	(.087)
Incumbents in 1980	−1.969		
	(1.718)		
Incumbents in 1990	−10.158***	−7.228***	
	(1.574)	(1.628)	
Incumbents in 2000	−3.964**	.182	8.185***
	(1.495)	(1.448)	(1.209)
Previous margin of victory	.617***	.434***	.459***
	(.029)	(.034)	(.041)
Republican incumbent	−14.305***		
in 1970	(1.405)		
Republican incumbent	−10.158***	−5.270***	−4.681**
in 1990	(1.574)	(1.513)	(1.529)
Seniority	−.233*	−.210#	−.175
	(.109)	(.114)	(.131)
Constant	30.111***	37.459***	34.113***
	(2.713)	(3.233)	(4.383)
Adj. R²	.573	.692	.695
N	1175	859	555

# p < .1 *p < .05 **p < .01 ***p < .001.

Notes

Dependent variable is the incumbent House member's margin of victory.

Robust standard errors in parentheses.

Model 1 includes the results for the 1970, 1980, 1990, and 2000 elections; Model 2 includes the results for the 1980, 1990, and 2000 elections; and Model 3 includes the results for the 1990 and 2000 elections.

insubstantial considering the mean difference between the incumbent's share of the vote and the challenger's share of the vote is about 31 points in this sample. This finding lends support to the hypothesis that elections contested in more populous jurisdictions invite greater competition.

The results in Model 2 buttress this conclusion. It introduces the campaign spending variables for the elections held in 1980, 1990, and 2000. This model shows that per capita challenger spending reduces the incumbent's vote margin, although the effect fades at higher levels of spending. The resources devoted to the campaign by the incumbent member of the House produce insignificant change in the outcome of the race. The size of the coefficient for district population actually increases in this specification (−1.642) and remains highly significant (p < .001). Even after spending is accounted for in this specification, incumbents win by 1.6 points less for every 100,000 citizens in the district. Model 3 displays an even stronger relationship when the results are just limited to 1990 and 2000, as the magnitude of district population exerts the most powerful effect. The size of the coefficient climbs to −2.28 when this smaller subset of cases is analyzed (p < .001).

To assess the robustness of this relationship across election cycles, individual models were tested for each individual election year. Table 3.3 contains the results of each of these models. This individual analysis reveals inconsistent findings. In the 1990 and 2000 elections district population had a significant negative effect on margin of victory at least at the .01 level. However, for 1970 district population has no significant impact and in 1980 the coefficient for this variable is insignificant and incorrectly signed. These discrepant results can possibly be attributed to the national Republican tide, especially in 1980, that may have lessened other peripheral influences like district population more than in the less volatile elections of 1990 and 2000.

On the whole, the chief evidentiary implication emanating from these results is that allowing House districts to continue to grow serves as a moderately positive stimulus for the competitiveness of elections. *Ceteris paribus*, an incumbent member of the U.S. House is worse off with thousands of extra constituents come election time. One must be cautious in drawing this inference based on the limited numbers of election cycles in this sample. Plus the inconsistency of the effects across election cycles suggests the relationship is a secondary factor in predicting House election outcomes. Nonetheless, the evidence presented here does suggest that surging district populations are a marginally positive influence on the level of electoral competition in U.S. House elections.

The Relationship between District Population and Probability of Defeat

The previous section examined the connection between constituency size and incumbent performance in House elections when tested in the context of margin of victory. However, simply because sitting members win by less in the

Table 3.3 Impact of district population size on the victory margins of incumbent House members by election

Independent variable	1970	1980	1990	2000
Challenger quality	−3.706*	−2.280	−2.755	−1.847
	(1.644)	(1.724)	(2.182)	(1.163)
Challenger spending		−28.970***	−31.941***	−12.393***
(per capita)		(3.725)	(6.536)	(1.680)
Challenger spending		6.048***	13.756***	1.626***
squared (per capita)		(1.395)	(3.506)	(.39)8
Democratic incumbent		−5.447***		
in 1980		(1.420)		
District partisanship	.233*	.584***	.135	.617***
	(.111)	(.087)	(.125)	(.078)
District population	−.477	.096	−3.398***	−1.776**
(in 100,000s)	(.864)	(.836)	(.908)	(.659)
Freshman	2.840	7.094***	9.668***	3.701***
	(2.790)	(1.996)	(2.822)	(1.205)
Ideological extremism	−6.117	−12.217**	−8.129	−9.178**
	(4.608)	(4.184)	(6.047)	(3.503)
Incumbent spending		.039	.981	.888
(per capita)		(2.148)	(2.010)	(1.107)
Incumbent spending		.189	−.181	−.111
squared (per capita)		(.265)	(.148)	(.096)
Previous margin of	.615***	.381***	.459***	.428***
victory	(.059)	(.056)	(.064)	(.049)
Republican incumbent	−14.172***			
in 1970	(1.4361)			
Republican incumbent			−4.514**	
in 1990			(1.490)	
Seniority	−.379#	−.284	−.366#	.126
	(.194)	(.217)	(.201)	(.149)
Constant	26.333***	32.194	41.744***	33.815***
	(4.382)	(5.552)	(6.514)	(4.713)
Adj. R²	.508	.718	.522	.856
N	316	304	275	280

# p < .1 *p < .05 **p < .01 ***p < .001.

Notes

Dependent variable is the incumbent House member's margin of victory.

Robust standard errors in parentheses.

most populated districts does not mean they are more prone to actually lose their seats because of this factor. Ultimately, if district population is going to meaningfully sway outcomes in House elections this relationship must manifest itself when the outcome is measured as a dichotomy, in this case whether the incumbent was re-elected. The next section of this chapter presents the

Table 3.4 Rare events logit models predicting the chances of defeat for incumbent U.S. House members

Independent variable	Model 1	Model 2	Model 3
Challenger quality	.914**	.726#	1.146#
	(.300)	(.417)	(.635)
Challenger spending		2.445***	3.205***
(per capita)		(.461)	(.732)
Challenger spending squared		−.260**	−.359***
(per capita)		(.089)	(.108)
Democratic incumbent in 1980	1.813*	1.558	
	(.782)	(1.049)	
District partisanship	−.036#	−.028	.033
	(.020)	(.029)	(.041)
District population	.023	.130	−.055
(in 100,000s)	(.170)	(.185)	(.314)
Freshman	−.953#	−1.060	−1.725
	(.493)	(.732)	(1.069)
Ideological extremism	2.121*	.380	−1.045
	(.825)	(1.322)	(1.697)
Incumbent spending		−.377	−.765#
(per capita)		(.431)	(.449)
Incumbent spending squared		.036	.074#
(per capita)		(.040)	(.039)
Incumbents in 1980	.466		
	(.887)		
Incumbents in 1990	.803	.617	
	(.661)	(1.160)	
Incumbents in 2000	.110	−1.206	−2.362*
	(.721)	(1.178)	(1.010)
Previous margin of victory	−.068***	−.023	−.032
	(.014)	(.018)	(.027)
Republican incumbent in 1970	1.414*		
	(.630)		
Republican incumbent in 1990	1.007	.617	.974
	(.640)	(.051)	(.823)
Seniority	.085*	.078	.041
	(.040)	(.051)	(.093)
Constant	−3.840***	−5.704***	−2.799#
	(1.126)	(1.451)	(1.527)
N	1175	859	555

# p < .1 *p < .05 **p < .01 ***p < .001.

Notes

Estimates are rare events logit coefficients with robust standard errors in parentheses.

Dependent variable is whether the sitting incumbent member of the U.S. House was defeated, coded 1 for members who lost and 0 otherwise.

Model 1 includes the results for the 1970, 1980, 1990, and 2000 elections; Model 2 includes the results for the 1980, 1990, and 2000 elections; and Model 3 includes the results for the 1990 and 2000 elections.

results of models investigating this relationship when the dependent variable is operationalized in a dichotomous fashion, coded 0 if the incumbent House member won re-election and 1 if the member was unsuccessful in the attempt at re-election.[53]

Table 3.4 lists the results of models estimating the probability that an incumbent will not win re-election. Model 1 includes the results from 1970, 1980, 1990, and 2000. It shows that facing a quality challenger, ideological extremism on roll-call votes, running as a Democratic incumbent in the Reagan landslide of 1980 and as a Republican in 1970, and longer tenure increased the probability of defeat. Conversely, higher previous victory margins and a more favorable partisan district makeup reduced the likelihood that incumbents would lose their seats in Congress. Of greatest relevance to the present study is that district population had no significant effect on whether an incumbent U.S. House member would suffer a loss in the general election.

Model 2 excludes 1970 and reintroduces the campaign spending variables. Challenger spending increases the probability of defeat, although the effects are reversed at higher levels of spending. The significance levels for some of the variables in the model change when comparing Models 1 and 2, but the story for district population is the same, as the effect of this variable remains insignificant.

Model 3 limits the analysis to 1990 and 2000 and reaffirms support for the null hypothesis. If an incumbent representative is toppled by a challenger at the polls, the population of the district is an inconsequential part of this dynamic. An enlarged constituency may cost a few extra points for the incumbent come election time, but its effect in House elections is not enough to ultimately tip the balance in favor of the challenger after traditional electoral factors are accounted for.

Conclusion

The findings presented in this chapter reinforce the validity of the results produced in earlier studies establishing a negative linkage between constituency population and the margin of victory incumbent politicians achieve over their challengers.[54] The chapter's major empirical contribution is to corroborate that this relationship exists in elections for the U.S. House. In a pooled regression analysis of four elections where current census estimates of district population levels were available, an increment of 100,000 citizens cost incumbents seeking re-election to the U.S. House 1.4 points off their margin of victory. Considering the mean House district population climbed from 469,087 in 1970 to 646,498 in 2000, this figure is not inconsequential. Though incumbents have additional votes to spare in most contests for the House, this development is one countervailing trend in modern congressional elections that introduces competition into the process. Still, other forces, such as residential migration patterns where individuals choose to live in closer proximity to like-minded partisans, creating more politically homogeneous districts; gerrymanders that protect incumbents; the lack of quality challengers with adequate financial resources to compete with incumbents; and the substantial institutional advantages that members of the House can bring to bear to enhance their reputation with their constituents to ward off potential competitors, all overwhelm the disadvantage of running in a larger constituency. The advantages that have accrued to incumbents in these other areas over the time frame investigated in this chapter have superseded the costs of running in more heavily populated districts for members of the U.S. House.

The paradox of rising constituency population levels and less competitive House elections can be understood with clarity when the other principal finding of this chapter is focused upon. A more bountiful number of constituents may shave a few points off their margins of victory but it does not raise the odds of representatives losing their seats in Congress. This observation supports previous research demonstrating the lack of consequence state population has for the likelihood an incumbent senator will win re-election.[55] State constituencies have expanded, yet Senate elections have become a bit less competitive, so it is reasonable to find a congruent development for the House as well. The upsurge in the ratio of population per representative of the U.S. House may not be a blessing for incumbents, although it is only a marginal dose of additional competition.

From a normative standpoint competitive elections are the lifeblood of representative democracy. The electoral process is essential for translating citizen preferences into public policy outputs. Incumbents forced to wage a competitive battle to retain their office may be more highly motivated to respect the wishes of their constituents than if they confront a certain path to victory.[56] Therefore, advocates of more competitive elections as crucial in improving responsiveness to the public can find something positive in maintaining the 435-seat limit for the U.S. House.

Does the evidence amassed in this chapter mean that increasing the size of the House to remedy the growth of House district populations would undermine representation? While these results seem to indicate that larger House constituencies generate greater electoral competition, it can be argued that this development should not be viewed in such a favorable light. Generally, competitive elections tend to be celebrated by pundits and political scientists alike. However, the work of political scientist Thomas Brunell has shown that they might not warrant such positive reviews.[57] He contends that as elections become more competitive the number of voters supporting the losing candidate in a district increases. The ultimate result is that more voters are less satisfied with the representation they receive when elections become closer. Therefore, the key finding of this chapter could be interpreted overall as a net negative for representation in the House rather than a positive. A larger average constituency size leads to closer elections, meaning that more citizens are casting their votes for candidates they will ultimately not approve of when they get elected.

The less favorable electoral fortunes of incumbents that are an outgrowth of more populated congressional districts may simply reflect the reality that voters are less satisfied with the performance of their incumbent House member as constituency size increases. House incumbents representing larger constituencies may have a more difficult time fulfilling the policy and services demands of the citizens in their districts. Hence, their less impressive electoral performance is potentially a manifestation of the struggle posed by representing thousands of additional people. Indeed Chapter 4 will further explore the empirical dimensions of this relationship.

Chapter 4

Constituents
How Many is Too Many?

Introduction

The mantra from critics of the rise in the mean House district population size is that it leads to a less intimate relationship between the representative and the constituent.[1] Beginning with the Anti-Federalists, the argument has been that it creates a situation where members are more likely to lose touch with people in their district. According to one former House member,

> If we keep adding tens of thousands of constituents to an individual Member of Congress. . . . through no fault of his own a Member would become unavailable and inaccessible, which is just the reverse of what the Founding Fathers envisioned when they drafted our Constitution.[2]

As outlined in previous chapters of the book, comparative legislative scholars citing the cube root law of national assembly size insist that the current ratio of population per representative creates an overly burdensome number of communication channels that interferes with the average House member's ability to interact with his/her constituents.[3] It is this rationale that has led comparative scholars to propose boosting the number of seats in the U.S. House to conform to the cube root law of national assembly size in order to mitigate these effects.[4] Yet in spite of these claims, there has yet to be empirical substantiation that the increase in constituency population size has interfered with the representational linkage in the U.S. House of Representatives.[5]

The objective of this chapter is to investigate whether variance in House district population levels has any ramifications for the quality of representation the populace receives from its national legislators. Relying on survey data from the American National Election Study (ANES) and the National Annenberg Election Survey (NAES), this chapter employs a series of multivariate models testing whether citizen contact with House members, perceptions of how helpful the House member is and how well he/she stays in touch with the district, and overall job approval are negative functions of constituency population size.[6] Answering these questions will lend empirical clarity to the normative debate over the wisdom of increasing the size of the House to offset population growth. The evidence confirms the existence of a negative relationship, extending support to the idea that a more representative House requires taking action to prevent the average number of persons in each congressional district from continuing its upward spiral.

Constituency Population Size and its Relationship to Contact and Approval

Empirical inquiry into the relationship between constituency population size and contact with legislators has concentrated on the U.S. Senate and state legislatures. For the U.S. Senate there has been consistent validation of the proposition that citizens in larger states are less likely to report having contact with their senator than their counterparts in smaller states.[7] Based on data compiled from the ANES Senate study, a number of works have shown that a higher state population level serves as a barrier for access to senators. Not only do citizens have less frequent contact with their incumbent senator in the most populous states, this research also verifies that they are less likely to initiate contact as well. The connection with perceptions of helpfulness is equivocal, with some studies reporting that large-state senators are viewed as less helpful[8] while others find no link at all.[9]

At the state legislative level the evidence also reveals a similar dynamic regarding contact. One survey of respondents in seven states found that district constituency size reduced the probability that a citizen had contact with a state legislator. The effect was even more significant than the degree of professionalism of the state legislature.[10] Even though legislators representing more citizens have a difficult task in remaining accessible, they do not report devoting extra time to this activity. A 1995 survey of state legislators failed to establish any significant connection between district constituency population size and time spent keeping in touch with the citizenry.[11] In 2002 a replication of this state legislative questionnaire produced a similar nonfinding.[12]

The evidence for a causal connection between constituency population level and approval ratings for politicians is not as conclusive. Generally, U.S. House members, who on average represent fewer constituents than U.S. Senators, tend to receive higher job approval ratings.[13] Both Krasno's and Hibbing and Alford's examinations of the ANES Senate election study came up with a null finding on whether the magnitude of a state's population and Senate approval ratings were related.[14] Contrary to this earlier research, Lee and Oppenheimer, employing an extended analysis of data from the 1988-1992 ANES Senate study, estimate that senators from California receive a job approval rating 20 points lower than their colleagues in the least populated states.[15] An alternative approach using polls from the Mason-Dixon Company also indicated senatorial approval is a negative function of population size after controlling for other variables.[16] At the state legislative level, district constituency population has little discernible relationship to the job performance of the legislature as an institution.[17] State population has not been shown to be a consistent predictor of gubernatorial popularity, having varying effects depending on the model specification used in particular studies.[18]

However, little work has been undertaken to determine whether constituency size matters for House members' approval ratings or contact with constituents.[19] It is logical to presume that a similar pattern exists in the House, but it still must be empirically borne out. The magnitude of population variance for House districts differs markedly from state legislative districts both across the country and at the state level. The nature and requirements of the job responsibilities do not mirror those of U.S. senators or state legislators. Therefore, asserting that the nature and strength of the relationship uncovered in the research on these other institutions are automatically the same for the House is conjecture. To get a full understanding of the implications of constituency size for representation in the U.S. House, it is critical to rely on survey data that elicit attitudes toward members of this institution.

Models Testing the Relationship Between District Population and Contact and Approval

Evaluating the interaction of district population levels, contact and approval run into the reality that precise estimates of population are only available once a decade. Notwithstanding this limitation, the relationship can be tested relying on a series of questions about members of the House the ANES asked respondents in 1980, 1990, and 2000. Pooling the data from these surveys can help to determine whether constituency population size has any influence on access to or perceptions of House incumbents. As was the case in previous chapters, district population estimates are taken from the U.S. Census Bureau and measured in hundreds of thousands.

To assess citizen-representative contact, this chapter will rely on responses from two ANES questions. The first investigates the link during the context of the campaign, asking respondents whether they have had any contact with candidates for the U.S. House, including actually meeting the candidate, attendance at a meeting with a candidate, contact with a staff member, or have received a mailing from the candidate, read about the candidate in the newspaper, heard the candidate on the radio, or seen the candidate on television. The second question asks whether citizens initiate contact with their House member. It asks, have you or anyone in your household ever contacted the representative or anyone in his/her office? While about 70% of respondents said they had some form of contact with their representative in the years this question was asked, less than one-third actually reported being inspired enough to contact their representative of their own volition. Including both questions in the analysis can parse out whether the population size of the House district interferes with vertical communication between the citizen and the legislator, both in cases when the member provided the stimulus for contact and when the constituent decided to make the effort. Unfortunately, the ANES did not include these survey items in 2000, so the analysis in this chapter is confined to responses in the 1980 and 1990 surveys.

There are four questions used to tap attitudes toward House members. (1) If you had a problem that your current representative could do something about, do you think he/she would be very helpful, somewhat helpful, not very helpful, or does it depend? (2) How good of a job would you say your representative does of keeping in touch with the people in your district: very good, fairly good, fairly poor, or poor? (3) In general, do you strongly approve, approve not strongly, disapprove not strongly, or disapprove strongly of the way your representative has been handling his/her job? (4) Using the feeling thermometer, how would you rate your current representative?

Collectively, these questions gauge to what extent an enlarged House district population impacts how representatives are perceived by the people they serve. There may be more contact with citizens in less populated districts but it does not necessarily follow that House members are evaluated any more favorably because of it. The approval and feeling thermometer questions were asked in each of the three elections under study. The question dealing with helpfulness was only asked in 1980 and 1990; the item probing whether the incumbent House member stays in touch was included as a part of the 1990 and 2000 studies.

A variety of other factors have been shown to predict variance in attitudes toward members of Congress, and several of these variables are controlled for to rule out spuriousness. Scholars have repeatedly demonstrated that partisanship is a primary determinant of political behavior.[20] One would expect that individuals will be more likely to have contact with and approve of their member of Congress if they share the same party affiliation. In this chapter, shared partisanship is coded 1 for respondents who profess the same party identification as their representative and 0 otherwise.

Descriptive representation can also influence political efficacy and support for one's representative.[21] Constituents who share demographic characteristics with their legislator may feel more connected to and express a greater level of support for them. Two central components of descriptive representation well documented by the political science literature are race and gender. When there is racial incongruity between a citizen and his or her member of Congress there tends to be a reduced likelihood that individuals will express higher levels of support and trust for and attempt to contact their representative in government.[22] To account for racial identity, respondents who share the same race as their representative are coded as 1 and 0 otherwise.[23] Gender has also been shown to play a more mixed role in the likelihood of citizen contact with and level of approval toward House incumbents. The sex of the candidate alone does not have a significant effect on whether constituents have contact with a member of Congress.[24] However, there is evidence that sex congruence may positively impact the evaluations and vote choice for incumbents.[25] To control for sex effects on the dependent variables used in this chapter, a dummy variable is created coded 1 for persons represented by someone of the same sex and 0 otherwise.

Certain characteristics of the respondent's House member could cause variation in the accessibility and approval measures. Fenno distinguishes between members of Congress based on the expansionist and protectionist stages of their careers.[26] In the former, they must work harder to cultivate support in the district before they can begin to start investing more time pursuing policy objectives and power within the institution. When the representative's career in Washington, D.C., advances such as when he or she assumes a party or committee leadership position, there is inevitably less time available for the member to devote to meeting with constituents back home. This development may reinforce perceptions that a representative has lost touch with the district. On the other hand, a longer tenure in Congress increases visibility and voter familiarity within the district.[27] Multiple independent variables are incorporated in this analysis to represent the impact of institutional status. Separate dummy variables are created coded 1 for respondents represented by a standing committee chair or ranking member and respondents represented by elected party leaders in the House, and 0 otherwise. Seniority is measured by the number of terms served by the respondent's member of the House. A dummy variable indicating freshman status is introduced since first-year members are particularly mindful of the need to spend time working to acquire support in their district because they are not as well known as more senior colleagues.

Campaign spending cuts in many ways as it may increase awareness of an incumbent's activities, but the most endangered incumbents are also forced to spend the most money. To control for spending effects, inflation-adjusted spending is included in this analysis, coded in hundreds of thousands.

Additionally, several demographic variables are likely to shape whether citizens have contact with their representative, especially if it is initiated by the citizen. Age, education, and income are strong correlates of political participation and efficacy.[28] Higher levels of interest in politics also predict the willingness of citizens to engage in the political process.[29] This variable is measured in this chapter through the ANES question asking respondents how closely they followed the campaign. All of these variables are included in the models exploring constituent-representative contact, and perceptions of whether the incumbent stays in touch and is helpful. When modeling approval, respondents' attitudes toward the U.S. Congress as an institution may color how they feel about their own member of the House, even if these two variables are only modestly related.[30] Thus, strength of approval toward Congress is entered into the various models estimating approval as well.

Finally, the geographic size of the district is likely to influence how much contact House members have with their constituents. Greater geographic dispersion can pose a substantial barrier for politicians seeking to interact with their constituents. To account for this possibility, each of the models includes the geographic size of the district measured in square miles.[31] Because of the positively skewed distribution of this variable in the sample a log transformation is employed in this analysis.[32]

Based on the prior research conducted on the impact of constituency population size, several hypotheses ought to be confirmed in this chapter even after these multivariate controls are introduced: (1) As district population increases citizens will be less likely to report having contact with their House member; (2) as district population increases citizens are less likely to initiate contact with their House member; (3) as district population increases citizens will be more likely to believe their House member does not do an adequate job of staying in touch with the district; (4) as district population increases it will be less likely that citizens will perceive their House member as able to assist them if they need help with a problem; (5) as district population increases the probability of citizens expressing disapproval of their representative will increase; (6) as district population increases citizens will give less favorable evaluations of their representative.

Congressional Contact with Constituents

Table 4.1 displays the results of a logistic regression model estimating the effects of district population on constituents' contact with their incumbent U.S. House member running for re-election in 1980 and 1990.[33] Here the dependent variable is coded 1 if the citizen had some form of contact and 0 otherwise. It shows that, consistent with prior research on the Senate, constituency population size is negatively related to citizen interaction with the incumbent. The coefficient is in the expected direction and is statistically significant (p < .05).

In order to evaluate the substantive impact of district population across a range of values in this sample, Figure 4.1 plots the predicted probabilities of

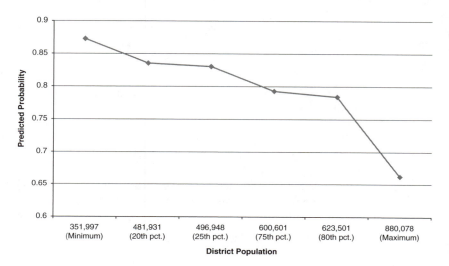

Figure 4.1 Probability of contact with incumbent House member by level of district population.

Table 4.1 Logistic regression model of constituent contact with incumbent House member

Independent variable	Coefficient	Robust S.E.
District population	−.237*	.105
(in 100,000s)		
Geographic size (log)	.177***	.051
Respondent characteristics		
Age	.013***	.004
Education	.096***	.018
Income	.038***	.604
Political interest	.604***	.078
Same party	.340*	.133
Same race	.079	.182
Same race*African-American	.758#	.412
Same sex	.135	.150
Member characteristics		
Committee leader	.771#	.416
Freshman	.009	.389
Incumbent's previous vote share	−.010	.006
Incumbent's spending (in 100,000s)	.059	.053
Party leader	−.951	.989
Seniority	.034	.038
Constant	−1.916	.879
Pseudo R²	0.101	
Log-likelihood	−1310.089	
N	2818	

#p < .1 *p < .05 **p < .01 ***p < .001.

Notes

Dependent variable is whether respondents had contact with their incumbent member of the U.S. House coded 1 for yes and 0 for no.

Data are from the 1980 and 1990 American National Election Studies.

respondents' contact with their House members, calculated holding all the other independent variables in the model at their appropriate means, medians, and modes.[34] An individual living in a district comprised of approximately 352,000 citizens (minimum value) has a predicted probability of about .87 of having some form of contact. The predicted probability at the maximum value of constituency size, about 880,000, is .66, a difference of 21 percentage points. The magnitude of this effect actually exceeds the differential for party congruence versus noncongruence, about five percentage points. In other words, the difference in the probability of a citizen having contact with the incumbent House member between the maximum value of district population and the minimum value of district population exceeds the difference between a citizen represented by a House member of the same party and someone who is not.

The previous section operationalized the dependent variable as whether the citizens had any form of contact with their representative. Table 4.2 breaks down which forms of contact are most affected by constituency size expanding. All of the coefficients for district population in these models are negative. The strength of the relationship is most pronounced for whether an incumbent has personally met his or her member of the U.S. House (p < .01). Logic would dictate that as the scale of district population increases, the chance that an incumbent would get to meet a constituent in the district is lessened.[35] This hypothesis is borne out from the results exhibited in Table 4.2.

Figure 4.2 shows that a citizen in the smallest district in the sample (352,000) has a predicted probability of about .24 of meeting his or her representative. This probability dips to about .06 in the most populous district in the sample (880,000). The fact that the number of citizens claiming to have personally met their House member is probably inflated mandates some perspective when evaluating this finding. Yet, it does illustrate to some extent that district population size does lessen the ability of legislators to interact on a one-to-one basis with their constituents. Representatives' time and energy are limited and they cannot make themselves available to all who wish to meet them. Having to serve thousands more constituents may create an impression in the district that officeholders are not as accessible as they should be, even if they are as dedicated as someone who serves a less populated district.

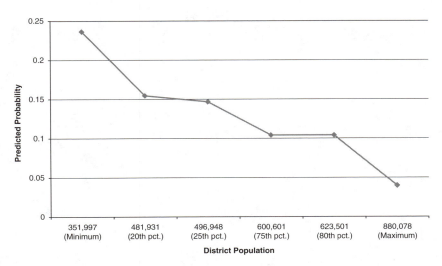

Figure 4.2 Probability of a constituent personally meeting with incumbent House member by level of district population.

Table 4.2 Logistic regression model predicting various forms of contact with incumbent House member

Independent variable	Met in person	Attended meeting	Talked to staff	Received mail	Read about	Heard on radio	Saw on T.V.
District population (in 100,000s)	-.398** (.137)	-.085 (.137)	-.218* (.095)	-.090 (.130)	-.114 (.104)	-.010 (.115)	-.102 (.149)
Geographic size (log)	.150*** (.031) .042	.139*** (.039)	.150*** (.043)	.004 (.046)	.008 (.038)	.126** (.047)	.106
Respondent characteristics							
Age	.016*** (.003)	.012*** (.004)	.004 (.005)	.019 (.004)	.010*** (.003)	.001 (.004)	-.004 (.004)
Education	.056# (.031)	.143*** (.035)	.144*** (.039)	.095 (.026)	.122*** (.023)	.023 (.037)	-.078* (.031)
Income	.012 (.012)	.008 (.014)	.000 (.015)	.030 (.010)	.031*** (.010)	-.001 (.011)	-.011 (.009)
Political interest	.627*** (.096)	.559*** (.125)	.745*** (.123)	.340 (.084)	.270*** (.078)	.183* (.090)	.195* (.086)
Same party	.239* (.117)	.466*** (.144)	.367* (.153)	.123 (.122)	.160* (.113)	.198# (.104)	.146 (.117)
Same race	.206 (.237)	.330 (.264)	.523 (.355)	.523 (.165)	.320 (.163)	.044 (.148)	-.492 (.189)
Same race* African-American	.068 (.451)	.234 (.593)	-.117 (.566)	-.450 (.495)	-.243 (.336)	.409 (.434)	.498 (.589)
Same sex	.199# (.120)	.238 (.173)	.440* (.186)	-.363 (.126)	.080 (.126)	.311* (.149)	.184# (.010)
Member characteristics							
Committee leader	.681** (.259)	.157 (.289)	.851** (.323)	-.340 (.388)	.478* (.240)	.766* (.381)	.324 (.355)
Freshman	-.717* (.280)	-.244 (.274)	-.490# (.264)	-.362 (.300)	.193 (.216)	-.085 (.313)	-.153 (.346)
Incumbent's previous	.009	.016**	.011*	-.006	.011#	-.002	.013#

	(1)	(2)	(3)	(4)	(5)	(6)	(7)
Vote share	.065	−.054	−.012	−.074	.014	.051	.150
	(.007)	(.006)	(.005)	(.007)	(.006)	(.007)	(.007)
Incumbent's spending (in 100,000s)	(.040)	(.046)	(.043)	(.050)	(.034)	(.046)	(.054)
Party leader	.203	1.009#	.246	2.414	1.183***	.784	Perfectly Predicts Success
	(.503)	(.535)	(1.014)	(.831)	(.367)	(.893)	
Seniority	−.034	.024	.002	−.010	.001	.023	−.022
	(.033)	(.024)	(.029)	(.036)	(.024)	(.038)	(.036)
Constant	−4.637***	−7.882***	−7.441***	−1.485	−3.081***	−2.152**	.188
	(.885)	(1.145)	(1.303)	(1.029)	(.829)	(.819)	(.892)
Pseudo R^2	.075	.090	.104	.077	.060	.025	.036
Log-likelihood	−899.856	−873.417	−708.799	−1313.397	−1388.898	−1411.6947	−1399.753
N	2212	2212	2212	2212	2212	2212	2200

#p < .1 *p < .05 **p < .01 ***p < .001.

Note

Data are from the 1980 and 1990 American National Election Studies.

Robust standard errors clustering on the House district in parentheses.

Citizens' Attempts to Contact Their Incumbent House Members

The previous analysis examined contact initiated by the representative rather than by the constituent. The model presented in Table 4.3 tests whether citizens' efforts to contact their representatives are a negative function of district population size. After controlling for the other variables in the model, the findings reported in Table 4.3 indicate that they are. The coefficient for district population is negatively signed and statistically significant ($p < .01$). Not only do citizens claim to have contact less often in heavily populated House districts, but they seem to try to make an overt effort to do so less frequently as well.

Shifting to the substantive effects of variation in district population, according to Figure 4.3, *ceteris paribus*, a respondent in a district at the minimum value of district population (352,000) has a predicted probability of .27 versus .9 at the maximum value (880,000). Constituency population size influences the

Table 4.3 Logistic regression model of constituents who attempt to contact their incumbent House member

Independent variable	Coefficient	Robust S.E.
District population (in 100,000s)	−.203**	.078
Geographic size (log)	.086**	.029
Respondent characteristics		
Age	.012**	.005
Education	.092**	.033
Income	.029**	.011
Political interest	.627***	.077
Same party	.173	.120
Same race	.246	.212
Same race*African-American	−.280	.668
Same sex	.193	.165
Member characteristics		
Committee leader	.203	.282
Freshman	−.363	.282
Incumbent's previous vote share	.008	.005
Incumbent's spending (in 100,000s)	.008#	.005
Party leader	.004	.667
Seniority	.056#	.031
Constant	−6.107	.949
Pseudo R²	.082	
Log-likelihood	−1080.524	
N	2795	

#$p < .1$ **$p < .01$ ***$p < .001$.

Notes

Dependent variable is whether respondents attempted to contact their incumbent House member coded 1 for yes and 0 for no.

Data are from the 1980 and 1990 American National Election Studies.

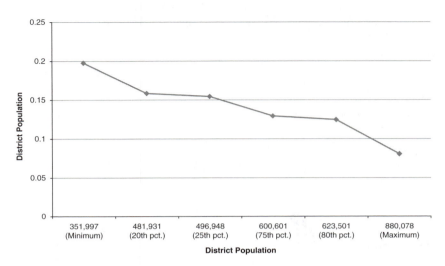

Figure 4.3 Probability of constituents attempting to contact incumbent House member by level of district population.

likelihood of an individual taking the step to reach out to a member of the House. In tandem with the results from the previous model, the evidence put forward here supplies confirmation that expanding district populations lessen the channels of communication between representative and constituent. Citizens in less populated districts are more likely to have had some access to their House member and a sense that he or she is more accessible, as is the case for the U.S. Senate.[36]

Perceptions of How Well House Members Stay in Touch

The data just presented demonstrate how the variability of constituency population can have an effect on the amount of contact between citizens and their members of the House. Merely because this evidence suggests less contact as the population in the district rises, it does not automatically follow that this dynamic will translate into how the member will be perceived by the constituents on other aspects of job performance. Citizens express a clear preference that their members of Congress avoid concentrating too much on happenings in Washington, and that they remain connected to the people in their districts.[37] In 1990 and 2000 the ANES asked respondents how well they felt their member of the House does at staying in touch? Table 4.4 depicts the results of an ordered probit model testing the extent to which constituency population size influences perceptions of the incumbent's ability to remain in touch with the people

Table 4.4 Ordered probit model of how good incumbent House member is at staying in touch

Independent variable	Coefficient	Robust S.E.
District population	−.196**	.065
(in 100,000s)		
Geographic size (log)	.079**	.030
Respondent characteristics		
Age	.017***	.002
Approval of congress	.179***	.027
Education	.015	.016
Income	.005	.007
Political interest	.202***	.051
Same party	.198**	.072
Same race	−.075	.092
Same race*African-American	−.265	.313
Same sex	−.119#	.069
Member characteristics		
Committee leader	.254	.165
Freshman	.019	.219
Incumbent's previous vote share	.007*	.003
Incumbent spending (in 100,000s)	−.010	.011
Party leader	.372	.233
Seniority	−.001	.019
Threshold 1	.249	.504
Threshold 2	.836	.499
Threshold 3	2.356	.498
Log-likelihood	−2160.978	
Pseudo R²	.065	
N	1984	

#$p < .1$ *$p < .05$ **$p < .01$ ***$p < .001$.

Notes

Dependent variable is how good of a job individual respondents feel the incumbent House member does keeping in touch with people in the district coded: 4 = Very Good, 3 = Fairly Good, 2 = Fairly Poor, 1 = Poor.

Data are from the 1990 and 2000 American National Election Studies.

of the district.[38] As was the case in the previous analysis, the sign of the coefficient is in the negative direction and highly significant ($p < .01$). Just as predicted by the Anti-Federalists and other critics of a larger House constituency size, there is a negative relationship between these two variables. Citizens in less populated districts feel their members of the House do a superior job of staying in touch with their constituents.

Figure 4.4 indicates that at the minimum value (396,000) of district population in this sample the probability of a respondent giving the incumbent a rating of very good is .17 versus .02 at the maximum value (1,062,000) of district population. This 15 percentage point differential in the likelihood of believing a representative does a poor job staying in touch is striking in its own right. That it

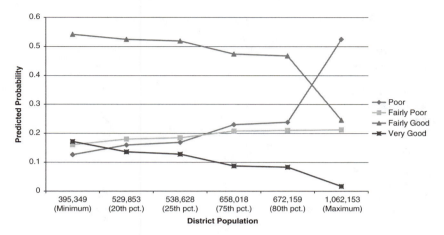

Figure 4.4 Probability of constituents rating incumbent House member as good at staying in touch by level of district population.

exceeds the five percentage point differential for the party congruence variable is also noteworthy. These data further corroborate the claims of scholars who maintain that failing to adjust legislative size to account for population growth does in fact undermine the representational relationship between lawmakers and their constituents.

Perceptions of House Members' Helpfulness

One of the key components in evaluating a legislator's responsiveness is how well that individual performs in the role of providing constituency service, also referred to as service representation.[39] People expect their representatives to provide assistance if they need help dealing with issues like a delayed social security check or a matter of local importance. In 1980 and 1990 the ANES asked respondents how helpful they believed their member of the House would be if contacted about some problem. Table 4.5 presents the results of an ordered probit model estimating the relationship between perceptions of a House member's helpfulness and the size of district population. To repeat a familiar refrain in this study, the direction of the coefficient for district population is negative and achieves statistical significance (p < .01). As constituency population increases, the likelihood the respondent's representative will be perceived as very helpful declines. One can conclude from this finding that it is a greater challenge to provide service representation as the numerical size of the district rises. Furthermore, it supports the assertions of House enlargement advocates who argue that increased staff and perquisites alone are insufficient to prevent a diminution in the quality of constituency service from the perspective of the citizenry.

Table 4.5 Ordered probit model of constituent perception of incumbent House member's helpfulness

Independent variable	Coefficient	Robust S.E.
District population	−.148**	.056
(in 100,000s)		
Geographic size (log)	.069**	.024
Respondent characteristics		
Age	.015***	.002
Approval of congress	.125***	.030
Education	.012	.015
Income	.004	.006
Political interest	.258***	.050
Same party	.185**	.063
Same race	−.011	.081
Same race*African-American	.010	.166
Same sex	−.065	.061
Member characteristics		
Committee leader	.364**	.119
Freshman	−.064	.140
Incumbent's previous vote share	.004	.004
Incumbent spending	.007	.031
(in 100,000s)		
Party leader	.507	.452
Seniority	−.013	.011
Threshold 1	.484	.453
Threshold 2	.576	.459
Threshold 3	2.133	.451
Log-likelihood	−2105.502	
Pseudo R²	.056	
N	2106	

$*p < .05$ $**p < .01$ $***p < .001$.

Notes
Dependent variable is how good of a job individual respondents feel the incumbent House member does keeping in touch with people in the district coded: 4 = Very Good, 3 = Fairly Good, 2 = Fairly Poor, 1 = Poor.

Data are from the 1980 and 1990 American National Election Studies.

The substantive effects of district population on perceptions of helpfulness are comparable with what was found for the in touch rating. Figure 4.5 reveals that a respondent residing in a district at the minimum population value has a .29 predicted probability of calling his or her member very helpful. In contrast, at the maximum value this drops to .09. For the not very helpful category, the probability is .15 for a respondent at the minimum value of district population compared to .39 for someone at the maximum value. This effect is greater than the corresponding differential for party congruence between the representative and the respondent, an additional sliver of empirical evidence lending credence to the idea that allowing the mean population size of House districts to rise is detrimental to representation.

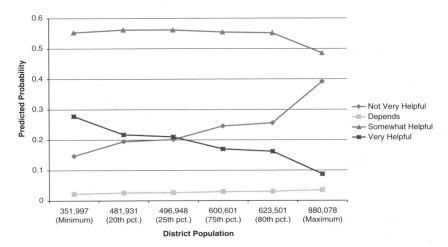

Figure 4.5 Probability of constituents describing incumbent House member as helpful by level of district population.

Approval of House Members

Citizens residing in House districts that encompass a wider sphere of population have less contact with their representative, view them as less helpful, and are more likely to see their member as out of touch. The next question investigated in this study is whether constituency population size carries any ramifications for the incumbent's overall job approval. Table 4.6 provides the results of an ordered probit model testing the strength of respondent approval as a function of district population with the appropriate multivariate controls. It offers confirmation for the hypothesis that House members representing more populated districts receive lower marks for their overall job performance. The significance level ($p < .05$) for the coefficient meets the conventional threshold required for rejecting the null hypothesis. Moreover, the substantive impact matches the effects of shared partisanship.

At the minimum value (352,000) of district population in the sample there is a .41 predicted probability that a respondent will strongly approve of his or her representative. At the maximum value (1,062,000) that value declines to .17. In contrast, a respondent who shares the party affiliation of his or her House member has a .49 predicted probability of expressing strong approval, compared to a .32 probability for someone who does not. These numbers show that constituency population size rivals party affiliation in its impact on approval, sharply reducing the likelihood that someone will voice approval of the job the representative is doing.

Table 4.7 bolsters this conclusion even further. In this analysis a regression model is employed where the dependent variable is the feeling thermometer

Table 4.6 Ordered probit model of incumbent House member's job approval

Independent variable	Coefficient	Robust S.E.
District population (in 100,000s)	−.121*	.056
Geographic size (log)	.049*	.023
Respondent characteristics		
Age	.010***	.002
Approval of congress	.180***	.030
Education	−.004	.012
Income	.001	.006
Political interest	.101*	.045
Same party	.464***	.060
Same race	−.044	.084
Same race*African-American	−.177	.384
Same sex	−.063	.064
Member characteristics		
Committee leader	.320**	.124
Freshman	−.050	.156
Incumbent spending (in 100,000s)	.011	.022
Party leader	−.221	.147
Seniority	−.004	.016
Threshold 1	−.748	.369
Threshold 2	−.269	.370
Threshold 3	1.046	.381
Log-likelihood	−2528.110	
Pseudo R²	.049	
N	2421	

*p < .05 **p < .01 ***p < .001.

Notes

Dependent variable is the respondent's job approval rating for the incumbent House member coded: 4 = Strongly Approve, 3 = Approve Not Strongly, 2 = Disapprove Not Strongly, 1 = Disapprove Strongly.

Data are from the 1980, 1990, and 2000 American National Election Studies.

measure of how favorable constituents feel toward their member of the House on a scale from 0 to 100. Inspecting the results in Table 4.7 reveals that for every additional 100,000 constituents in the House district the feeling thermometer rating declines 2.4 percentage points, holding the other variables in the model constant. It appears that having to contend with representing more people in the House district causes members to be evaluated less warmly than would otherwise be the case. Citizens residing in more heavily populated congressional districts feel perceptibly less favorable toward their incumbent House member, further empirical verification of the proposition that an expansion of constituency size weakens the level of support citizens extend to their representatives.

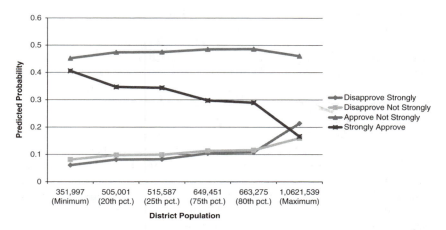

Figure 4.6 Probability of strong constituent approval toward incumbent House member by level of district population.

Table 4.7 Regression model of constituent feeling thermometer ratings of incumbent House members

Independent variable	Coefficient	Robust S.E.
District population (in 100,000s)	−2.441*	1.039
Geographic size (log)	.889*	.428
Respondent characteristics		
Age	.188***	.033
Approval of Congress	2.903***	.540
Education	−.405	.303
Income	.0489	.108
Political interest	1.808*	.900
Same party	8.688***	1.046
Same race	1.785	2.167
Same race*African-American	4.395	5.786
Same sex	−.878	1.029
Member characteristics		
Committee leader	10.901***	2.861
Freshman	−3.839	3.077
Incumbent spending (in 100,000s)	−.172	.439
Party leader	−2.930	4.107
Seniority	−.367	.266
Constant	55.446	8.053
Adj. R²	.111	
N	2635	

*p < .05 **p < .01 ***p < .001.

Notes

Dependent variable is how warm respondents feel toward their incumbent House members.

Data are from the 1980, 1990, and 2000 American National Election Studies.

Thus far this chapter has scrutinized the impact of district population at the individual level. Because the number of respondents per House district in the ANES is extremely limited it is next to impossible to draw inferences about whether any relationships at the individual level hold up in the aggregate. However, the 2000 National Annenberg Election Survey (NAES) has over 20,000 respondents who rated how favorable they were toward their incumbent House member on a scale of 0, very unfavorable, to 100, very favorable.[40] By aggregating these responses by congressional district where there are at least 40 respondents, any relationship between district constituency population size and job approval gains added confirmation. Previous studies have relied on the NAES to investigate issues of representation at the House district level.[41] In this sample there are 184 districts with at least 40 respondents who answered this question. This analysis supplements the findings already presented and helps to reduce the possibility that the individual findings are a product of errors resulting from the sample of individual cases included in the ANES data.

Table 4.8 presents the results of a regression model predicting the favorability rating of the incumbent member of the U.S. House at the district level.[42] These data affirm that negative affect toward the incumbent in more populous districts is not solely an individual-level phenomenon. After controlling for the other variables in the model, including race, sex, and tenure, an upward shift of 100,000 constituents corresponds with a one percentage point decline in the incumbent's favorability rating in the district ($p < .01$). The difference between an incumbent in the most populous district and the least populous district is

Table 4.8 Regression model of incumbent's favorability rating by House district

Independent variable	Coefficient	S.E.
African–American	−.331	1.933
Committee leader	−1.065	1.759
District population (in 100,000s)	−1.097*	.476
Female	−1.574	1.329
Freshman	−2.441#	1.459
Hispanic	−1.183	3.737
Ideological distance from District	−6.277**	2.311
Party leader	−4.600	3.181
Seniority	.237	.149
Constant	70.098***	3.348
Adj. R²	.117	
N	184	

#$p < .10$ *$p < .05$ **$p < .01$ ***$p < .001$.

Note

Dependent variable is the mean favorability rating of the incumbent member of the House based on aggregated responses from the 2000 National Annenberg Election Survey.

Ideological Distance is the difference between the predicted value of the member's DW-NOMINATE score and the actual value as predicted by the mean self-reported ideology within the district.

almost six percentage points. As the population size of the district rises, the incumbent is held in lower regard by people in the district. Having to satisfy an additional number of constituents can make a representative's job more difficult and places downward pressure on the House incumbent's favorability rating. The caveat has to be offered that this is only a sampling of House districts from one election year and that these results could be idiosyncratic. However, considering that the pattern is so consistent throughout the analysis in this chapter and is consistent with prior studies on senatorial approval, one can have some degree of confidence in the strength of this relationship.[43]

Conclusion

This chapter has examined whether district population size hampers the accessibility and approval of U.S. House members. The findings unearthed from a collection of survey items for multiple years indicated that this was indeed the case. Citizens are less likely to report having contact with and attempting to contact their House incumbent as the population in the district escalates. There also is a higher probability of them claiming their member is out of touch with the district and then have a greater propensity to believe their House member would not be helpful if they needed assistance. Finally, constituents in larger House districts evaluate the performance of their representatives less favorably and feel less warmly toward them. This evidence fits rather well with earlier research on U.S. senators and constituency size.

Collectively, the portrait painted here is one of damage to the representational linkage that has resulted from permitting the mean congressional district size to grow. It offers additional ammunition to the proponents of enlarging the U.S. House who insist that it will enhance the quality of representation the U.S. citizenry receives. Technological advancements, additional staff, and other perquisites of office have expanded simultaneously with the jump in the ratio of citizens per House district.[44] Representatives are not shy about exploiting the institutional advantages of their office and advertising their efforts to the voters.[45] The rise of the internet as a staple of the communications apparatus of House members both on the official government side and in the campaign may foster a closer relationship with constituents.[46] Yet all of these developments cannot fully militate against the demands that a more populous district brings, as there has been a downward trend in the ratings citizens give to their House members on district service and attention.[47] Americans want expanded access to their House members and expect them to maintain a connection to their districts.[48] A larger constituency impinges on the representative's ability to fulfill this expectation.

Overall, House members remain quite popular with their constituents even if the institution in which they serve is held in lower regard.[49]. This reality has not been fundamentally altered by the surge in constituency size that has materialized over the decades. The standing of the typical representative is such that he or she can afford a slight loss in his or her job rating. Most citizens can get access to a representative in one way or another and have their problems dealt with in a satisfactory manner. What this chapter shows is that it becomes progressively more challenging to do so as the number of citizens representatives serve rises and voters appear to notice. If present trends in population growth persist over the next couple of decades, evaluations of House members' performance may decline to the point that they begin to suffer noticeably for it.

A larger constituency encroaches on the representative's ability to fulfill this expectation, and more staff and improvements in technology are not sufficient to ameliorate this condition. As predicted by the cube root law of national assembly size, failing to account for this population surge by not increasing the size of the House in line with population growth has interfered with channels of communication between representatives and their constituents. A continued refusal to adjust the size of the chamber as the population expands will further undermine the representational character of this institution. Conversely, increasing the size of the House according to the cube root of population would reduce the burden interacting with citizens imposes on representatives moving forward. Chapter 2 included a quote from Rep. Alcee Hastings of Florida asking his colleagues whether they could serve as effectively when representing thousands of additional citizens in their districts.[50] His fellow House members may not have openly responded to this query, but their constituents seem to have reached a conclusion, and the answer is no.

Chapter 5

House Constituency Size and Voting Patterns

Introduction

Of the many forms of representation an elected official can provide, the most frequently studied by scholars of legislative behavior is policy responsiveness.[1] This representational component draws the bulk of scholarly attention because it is substantive policy outcomes that have the greatest potential influence on the citizenry. Other forms of representation are not unimportant, but ultimately it is representatives' broad decisions about the role of government that touch the widest number of people. The translation of citizen preferences into policy outcomes is one of the signature features that distinguish democratic political systems from other forms of government.[2]

One unmistakable trend in policy activity at the national level is that the U.S. Congress has become more ideologically extreme when the outcomes of roll-call votes are examined. The U.S. House especially has become an increasingly polarized institution in recent decades. A legion of studies has demonstrated that the ideological differences between the congressional parties have widened and the ideological homogeneity within the parties has strengthened dramatically since the collapse of the textbook Congress nearly three decades ago.[3] Democrats are more consistently liberal and Republicans are more consistently conservative when roll-call votes are examined using a variety of different measures. Both political scientists and journalists have derided this polarization as unhealthy for representative government since elites are more polarized than the mass electorate.[4]

The explanations for the rise of polarization in the House are linked to both internal procedural forces and changes in the political composition of the districts members of Congress represent, among other factors. One causal factor that has not been widely considered is the surge in the mean constituency size over this period. Rising extremism in the U.S. House has occurred simultaneously with the growth of House district constituency populations. Chapter 2 presented arguments, from political theorists and legislators alike, that a larger constituency size makes it less likely representatives will reflect the views of their constituents. This chapter investigates whether the failure to increase the size of the U.S. House in line with national population growth has had any bearing on the voting patterns of its members by pushing them in a more extreme direction. Multivariate models are formulated to ascertain the impact of district population size on the relationship between constituency opinion and the policy representation House members provide. The evidence indicates that as House members represent more populous constituencies they have more extreme voting records that diverge from the median voter in their districts. The findings reinforce the proposition that a larger House would improve the policy representation its members provide.

Constituency Size and Policy Representation

The American political system is highly responsive to public opinion.[5] Still, some observers allege that politicians are increasingly willing to ignore popular opinion in favor of the preferences of elites.[6] Contrary to this view, the most systematic analyses of aggregate outcomes in the U.S. political system demonstrate that mass preferences are translated into public policy outcomes. This evidence indicates politicians are highly responsive and often anticipate the public mood and respond accordingly. Furthermore, members of the U.S. House tend to be the most sensitive to changes in public opinion, as they face re-election every two years.[7] Even from a dyadic perspective, members of the U.S. House largely reflect contours of public opinion in their district.[8] There is good reason for House members to heed the policy desires of their voters, as several studies have shown that legislators suffer a decline in electoral support as they deviate further from the median voter of their district.[9] Though most House members provide policy representation in accord with their constituents' wishes, political scientists have demonstrated a greater tendency for congressional candidates to veer toward the extremes in the last three decades.[10] This propensity for candidates to move away from the center has coincided with an escalation in mean population size of U.S. House districts.

Despite the fact that it may be a highly responsive institution, members of the House are clearly more polarized than the mass electorate.[11] There has been a general upward trajectory in the number of citizens asserting they dislike the policy positions of their House incumbent.[12] Could the divergence between constituents and representatives on policy outcomes be in some way influenced by constituency size? As Chapter 2 described, the Anti-Federalists made the case that as the ratio of population per representative ascends, the likelihood that a legislator would represent the views of the constituency would decline.[13] This result materializes because the connection between citizen and legislator would be less intimate; legislators would possess the freedom to pursue polices that represented elite interests rather than the those of masses. During the course of debates over the institution's size, some members of the House predicted that as constituency size drifted upward the ability of constituents to influence their national legislators would be reduced.[14] Even advocates of smaller legislative chambers concede that as the ratio of persons per district rises the ability of constituents to exert control over their representatives is diminished.[15]

These views are congruent with the theoretical expectations delineated by scholars of institutional size. This perspective holds that as the scale of population expands so does the heterogeneity of a district. As a consequence, the likelihood that representatives will mirror the views of the citizenry is diminished. Dahl and Tufte describe this dynamic in greater detail:

> Size also creates barriers for representation of views. The greater homogeneity of the smaller community increases the chances that an elected representative will hold the attitudes of his constituents—even without any further communication after he has been elected. Any increase in the number of constituents makes it more difficult to achieve an accurate match between the views of voters and politicians.[16]

A more heavily populated legislative district imposes an onerous burden on representatives when monitoring the beliefs and attitudes of their constituents. The costs in time and resources that must be devoted to the task inevitably escalate. As a result, the flow of communication between legislator and citizens is disrupted by the expanding number of citizens whose views must be ascertained and accommodated. Ultimately, a larger constituency size makes explanation of policy positions a greater struggle as well.[17] The end result is an increase in the probability that the representative will deviate from district-wide constituency preferences.

There are empirical grounds for believing the expansion of the ratio of citizens per representative may foster detachment from the constituency and thus greater extremism in policy representation. A 1995 survey of state legislators throughout the U.S. found that district population size was negatively related to legislators' willingness to follow the preferences of their districts.[18] On the other hand, it could force representatives to modify their voting records to attract a broader segment of voters. Studies have shown that U.S. House members may alter their voting records to appeal to a wider cross-section of the state's electorate when they have plans to run for the U.S. Senate.[19]

The top priority of most officeholders is to get re-elected to their current positions.[20] To achieve this objective they must balance the need to appeal to the median voter as well as to their most loyal supporters.[21] In doing so politicians representing a larger constituency cannot satisfy both demands, and often opt to skew their voting records in favor of their electoral base rather than the center of the electorate.[22] Indeed, in some instances House members have been shown to faithfully represent the views of sub-constituency preferences within their districts better than they do those of the centrist voter.[23] Therefore, if larger constituency populations are more politically competitive, as has been well chronicled,[24] the upward trend in the ratio of population per representative should create a scenario where House members are further away from ideological moderation in their roll-call voting behavior. This hypothesis is formally stated by Dahl and Tufte: "The greater the number of constituents a representative has [the greater the likelihood there is] divergence in policies between representative and constituents."[25] Based on previous research showing that legislators representing heterogeneous districts tend to become heavily dependent on their core supporters, this divergence ought to be manifested in a voting record that caters to the extreme.[26]

This extremism-divergence hypothesis is empirically tested in this chapter with the individual representative as the unit of analysis in the 92nd, 97th, 102nd, and 107th Congresses.[27] If this hypothesis is correct, House members representing more heavily populated districts ought to have extreme voting records at odds with what would be predicted by the ideological composition of opinion within their district. To corroborate this expectation, a multivariate model predicting roll-call voting behavior must be specified that demonstrates that representatives serving more populous districts are less moderate than other members after other variables are controlled for. After establishing that House members are more extreme when representing larger constituencies, a second model is formulated to test the hypothesis that members are more likely to diverge from constituency opinion. Based on the expectations of previous scholarship, constituency size should be positively related to both extremism and divergence in roll-call outcomes.

Models Predicting Policy Extremism and Divergence

Constituency size alone does not shape outcomes on roll-call votes. Otherwise U.S. senators from the same state would mirror each other on the ideological continuum. An assortment of other variables also helps determine why a legislator may be more likely to amass a voting record divergent from the center. For the most part, House members tend to reflect the views of their constituents. More liberal members are elected from highly liberal districts and more conservative members originate from districts leaning furthest to the right. Moderate members tend to come from districts where the distribution of public opinion is most balanced.[28] Nevertheless, incongruities do exist between members of the U.S. House of Representatives and their constituents.[29]

Ideally survey data estimating public opinion within House districts would be used to determine the ideological makeup of a representative's constituency. However, due to the limited number of cases in each House district in surveys like the American National Election Study, getting aggregate estimates of constituency opinion for the U.S. House is problematic.[30] For instance, Miller and Stokes tried to draw inferences about constituency opinion based on an average sample size of 13 constituents per district.[31] Because it contains a larger number of cases per district, the National Annenberg Election Survey (NAES) has been utilized for this purpose in recent studies.[32] However, these data are not available for all the time points covered in this study. Another tactic is to use simulated estimates of district ideology through demographic data,[33] although these simulated estimates are also undermined by shortcomings like unknown errors and measurement assumptions.[34]

The approach most frequently used to measure ideology for U.S. House constituencies is to rely on aggregate election returns from the presidential contest at the district level.[35] Though it has limitations, the percentage of the two-party presidential vote serves as a reasonable proxy of the ideological composition of a House member's district. Furthermore, it may be an increasingly reliable estimate of district ideology than it has been in years past.[36] This method of measuring district preferences is utilized in the models formulated in this chapter. Specifically, in the first model predicting roll-call extremism, the percentage of the two-party vote received by the presidential candidate of the incumbent's party in the previous election serves as the estimate of district ideological extremism of the district constituency. For the second model, predicting divergence, the percentage of the two-party vote received by the presidential candidate of the Democratic Party in the previous election serves as the estimate of constituency liberalism in the district. A higher percentage of the vote signifies a more liberal district.

This chapter employs the most widely used measure of roll-call voting behavior in legislative studies, Poole and Rosenthal's first-dimension DW-NOMINATE scores, as the estimate of legislators' ideology.[37] These scores provide an estimate of a member's relative liberalism or conservatism on all nonunanimous roll-call votes, not just within one Congress but across time. Poole and Rosenthal introduce strong evidence that a single left-right dimension most effectively captures the structure of roll-call voting behavior throughout most of the nation's history.[38] For this study, two dependent variables are utilized to capture extremism and divergence in representatives' voting records. The operationalization of the level of extremism in the representative's voting record is the absolute value (.00 to 1.00) of these scores rather than the liberal-conservative (−1.00 to 1.00) formulation commonly used. A higher value is indicative of a more extreme voting record.

To measure divergence, the second dependent variable relies on the traditional left-right continuum as the estimate of roll-call ideology. In this specification ideological divergence from the constituency is operationalized by taking the absolute value of the difference between the predicted value and the actual value of the representative's first-dimension DW-NOMINATE score. This estimate of the predicted value is generated from an OLS regression equation predicting the member's DW-NOMINATE score as a function of the percentage of the two-party vote for the Democratic presidential candidate in the last election. This measure allows for an interpretation of how far each House member deviates from the median voter in the constituency. A higher value signifies the representative is more ideologically distant from citizen preferences.

Another determinant of roll-call voting patterns is electoral marginality. Most research on the link between these two factors has shown that incumbents who win by a narrower margin in the previous election tend to be more extreme after controlling for other factors. Rather than demonstrate moderation, political vulnerability may drive legislators to deviate further from the center and toward the extremes due to a greater need to pursue the support of their most committed political supporters.[39] To control for the electoral context that shapes a member's voting record, the models incorporate the share of the two-party vote obtained by the incumbent in the last election. Other electoral factors that may be influential are members deciding to leave the House voluntarily by retirement, resignation, or the decision to run for another office. Representatives not seeking re-election to the House may alter their behavior as a result.[40] Members running for higher office may have a strategic incentive to alter their voting records to appeal to a broader constituency.[41] One variable in this model indicates whether the representative resigned during or retired at the end of the Congress. Another dummy variable, coded 1 if the member sought higher office and 0 otherwise, is also a part of the model.

The South is a unique region of the country and its political distinctiveness has powerfully shaped coalitions within the House. Despite being elected under the banner of the more liberal of the two national parties, Southern Democrats have historically been more conservative than other members of their party in the House. Though Southern Democrats gradually began to gravitate towards the position of the rest of the Democratic Caucus,[42] they still are among the most moderate members in the House. As more Southerners joined the ranks of the Republican Conference, they have generally been some of the most conservative members of the House.[43] Two dummy variables are created for the models to account for the moderation of Southern Democrats and the conservatism of Southern Republicans.[44]

The sex and race of legislators may play a role in whether legislators vote in a more extreme fashion. African-American members of the House have consistently had some of the most liberal voting records in Congress,[45] sometimes even to the left of their constituents on issues like welfare reform.[46] Hispanic lawmakers have also been found to be more liberal than their colleagues, though not to the same extent as members of the Congressional Black Caucus. To capture the effects of these minority legislators, separate dummy variables are included in the model representing members who are African-American and Hispanic.

Research looking into whether female House members are more liberal than their colleagues is less conclusive. Some research uncovers greater liberal tendencies among women in the House, especially on women's issues.[47] Other recent studies have not found any significant gender differences on the liberal-conservative roll-call continuum after other characteristics are controlled for.[48] The role of gender in predicting roll-call outcomes in its own right may be in doubt. However, when gender interacts with party, a reasonable expectation is that Republican women are likely to be more moderate than other members of the House and Democratic women may tend toward the liberal extreme of the Democratic Caucus. Therefore, a pair of dummy variables coded 1 for female Republicans and female Democrats and 0 otherwise is added to the models in this chapter.

Majority party status may dictate how extreme a representative's voting record happens to be. The majority party controls the power to set the agenda in the House and has the capacity to structure the agenda to further the party's objectives.[49] Greater cohesion in the majority party may translate into more extreme voting records than is the case for representatives in the minority.[50] Partisanship alone may be a factor as well. Scholars have observed that Republicans in Congress have shifted further to the right than Democrats have to the left.[51] If this contention has merit, Republicans ought to have records closer to the ends of the ideological continuum, all else equal. Though Republicans were in the minority for three of the four Congresses in this study, the Democrats' minority status in the 107th provides enough variation to control for minority status as well as party. To test the effect of party and minority status, two dummy variables are formulated: the first with Republicans coded as 1 and 0 otherwise, the second coded 1 for members of the minority party and 0 otherwise.

Institutional factors such as tenure and leadership need to be controlled for as well. Members who serve as elected party leaders or committee chairs or ranking members are likely to have voting records further from the median position in the House.[52] This outcome is has only been enhanced by the 1974 reforms subjecting the election of committee chairs to the entire Democratic conference and the Republicans' more forceful attack on the seniority rule upon taking majority control in the 104th Congress.[53] There is evidence that members may become slightly more moderate as they serve additional terms in the House.[54] Tenure effects are measured the same way as in previous chapters, with variables for the number of terms served by the representative and a dummy variable indicating freshman status. Consistent with prior chapters the key independent variable in this analysis is district population measured in hundreds of thousands. Finally, a set of dummy variables representing individual Congresses are adopted for the pooled models.

Relationship between District Population and Extremism

The first model investigates what factors predict whether legislators will be positioned further toward the ends of the ideological spectrum in the House. The results found in Table 5.1 show that several of the variables have the anticipated effects on roll-call extremism. House members from more liberal or conservative districts, African-American members, Southern Republicans, and members of the 107th Congress exhibit more extreme voting patterns. Conversely, Republicans, female Republicans, members of the minority party,

Table 5.1 Impact of district population on ideological extremism for the 92nd, 97th, 102nd, and 107th Congresses

Independent variable	Coefficient	S.E.
African-American	.107***	.018
Committee leader	.004	.013
District population (in 100,000s)	.020***	.004
Female democrat	−.006	.017
Female Republican	−.096***	.023
Freshman	.014	.011
Hispanic	.034	.023
Minority party	−.060***	.008
Previous vote share	−.001***	.000
Party leader	.021	.023
Presidential vote	.006***	.000
Ran for higher office	−.008	.020
Republican	−.030***	.010
Retired	−.021	.013
Seniority	.001	.001
Southern democrat	−.143***	.010
Southern republican	.043***	.012
107th Congress	.035***	.010
102nd Congress	−.018#	.011
97th Congress	−.015	.010
Constant	−.006	.036
Adj. R^2	.392	
N	1750	

***p < .001 **p < .01 *p < .05 #p < .10.

Notes
Dependent Variable is the absolute value of each member's first dimension DW-NOMINATE score for the 108th Congress.

Entries are unstandarized regression coefficients.

members garnering a greater share of the two-party vote in the last election, and Southern Democrats tend to vote in a moderate fashion. There is no statistically significant relationship for the variables representing Hispanic members, female Democrats, committee chairs or ranking members, party leaders, more senior members, and members retiring or running for higher office.

Focusing on the principal variable of interest in this study, the coefficient for district population signifies that House members representing larger constituencies tend to be more extreme (p < .001). Controlling for the other variables in the model, a 100,000 increase in district population corresponds with a shift of .02 units in the absolute value of DW-Nominate scores. To interpret this statistic another way, a member representing 100,000 additional citizens is about 2 percent more extreme, *ceteris paribus*.[55]

When House members vote in a more extreme fashion it is because it reflects the preferences of their district. However, after the other variables in this model are accounted for, constituency population size appears to lead to less centrist outcomes. Although the substantive impact is modest, the key finding emanating from these data is that district population is positively linked to members having extreme voting records. Rather than producing moderation, thousands more constituents in the House district leads to the election of members prone to gravitating toward the edges of the ideological continuum.

Relationship between District Population and Ideological Divergence

The previous models showed that, in line with expectations, members serving a larger constituency are more extreme. This section of the chapter presents the results of a model exploring whether there is a link between ideological distance of representatives and their constituents due to constituency size. The results presented in Table 5.2 show that several of the variables have significant

Table 5.2 Impact of district population on ideological divergence for the 92nd, 97th, 102nd, and 107th Congresses

Independent variable	Coefficient	S.E.
African-American	−.023	.017
Committee leader	.010	.014
District population (in 100,000s)	.013**	.005
Female democrat	−.042*	.018
Female republican	−.057*	−.025
Freshman	.011	.011
Hispanic	−.042#	.024
Minority party	−.094***	.009
Previous vote share	−.003***	.000
Party leader	.025	.025
Ran for higher office	−.003	.022
Republican	.001	.010
Retired	−.014	.014
Seniority	−.001	−.027
Southern democrat	−.042***	.011
Southern republican	.022#	.013
107th Congress	.048***	.013
102nd Congress	.011	.011
97th Congress	.009	.010
Constant	.405***	.031
Adj. R^2	.169	
N	1750	

***p <. 001 **p < .01 *p < .05 #p < .10.

Notes
Dependent variable is the degree to which the incumbent House member's voting record diverges from constituency preferences.

Entries are unstandardized regression coefficients.

effects on roll-call divergence. Southern Democrats, female Democrats, female Republicans, Hispanic members, and members of the minority party are more responsive to constituency opinion. Conversely, Southern Republicans and members of the 107th Congress are more likely to diverge from their constituents' views. There is no statistically significant relationship for African-American members, Republicans, committee chairs or ranking members, party leaders, more senior members, or members retiring or running for higher office.

Concentrating on the main variable of interest in this study, the coefficient for district population signifies that House members representing larger constituencies tend to be more ideologically distant from their constituents (p < .007). Controlling for the other variables in the model, a 100,000 increase in district population corresponds with a shift of .013 units in the degree of divergence from the constituency opinion. To interpret this statistic another way, a member representing 100,000 additional citizens is about 1.3% more divergent, *ceteris paribus*.[56] The difference in the level of divergence exhibited for a member at the maximum and the minimum value of constituency size in the sample would be around seven percentage points. For some observers the magnitude of these substantive effects might not seem all that impressive, but by the middle of this century, with the mean constituency size pushing about a million per House district, the divide between representatives and their constituents will exceed even what is reported here.

While the impact of this relationship should not be exaggerated, an expanding constituency size is not an insubstantial contribution to House members' level of ideological divergence from their constituents. After the other variables in this model are accounted for, constituency population size appears to lead to less responsive outcomes. This result supports the divergence hypothesis advanced by the Anti-Federalists and institutional scholars. Constituency population size is not the sole reason why members might vote in this fashion, but it does appear that members are a bit less responsive to the median voter as the population of the district rises. District population does provide more explanatory power in predicting divergence in the House than institutional forces, such as leadership and committee status and seniority. Altogether, the evidence presented in this chapter supplies empirical weight to the notion that the ideological distance between representative and constituency is widened as the scale of district population expands.

Conclusion

Chapter 5 has explored whether constituency population size has any discernible impact on policy representation for the U.S. House of Representatives. The findings uncovered in this chapter suggest that it does. The size of the population in the average House member's district is not the strongest factor in predicting the degree of responsiveness evident in the representative's voting record, but it is meaningful nonetheless. The presence of a considerable number of additional citizens in the district has the effect of nudging the member toward the extreme. The result is representatives who are more ideologically distant from the district's median voter. House district constituency size appears to have modestly exacerbated the polarization in the House rather than acting as a moderating influence on House members' roll-call behavior. This research effort lends some evidentiary basis for observers who have expressed dismay at the trend toward rising elite polarization to have reason for concern. As population in the district rises, national representatives have a greater incentive to appeal to members of their political base, who are becoming increasingly extreme.[57] If the average House district population continues to expand, the prospect for greater divergence between constituency preferences and policy responsiveness will be heightened. Enlarging the U.S. House of Representatives could serve as an antidote to the polarization that has gripped this institution in recent years and bring House members more closely into alignment with the views of their constituents.

The responsiveness of elected officials to centrist opinion is a conditional phenomenon and fluctuates according to temporal trends.[58] The proclivity of House members to display moderating tendencies can vary regardless of the ratio of constituents per congressional district. In fact Congress was at least as polarized in the late nineteenth and early twentieth centuries, when House districts contained far fewer citizens. Many other factors have combined to drive the extremism exhibited by House members in contemporary Congresses. Such forces include redistricting plans consciously designed to group like-minded partisans into the same districts, the change in the nomination process of congressional candidates that has driven politicians away from centrist voters toward satisfying the wishes of political activists who demand ideological purity, and the ideological realignment of the U.S. electorate.[59] Many of the reforms proposed to remedy these developments, such as campaign finance reform, nonpartisan redistricting commissions, and changes to the nomination process, all have a higher probability of being successfully enacted than does changing the size of the House to offset population growth. Therefore, the impact of constituency size should not be overstated. Nevertheless, the population levels of U.S. House districts should be mentioned as a part the equation explaining what factors are driving elite and mass preferences further apart.

Overall, the association between constituency size and policy divergence is modestly positive. The greater the size of the district's population, the less likely representatives are to reflect opinions of the median voter. In smaller, ideologically cohesive constituencies it is easier for legislators to satisfy the policy desires of the citizenry. The growth in House district populations seems to have increased the distance between representative and constituents in the area of policy representation, as democratic theorists and numerous legislators predicted.[60] This empirical reality is another consequence of maintaining the 435-seat limit on the size of the U.S. House while the population expands, a divide that will only continue to grow if the status quo is maintained. In the domains of both service and policy, representation has been undermined by the decision to discontinue further enlargements House. While increasing the size of the House to account for population growth in line with cube root law of national assembly size would not be a cure-all for remedying the lack of responsiveness of House members to their constituents' policy views, it would certainly make a contribution toward bridging the divide that currently exists.

Chapter 6

Public Opinion on the Size of the House

Introduction

The previous chapters dissected the effects of the representational tradeoff that have emerged from the 435-seat limit and the subsequent growth in the ratio of citizens per House district. The evidence uncovered indicated there have been some measurable costs to representation. Advocates of enlarging the House can cite these findings in the areas of policy responsiveness, service representation, and citizens' attitudes toward their representatives to bolster their claims that an increase in the institution's size would improve the overall quality of representation its members provide. Notwithstanding these effects, it is unclear whether the U.S. public would favor an enlargement of the House, the ultimate barometer of whether lawmakers are responsive to the wishes of their constituents on this matter. Public attitudes toward numerous aspects of American political institutions are limited in scope. Institutional size is a domain that has been especially ignored by survey researchers. Moreover, there has been a complete absence of survey data probing attitudes about the size of the U.S. House and the number of persons per congressional district. So a question remains to be answered about whether the public would embrace the increase in the size in the House called for in this book.

This chapter fills this void by presenting the responses to questions on these topics from a national survey administered by Knowledge Networks of 1020 Americans. These three survey items deal with various components of the debate surrounding whether to add to the number of seats allocated for the U.S. House. The first question probes whether the U.S. public is willing to accept an increase in the size of the House to offset the growth in constituency size in order to improve the quality of representation, even of it means a less efficient legislative process. A second question asks whether the public would support increasing the size of the House to prevent states from losing representation in the House. A third question deals with descriptive representation by asking citizens if they would support enlarging the size of the House to increase the number of opportunities that women and minorities have to be elected to the institution. The final analysis includes an examination of support for increasing the size of the House based on at least one of the three questions in the survey. The responses to these questions can give some measure of how the American people feel about the size of the people's House. These findings offer unprecedented insight into public attitudes toward a critical aspect of the representational character of the institution in the national government closest to the citizens. This chapter makes strides toward answering the fundamental question of whether an alteration in the number of seats would improve perceptions of the U.S. House of Representatives or would inflict further damage on the reputation of the institution. It provides a more exhaustive analysis of these results, building on previous work I have done examining public opinion on this topic.[1] The data indicate that while there is not a majority in favor of increasing the size of the House when the responses to each of the questions are examined, approximately 56% of respondents expressed support for an increase based on at least one of the three justifications included in the survey. This evidence suggests that while increasing the size of the House may not be a wildly popular idea, it would not engender enormous opposition either.

Expectations Regarding Public Attitudes toward the Size of the House

Although it may enhance representation, there are sound reasons to believe that an upward adjustment in the size of the U.S. House might draw opposition from a majority of the U.S. public. Of the three branches of government, the U.S. Congress is consistently viewed the least favorably.[2] Approval of Congress fluctuates along with factors such as the economy, scandal, and other political events, but typically it gets low marks from the U.S. public.[3] While individual members of Congress are generally perceived positively by their constituents, there is a great deal of consternation about the collective membership of the body as a whole.[4] Richard Fenno discovered in his observation of U.S. House members in their districts during the 1970s that they routinely derided the institution in which they served as a tactic to gain support among their constituents.[5]

Dissatisfaction with the nature of the political process is a primary driver of the low regard most politicians are held in by the public.[6] American citizens think their representatives in Washington are compensated at an exorbitant level, have an overabundance of staff persons at their disposal, and are principally concerned about their own self-interest and the concerns of well-connected special interest groups.[7] Despite a surge in good feeling toward all political actors in the wake of the 9/11 attacks, many Americans harbor a strong sense of distrust toward the political system at the national level.[8] Most of the public dislike the contentious nature of political debate that goes on in Congress, as well as what is perceived as the sacrificing of principles that occurs when compromise is reached to pass legislation.[9]

Asking the public to get behind an increase in the number of politicians whom they hold in low regard does not seem like it would meet with a positive response. Even advocates of the idea admit that the rallying cry "Enlarge the House" is unlikely to evoke broad support.[10] At the state level the most recent instance of voters expressing their will on the issue of legislature size confirms this proposition. In 1994, as a response to a spate of scandals in state government, Rhode Island voters approved an initiative that reduced the membership of both houses of the Rhode Island legislature.[11] It is a not far-fetched notion to think that a sizable portion of the populace might favor a reduction in the size of the U.S. House of Representatives.

Despite the antipathy that most Americans feel toward members of Congress, they do evaluate the institutions of government separately from the politicians who serve in them.[12] Therefore, if it was framed as a way to strengthen the institution and make it more responsive, Americans might not be so hostile to the idea of enlargement. Furthermore, there is a desire among the public to have more access to their representatives and for those representatives to do a better job staying in touch with their districts. They crave more attention from and want to see that their representatives in Washington put forth a concerted effort to make themselves visible to the constituents in their district.[13] If it was couched as a way to improve representation, support could be found for lifting the 435-seat limit. Thus, it is not out of the question that Americans might rally behind a proposal to enlarge the House.

The numerical composition of seats for the House is not likely to be a salient issue for most citizens. Many Americans may be indifferent on a question like this one involving institutional structure. The level of political knowledge displayed by the average U.S. citizen is extraordinarily weak. Very few individuals can even recall basic facts about civic institutions and processes. For instance, only 30 percent of people even know the length of the term a House member serves.[14] Still, public attitudes toward the functioning of democratic institutions can stir a passionate response. There are strong feelings among many in the public that changes to the political process ought not to reward special interests or enrich politicians.[15] If Americans perceived that any proposed increase in the size of the House was being pushed to serve the needs of politicians, there could be an intense backlash. On the other hand, if convinced that such a move would enhance representation and bring House members closer to the people there could be openness toward the idea.

One of the key reasons to gather systematic data on this issue is to better understand public reaction to raising the 435-seat ceiling on the size of the House. It could have positive consequences for the representational linkage between representative and citizen, but if the public opposed this policy shift it could actually further undermine Americans' trust in government. Most proponents of a larger House fail to account for public opinion on the matter of national legislative size. They tout the potential benefits for representation but there is little consideration of whether the citizens being represented would actually have a favorable impression of this policy direction. Of course public opinion is not always reasoned and should not necessarily be followed in all instances. An increase in the size of the U.S. House may be a wise policy decision in spite of what the public thinks. Conversely, if a majority of the public were to endorse raising the 435-seat cap, then such a result would lend even greater support to advocates of an increase to enhance representation and make it easier to achieve this policy objective. To do so would ultimately fulfill the will of the people and demonstrate policy responsiveness. As Hibbing and Theiss-Moore point out, "The very nature of institutions and the processes they are seen to embody affect the way citizens feel about their political system."[16] There are very few subjects more fundamental to the character of an institution than its numerical size. If this policy course is one that either undermines or uplifts Americans' faith in the Congress or the broader political system, it would be useful information for policymakers and academics to have at their disposal in order to grasp the full ramifications of an enlargement of the House.

Questions Utilized for this Study

In undertaking an effort to empirically investigate attitudes toward the size of the U.S. House and its impact on the mean congressional district population size, there are no benchmark survey questions from which to take guidance. Therefore, this study will chart new territory in assessing public opinion on this aspect of institutional size. Ideally an extensive battery of questions would be utilized to fully probe the complete dimensions of public perceptions on this matter. However, unlimited resources were not available for this purpose, so only a handful of survey questions can be administered. Nevertheless, the survey conducted by the organization Knowledge Networks can tap into public sentiment on the basic research questions at the heart of this study. These questions deal with the tradeoff between representation and governance, the loss of representation for the states, and descriptive representation for minorities and women in the House.

Prior to a delineation of the rationale for the choice of questions, a brief explanation of the survey methodology employed by Knowledge Networks is in order. Knowledge Networks creates a panel using probability sampling techniques. Recruited by random-digit dialing over the telephone, the Knowledge Networks panel is the only online consumer panel that represents those who do not have internet access as well as those who do. Knowledge Networks supplies internet technology to the roughly 30% of panel members who do not have internet access at home. Research by Stanford University and others has shown that Knowledge Networks' panel data are often more reliable than findings from other research companies using traditional survey techniques.[17] Survey results gathered by Knowledge Networks have been used in a number of political science studies in recent years.[18] Thus one can have confidence that the results reported here are an accurate estimate of public opinion on this topic. From September 13 to September 19, 2006, Knowledge Networks administered the survey to 1425 of its members. The results presented in this chapter are based on responses from the 1020 panel members who completed the survey, representing a 71.6% response rate.[19]

Ideally, a vast array of questions would be available to extensively probe public attitudes toward increasing the House, but the funding for this study was not limitless. Therefore some questions related to this topic will have to be left for future research endeavors. While this book makes the case on behalf of increasing the House to improve representation, I intentionally tried to formulate questions that would try to achieve a balanced perspective in this debate. The overarching theme pursued in the previous chapters revolved around the tradeoff that exists between a small legislative chamber and a larger constituency size and a large legislative chamber and a smaller constituency size. A small chamber may facilitate a more efficient legislative process, while a larger chamber is more representative.[20] This tradeoff involving all facets of legislative structure forms the basis for the first question included in the survey.[21] Because of the rudimentary knowledge many U.S. citizens display about U.S. institutions, the first question is introduced with a brief explanation of the changes in the size of the U.S. House and the growth of congressional districts. In doing this, each side of the tradeoff debate is also included. The text of the question follows:

> When the U.S. House of Representatives was first constituted it consisted of 65 members with each congressional district having approximately 30,000 people. As you may know, the House of Representatives has grown to 435 members with each member representing approximately 640,000 people. Some have argued that the number of representatives should be increased so that each member would represent fewer people, would be closer to the people and provide better representation. Others have argued that a House of Representatives with greater than 435 members would be more costly and make the legislative process less efficient. In your opinion, should the size of the House be: (1) increased, (2) kept at its current size, (3) decreased.

By providing a detailed question that offers each of the major arguments on both sides of the debate, this approach allows for a nuanced understanding of public attitudes to be elicited. Those citizens inclined toward wanting to see a greater emphasis on additional representation through institutional reforms should support an increase, while those citizens concerned with gridlock and the cost of government may prefer to maintain the status quo or even voice support for a reduction. Though most of the debate centers on an increase beyond 435 members, many Americans may find a reduction an appealing option. Indeed, a few commentators have urged consideration of cutting back on the size of the U.S. House.[22]

The remaining survey items investigate two of the other representational issues that have arisen from a permanent freeze in the size of the U.S. House that have yet to be examined in great detail in this book. First, as was detailed in Chapter 1, one of the most conspicuous consequences of the 435-seat limit pertains to geographic representation. Several states have lost seats in the House over the past century. Preventing this practice from continuing has been one of the most prominent arguments advanced by promoters of House enlargement.[23] Even rapidly growing states do not receive an allocation of seats that is commensurate with their population gains. Yet there has been a visible decline in the actual number of seats for Midwestern and Northeastern regions despite the fact the population of these states has continued to rise. For the purposes of this study the absolute losses of seats for states is focused on here, since this norm once played a pivotal role in determining how many seats ought to be apportioned for the House. Would Americans favor a return to a process where apportionment no longer allows states to suffer a reduction in the number of seats allocated for the U.S. House?

The question gauging support for this proposition reads: "After the U.S. census is taken, every ten years, some states lose seats in the U.S. House of Representatives because their population growth is slower than the national rate. Would you support increasing the size of the House to prevent states from losing any seats?" This question serves as a straightforward way to assess to what extent Americans are concerned about the fact that many states are losing representation in the House due to the 435-seat limit. One plausible expectation in relationship to opinion in this area is that residents from the Northeast and Midwest may be more inclined to support an increase for this purpose than would citizens in the other regions of the country, especially citizens from states suffering a loss of at least one House seat following the last round of reapportionment.

One of the major claims advanced by advocates of an upward adjustment in the size of the House is that it would increase representation for women and minorities.[24] The logic behind this argument is that most members are elected to the House not by defeating a sitting incumbent, but rather when a seat becomes open by retirement, resignation, or death.[25] There is a greater likelihood that women will run for office and emerge victorious in open-seat races.[26] Women have traditionally made noticeable gains in the first election following reapportionment.[27] After each census, the number of new seats apportioned would rise, creating additional opportunities for women and minority to run successfully for the House. For African-Americans and Latinos, less populated congressional districts would make it easier to create majority-minority districts likely to elect members of these underrepresented groups.[28] As was discussed in Chapter 2, descriptive representation has long occupied a place in this debate. The Anti-Federalists were highly critical of the original size of the House because they felt it failed to ensure that a wide cross-section of individuals in society would get adequate representation in the national legislative body closest to the people.[29]

While the concept of descriptive representation is frowned upon by many normative political theorists, as Mansbridge observes, it may allow for unarticulated interests to be heard in the deliberative process and may grant the chance for members of groups systematically excluded from full participation in politics to demonstrate their ability to participate effectively in the governing process.[30] Furthermore, when constituents share the same race as their member of Congress, they are more likely to express approval of their representatives, all else being equal.[31] The same relationship is present for women represented by a female member of Congress as well.[32] Thus, increasing the size of the House might have the effect of increasing the level of political efficacy some citizens would feel toward the political system were they to see more people like themselves serving in government. To discern whether there is support for increasing the size of the House on this basis, a third question was asked in this survey:

> Some argue that increasing the numerical size of the U.S. House of Representatives would create more opportunities for members of under-represented groups such as women and racial minorities to get elected. Would you be very supportive, somewhat supportive, somewhat opposed, or very opposed to increasing the size of the House for this purpose?

Even if there is opposition among the broader public to an increase on these grounds, if certain segments of society who have faced historical systemic barriers to full participation in the electoral process communicate support for an increase, it could be a meaningful way to help build political efficacy among these groups of citizens. In reviewing the responses to these questions, particular attention will be paid to answers given by women, African-Americans, and Hispanic respondents.

To reiterate, a much broader set of questions would be needed to encompass public attitudes on all of the arguments put forward on behalf of raising the 435-seat limit on the size of the House. Notwithstanding these constraints, the survey items administered for this study touch on some of the main considerations that have been raised in this debate.

Support for Increasing the Size of the U.S. House in the Context of the Legislative Tradeoff

The first set of results gauges public support for an increase in the size of the U.S. House in the context of the legislative tradeoff between governance and representation. Table 6.1 reveals that Americans are solidly behind keeping the House at its present size. Overall, 61.9% of those individuals surveyed selected that option, while only 18.9% favored an increase and just 19.3 supported a reduction in the membership of the body.[33] There is some degree of variation across the subgroups listed in Table 6.1. Conservatives, Republicans, and older

Table 6.1 Support for an increase in the size of the U.S. House to improve representation

Respondents	Increase	Keep at present size	Decrease
All	18.9	61.9	19.3
	(188)	(618)	(192)
Party ID			
Republicans	11.3	70.2	18.5
	(42)	(262)	(69)
Democrats	23.7	58.0	18.3
	(104)	(254)	(80)
Independents/other	22.7	54.3	23.0
	(43)	(102)	(43)
Ideology			
Liberal	27.0	55.8	17.3
	(68)	(141)	(44)
Moderate	20.7	58.4	20.9
	(80)	(226)	(81)
Conservative	11.7	71.0	17.3
	(39)	(238)	(58)
Gender			
Men	16.5	59.6	23.9
	(80)	(289)	(116)
Women	21.2	63.9	15.0
	(109)	(329)	(77)
Race			
White	15.5	64.6	19.9
	(109)	(454)	(140)
Black	28.0	57.9	14.0
	(30)	(62)	(15)
Hispanic	23.4	56.5	20.2
	(29)	(70)	(25)
Education			
Less than high school	18.1	63.2	18.8
	(26)	(91)	(27)
High school	16.6	57.2	26.2
	(52)	(179)	(82)
Some college	22.1	59.0	18.8
	(60)	(160)	(51)
Bachelor's degree or higher	18.6	69.5	11.9
	(50)	(187)	(32)
Household income			
Less than $50,000	20.6	59.1	20.2
	(130)	(373)	(128)
$50,000–75,000	15.0	64.7	20.3
	(26)	(113)	(36)

Table 6.1 (Continued)

Respondents	Increase	Keep at present size	Decrease
$75,000–100,000	14.3	74.0	11.7
	(15)	(79)	(12)
$100,000 or higher	19.9	60.8	19.3
	(17)	(52)	(17)
Region			
Northeast	19.7	55.9	24.4
	(36)	(102)	(45)
Midwest	17.5	66.2	16.3
	(39)	(148)	(36)
South	18.1	63.6	18.3
	(66)	(233)	(67)
West	20.7	59.7	19.6
	(47)	(135)	(44)
Age			
18–24	24.1	62.7	13.2
	(21)	(54)	(11)
25–34	21.8	62.2	15.9
	(49)	(140)	(36)
35–44	19.1	60.3	20.6
	(35)	(111)	(38)
45–54	17.7	61.5	20.8
	(34)	(117)	(40)
55–64	21.6	59.2	19.1
	(33)	(90)	(29)
65 and higher	10.4	65.7	23.9
	(17)	(106)	(39)

Note
Cell entries represent the percentage of respondents who fall within each category.
The number of cases is in parentheses.

citizens are less likely to favor an increase. Conversely, liberals, African-Americans, Hispanics, women, and younger people express the highest levels of support for an increase.

It has to be noted, however, that for each of these groups the support for an increase is less than 30 percent and the disparities between them are quite modest. A majority in all categories favor maintaining the present size of the House. There is minimal regional variation contained in the results as well.

Despite the extremely dim appraisal of the job Congress was doing at the time of this survey, Americans of all political stripes do not want to reduce the number of politicians they send to Washington. These results buttress the conclusions of prior scholarship by illustrating strong support for the House as an institution, despite the hostility toward the actions of the members who run and occupy it.[34] On the other hand, citizens are not willing to go along with an increase even if it would lead to an improvement in representation.

In order to get a better handle on which groups of citizens are most likely to support increasing and decreasing the size of the House, a multinomial probit model was formulated to predict responses to this question.[35] The reference category in this model was support for maintaining the House at its present size. Several independent variables were employed as predictors in the model, including political ideology, dummy variables for African-Americans and Hispanic respondents, dummy variables for Republicans and independents, and a standard set of demographic variables, including age, education, income, and marital status. Dummy variables were also created for residents in the Northeast, Midwest, and West, with the South as the omitted category. Another variable was entered into the model measuring how closely respondents follow politics. Finally, this analysis incorporates a variable, indicating whether the respondent is personally acquainted with a member of Congress, state legislator, or local elected official. This variable was used to tap the positive sentiments of citizens who personally know politicians, since they may feel more positively toward them in general, raising the likelihood that they would favor an increase.

Table 6.2 reports the results of this analysis. First, examining the predictors of support for an increase versus support for maintenance of the status quo reveals that politically interested citizens are more inclined to support an increase, as are individuals who are personally acquainted with a politician. As expected, conservatives, Republicans, and wealthier and older citizens are less likely to favor an increase.[36]

Members of these subgroups are less concerned with bolstering the representational relationship that would come from increase, and are more troubled by the cost and greater legislative inefficiency that might ensue. The coefficients for the other variables in the model were not significant at better than the .10 level.

Scrutinizing the data on support for a decrease in the size of the House versus keeping it at 435 seats, one finds that married respondents are the only group significantly more likely to support a decrease in the size of the House. Conversely, women and highly educated citizens are significantly less likely to favor a decrease. The latter relationship is consistent with earlier work showing that more educated citizens tend to rate Congress more highly as an institution,[37] which may translate into less willingness to endorse a reduction in House membership.

None of the other variables are significantly related to opposition to a decrease. Women and highly educated citizens are more concerned about the loss of representation that would come from a reduction in House membership, whereas married voters do not share the same apprehension. Overall, however, the responses to this question paint a picture of public satisfaction with the size of the House. In spite of the possible enhancement of representation that might result from an increase, the American people are not willing to accept the tradeoff of a more costly and less efficient legislative operation in the House. However, there still may be support for an increase on other grounds.

Table 6.2 Multinomial probit model estimating support for increasing or decreasing the size of the House

Independent variable	Increase	Decrease
African-American	.269	−.236
	(.257)	(.278)
Hispanic	.297	.063
	(.284)	(.281)
Female	.201	−.377*
	(.157)	(.160)
Republican	−.399#	−.088
	(.207)	(.202)
Independent	.123	.123
	(.226)	(.226)
Ideology (conservative)	−.128*	−.086
	(.060)	(.061)
Age	−.009#	.004
	(.005)	(.005)
Education	.016	−.110*
	(.055)	(.050)
Income	−.040#	−.027
	(.022)	(.022)
Married	−.168	.442**
	(.164)	(.171)
Political interest	.188*	−.007
	(.089)	(.091)
Personally acquainted with a politician	.372#	.218
	(.214)	(.207)
Northeast	.195	.216
	(.235)	(.214)
Midwest	.089	−.198
	(.215)	(.207)
West	.205	.057
	(.209)	(.216)
Constant	−.376	−.160
	(.470)	(.466)
N	978	978

#p < .10 *p <.05 **p < .01.

Note
Dependent variable is the respondent's support for increasing or decreasing the size of the U.S. House, with "keep the same size" the omitted category.

Support for Increasing the Size of the House to Prevent States from Losing Seats

The loss of seats by states in the Northeast and Midwest has been one of the centerpieces of the case advanced by advocates of increasing the size of the U.S. House. Do the American people express any concern about this impact on the geographic representation? This section of the chapter provides the results of the survey question ascertaining whether U.S. citizens are in support of enlarging the House to prevent states from losing seats in subsequent rounds of reapportionment. According to the data contained in Table 6.3, Americans

Table 6.3 Support for increasing the size of the House to prevent states from losing seats in the House

Respondents	Support	Oppose
All	33.6	66.4
	(336)	(665)
Party ID		
Republicans	26.2	73.8
	(96)	(271)
Democrats	39.2	60.2
	(176)	(266)
Independents/other	33.4	66.6
	(64)	(128)
Ideology		
Liberal	41.2	58.8
	(104)	(149)
Moderate	36.2	63.8
	(142)	(250)
Conservative	25.2	74.2
	(87)	(249)
Gender		
Men	24.8	75.2
	(120)	(362)
Women	41.7	58.3
	(217)	(303)
Race		
White	30.2	69.8
	(213)	(491)
Black	52.7	47.3
	(58)	(52)
Hispanic	33.7	66.3
	(42)	(83)
Education		
Less than high school	39.9	60.1
	(57)	(86)
High school	34.8	65.2
	(111)	(208)
Some college	36.9	63.1
	(100)	(171)
Bachelor's degree or higher	25.4	74.6
	(68)	(200)

Table 6.3 (Continued)

Respondents	Support	Oppose
Household income		
Less than $50,000	35.6	64.4
	(223)	(404)
$50,000–75,000	32.2	67.8
	(58)	(122)
$75,000–100,000	31.1	68.9
	(34)	(75)
$100,000 and higher	25.2	74.8
	(22)	(64)
Region		
Northeast	34.4	65.6
	(65)	(123)
Midwest	36.0	64.0
	(79)	(141)
South	30.2	69.8
	(110)	(255)
West	36.1	63.9
	(82)	(145)
Age		
18–24	43.4	56.6
	(37)	(49)
25–34	36.5	63.5
	(84)	(146)
35–44	37.9	62.1
	(70)	(115)
45–54	28.0	72.0
	(53)	(137)
55–64	27.8	72.2
	(42)	(110)
65 and higher	31.2	68.8
	(49)	(108)

Note
Cell entries represent the percentage of respondents who fall within each category.
The number of cases is in parentheses.

do not perceive this development as a compelling rationale to alter the size of the institution. Altogether, 66.4% of respondents are against the idea for this purpose. This view is consistent among a broad cross-section of groups in society. Only African-Americans give majority support for an increase to preserve representation for the states. A sizable racial gap is present in public opinion on the question, with Whites 22.5 points less supportive than African-Americans. This finding is consistent with the actions of members of the Congressional Black Caucus, such as Rep. Alcee Hastings of Florida, who have called for a re-examination of the size of the House. Considering the question does not explicitly touch on the subject of race, this divide among African-Americans and Whites is quite startling. While both liberals and conservatives are against the idea, there is a 15-point difference in the level of opposition, with conservatives more uniformly against it. Most women are also opposed, but there is a substantial gender gap, with female respondents approximately 17 points more supportive than men. As with the first question, younger people are more sympathetic to the cause of precluding states from losing representation in the House.

One striking aspect of the results contained in Table 6.3 is the negligible regional variation. One might expect that respondents in areas that have experienced modest population growth would be predisposed to support an increase for this purpose, but that supposition is not corroborated. Southerners are slightly more opposed than individuals living in other regions of the country; however, residents of the Midwest and Northeast stand solidly in opposition. Residents in these regions may not be familiar with the size of the House delegation in their states, but they should have some knowledge that slower population growth is decreasing their political influence. Just as House members have been willing to accept this outcome of the 435 seat-limit, the people they represent express little concern as well.

To gain further leverage on variance in public opinion on this question, a logistic regression model was formulated for this analysis. Most of the independent variables in this model are similar to the previous multivariate analysis, with one addition. To parse out whether any systematic geographic differences were overlooked in the cross-tabular analysis, a dummy variable was included in the model, coded 1 for residents in the ten states that lost a seat following the 2000 census and 0 otherwise. The results of this model are contained in Table 6.4. The previous analysis is largely confirmed. There is no significant regional variation, and residents from states losing seats after the last census are not more likely to support an increase the size of the House for this purpose. Alternative model specifications with interaction terms for state seat loss in tandem with region, education, and political interest also uncovered no support for the state interest hypothesis. Put another way, even highly educated, politically attentive citizens in these states are not significantly more likely to back an increase.

The impact of party identification washes out after the other variables are controlled for in the multivariate analysis, although conservative ideological identification is marginally associated with greater opposition. Older persons are significantly less likely to back an increase to enhance state representation. The pattern of support from African-Americans and women holds in this analysis as well. The coefficients for these variables are significant at better than the .01 level. Members of these groups are the most concerned about the representational costs of the size of the House failing to expand in line with the U.S. population. Altogether this evidence suggests that Americans are not bothered by the loss of representation for the states and do not find that it is a persuasive justification for an upward adjustment in the number of House seats.

Table 6.4 Logistic regression model predicting support for increasing the size of the House to prevent states from losing seats in the House

Independent variable	Coefficient	S.E.
Northeast	.387	.301
Midwest	.471	.299
West	.324	.241
Respondent's state lost a house seat in the 2000 census	−.106	.272
Republican	−.284	.220
Independent	−.217	.257
Ideology (conservative)	−.122#	.066
Age	−.012*	.005
Education	−.105#	.063
Income	−.017	.024
Political interest	.048	.101
African-American	.781**	.296
Hispanic	−.026	.315
Female	.772***	.174
Married	−.233	.184
Constant	.373	.506
Log-likelihood	−584	.604
Pseudo R²	.072	
N	984	

#p < .10 *p < .05 **p < .01 ***p < .001.

Note
Dependent variable is the respondent's support for increasing the size of the House to prevent states from losing seats, coded 1 for support and 0 otherwise.

Support for Increasing the Size of the U.S. to Enhance Descriptive Representation

Thus far the evidence presented in this chapter indicates that there is no public enthusiasm for increasing the size of the House to improve the quality of representation House members provide or to end the practice of subtracting from the apportionment of seats from states with lagging population growth. This analysis explores whether Americans are receptive to enlarging the numerical composition of the House to enhance the prospects for women and minorities to gain additional opportunities to be elected and serve in the body. As shown in Table 6.5, there is almost a split decision on this question: 15.5% of respondents are very supportive of the idea, 33.1% are somewhat supportive, 29.6% are somewhat opposed, and 21.8% are very opposed. Combining the response categories produces a figure of 48.6% in support, just short of a majority.

Though a slight majority remains opposed to an increase, the cause of descriptive representation generates the largest reservoir of support from the U.S. public on behalf of taking this policy action. Giving members of underrepresented

Table 6.5 Support for an increase in the size of the House to increase the chances of women and minorities getting elected

Respondents	Very supportive	Somewhat supportive	Somewhat opposed	Very opposed
All	15.5	33.1	29.6	21.8
	(154)	(328)	(294)	(216)
Party ID				
Republicans	8.2	25.7	35.2	30.9
	(30)	(95)	(131)	(114)
Democrats	22.2	37.5	27.1	13.1
	(98)	(165)	(119)	(58)
Independents/other	14.0	37.5	24.4	24.0
	(25)	(68)	(44)	(44)
Ideology				
Liberal	24.7	37.1	24.1	14.0
	(62)	(93)	(61)	(35)
Moderate	14.5	42.7	24.3	18.5
	(55)	(163)	(93)	(71)
Conservative	10.4	20.5	38.4	30.7
	(35)	(69)	(129)	(103)
Gender				
Men	12.8	28.0	33.6	25.6
	(61)	(134)	(160)	(123)
Women	18.0	37.8	26.0	18.1
	(93)	(194)	(134)	(93)
Race				
White	11.0	31.3	32.2	25.5
	(77)	(219)	(226)	(179)
Black	33.9	42.9	15.7	7.5
	(37)	(47)	(17)	(8)
Hispanic	23.6	31.6	27.8	17.0
	(29)	(39)	(34)	(21)
Education				
Less than high school	16.1	37.1	27.2	19.6
	(24)	(54)	(40)	(29)
High school	13.3	33.9	30.4	22.4
	(42)	(107)	(96)	(70)
Some college	19.0	28.9	32.0	20.1
	(51)	(78)	(86)	(54)
Bachelor's degree or higher	14.1	34.2	27.7	24.0
	(37)	(89)	(72)	(63)
Household income				
Less than $50,000	16.6	34.9	30.7	17.8
	(103)	(216)	(190)	(110)
$50,000–75,000	14.1	33.0	26.2	26.7
	(25)	(58)	(46)	(47)

Table 6.5 (Continued)

Respondents	Very supportive	Somewhat supportive	Somewhat opposed	Very opposed
$75,000–100,000	11.2	33.1	28.9	26.7
	(12)	(36)	(32)	(29)
$100,000 and higher	15.6	20.5	30.3	33.6
	(13)	(18)	(26)	(29)
Region				
Northeast	14.8	27.5	31.2	26.5
	(27)	(50)	(57)	(48)
Midwest	12.0	34.1	31.6	22.3
	(26)	(75)	(69)	(49)
South	17.2	34.3	29.9	18.6
	(63)	(125)	(109)	(68)
West	16.7	34.8	26.0	22.5
	(37)	(78)	(58)	(50)
Age				
18–24	31.1	33.0	21.0	15.0
	(27)	(29)	(18)	(13)
25–34	15.1	38.3	35.4	11.2
	(34)	(86)	(80)	(25)
35–44	14.3	38.6	26.5	20.5
	(26)	(70)	(48)	(37)
45–54	13.4	41.3	24.3	21.0
	(25)	(77)	(45)	(39)
55–64	17.1	20.9	30.4	31.5
	(26)	(32)	(46)	(46)
65 and higher	9.9	21.7	35.4	32.9
	(16)	(35)	(57)	(53)

Note
Cell entries represent the percentage of respondents who fall within each category.
The number of cases is in parentheses.

groups more opportunities to serve in the House finds a receptive audience among some Americans not persuaded about the need for an increase for other reasons. In fact, about 17 % of all respondents backed an increase for the purpose of enhancing descriptive representation, but did not voice support when answering either of the first two questions.

One must be cautious in interpreting these results because, due to the nature of this question, social desirability effects may be at work. Some individuals may simply be voicing support for this idea because they do not want to openly express their opposition to this cause for fear of being perceived as sexist or racially insensitive. A large body of academic literature has documented the social desirability phenomenon.[38] However, in the case the possibility is not as worrisome since Knowledge Networks conducts it surveys via the internet, lessening the chances that interview effects are at work.[39]

Unlike for the previous two questions utilized for this chapter, there are some major systematic differences in public opinion among various segments of the population. These results confirm the ideological realignment that has transpired in the electorate over the past generation.[40] Conservatives and Republicans are the least supportive of a House size increase to improve descriptive representation, while liberals and Democrats take a diametrically opposite position. Approximately two-thirds of Republicans and conservatives are against an increase on this basis, compared to about 60 percent of Democrats and liberals who express some form of support. The partisan and ideological polarization on this issue suggests that if policymakers tried to propose an increase for purposes of descriptive representation, a bipartisan consensus on the matter might not emerge. These data also lend credence to the notion that race is still an important cleavage dividing party followers in the electorate,[41] contrary to the conclusions of some scholars who contend it has faded in importance.[42]

A further inspection of these data brings to light that a gender gap exists on this question, just as it does on other policy issues as well.[43] About 55.8% of women are behind the idea, compared to only 40.8% of men. This gap is substantial but it pales in comparison with the racial gap that exists on this question. Over three-quarters of African-Americans want to see the House enlarged to enhance descriptive representation, and slightly more than 55% of Hispanics are in favor as well. In contrast, only about 42% of Whites offer some degree of support. This cavernous divide, particularly between Blacks and Whites, is highly illustrative of the different conceptions of matters of race and representation that are still present in U.S. society. African-Americans still feel there are strides that need to be made in opening up the political process, while most White Americans do not see the same need to alter institutional arrangements to help the electoral prospects of women and minorities.[44] This question is another area where racial division is present in public opinion just as it is on a variety of other issues.[45]

Age differences also exist in attitudes toward a House size increase for better descriptive representation, especially at the two ends of the age spectrum. The youngest age cohort, 18–24 years old, expresses 64.1% support, compared to 30.2% support from individuals over 65. There are some slight regional differences in reactions to this question but not necessarily what would be anticipated. Solid majorities of residents in the Northeast and Midwest reject this idea, while a majority of Southerners and Westerners are in favor. However, this finding could be a function of the high concentrations of minorities in parts of the South and West.[46]

To rule out the possibility that the preceding analysis consisted of any spurious relationships, a multivariate analysis employing an ordered probit model was undertaken. The independent variables utilized in this analysis are similar to the previous multivariate models presented in this chapter, with one addition. A dummy variable indicating a respondent's status as a gay, lesbian, or bisexual American was incorporated to account for the possibility that members of this community may be more receptive to enhancement of descriptive representation. Table 6.6 generally bolsters the conclusions of the study thus far.

Table 6.6 Ordered probit model of support for increasing the size of the House to increase representation for women and minorities

Independent variable	Coefficient	Robust S.E.
African-American	.553***	.142
Hispanic	.216	.165
Female	.290***	.083
Republican	−.376***	.108
Independent	−.264*	.135
Ideology (conservative)	−.110**	.035
Age	−.011***	.003
Education	.035	.029
Income	−.035**	.013
Married	−.199*	.086
Gay/Lesbian/Bisexual	−.693#	.402
Political interest	−.050	.049
Northeast	−.064	.119
Midwest	.003	.106
West	−.056	.119
Threshold 1	−2.310	.266
Threshold 2	−1.394	.262
Threshold 3	−.274	.255
Pseudo R²	.080	
N	980	

#p < .10 *p < .05 **p < .01 ***p < .001.

Note
Dependent variable is the respondent's level of support for increasing the size of the House to increase representation for women and racial minorities, coded: 4 = Very Supportive, 3 = Somewhat Supportive, 2 = Somewhat Opposed, 1 = Very Opposed.

Republicans, conservatives, older persons, and married individuals are all significantly less likely to support an increase to help more women and minorities get elected. Consistent with the class divide present in the American political landscape,[47] wealthier citizens have a lower inclination to support House size expansion to aid descriptive representation. Political independents are also less likely to lend their support to an increase. Contrary to expectations, gay, lesbian, or bisexual status is negatively related to higher levels of support. In contrast, the two strongest predictors of support were status as a woman or an African-American. These two subgroups have been the most consistent supporters of representation in the context of the size of the U.S. House.

To expand on this premise, Figure 6.1 depicts the predicted probabilities of the level of support for white male and female Democrats, White male and female Republicans, and African-American male and female Democrats, holding all the other variables in the model at their appropriate means, medians, and modes.[48] The average African-American female Democrat has a predicted probability of .40 of being very supportive or somewhat supportive of an increase. The corresponding figures for African-American males are .30 and .40,

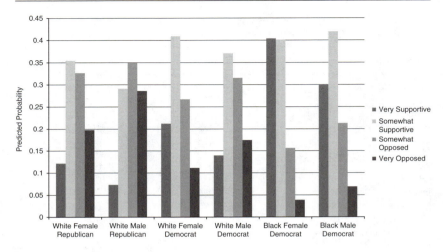

Figure 6.1 Probability of support for increasing the size of the U.S. House to increase the chances of women and minorities getting elected.

respectively. The numbers for white male Republicans are completely at odds with the story for African-Americans. For the typical member of this group the predicted probability of being very supportive is .07, and .29, for the somewhat supportive category. The estimates for White female Republicans are .12 and .35 for the same categories. The average White male Democrat is notably more supportive than a Republican with the same characteristics but more likely to voice some form of opposition than an African-American Democrat (Very Supportive = .14; Somewhat Supportive = .37). The role of gender is evident, with the predicted probabilities for White female Democrats .21 for the very supportive category and .41 for the somewhat supportive category.

These numbers are indicative of the importance party, gender, and race play in determining the role that representation should play in the institutional design of the national legislature. The groups in society that are most under-represented in the nation's political system are the citizens most likely to embrace enlarging the institution to further the cause of descriptive representation. These results supply more evidence of the representational benefits that would be spawned for certain segments of society by enlarging the size of the House. African-Americans and women are generally more favorable to the type of representation they receive when there is racial and gender congruence with their member of Congress.[49] Allocating extra positions in the U.S. House could elevate the likelihood that women and minorities would be represented by someone like themselves and potentially feel that the broader political system is more efficacious. There are already intense partisan and ideological disagreements about the propriety of overt government efforts to aid women and minorities, and these fault lines are only heightened even further when race and sex become a part of the equation. Not surprisingly, it is the politics of race and the rights of women that most polarize the U.S. public on the underlying principles that warrant an increase in the size of the House.

Support for Increasing the House Based on at Least One Justification

Thus far, support for increasing the House has been gauged by examining the responses to each individual question. This final analysis reviews support across questions by combing the responses to all three questions and calculating the number of respondents who voiced support for increasing the House on at least one question. Viewed from this perspective House enlargement is reflective of the public will. According to the data in Table 6.7, overall 55.6 per cent of respondents surveyed said they would support increasing the House for at

Table 6.7 Support for increasing the size of the House on at least one question

Respondents	Support on at least one question	Oppose on all three questions
All	55.6	44.4
	(544)	(435)
Party ID		
Republicans	43.2	56.8
	(159)	(209)
Democrats	65.8	34.2
	(283)	(147)
Independents/other	56.7	43.3
	(102)	(78)
Ideology		
Liberal	68.0	32.0
	(168)	(79)
Moderate	61.3	38.7
	(231)	(146)
Conservative	41.9	58.1
	(140)	(194)
Gender		
Men	46.6	53.4
	(221)	(253)
Women	64.0	36.0
	(322)	(181)
Race		
White	49.6	50.4
	(347)	(352)
Black	78.6	21.4
	(81)	(22)
Hispanic	64.4	35.6
	(76)	(42)

Table 6.7 (Continued)

Respondents	Support on at least one question	Oppose on all three questions
Education		
Less than high school	64.1	35.9
	(91)	(51)
High school	54.7	45.3
	(170)	(141)
Some college	56.1	43.9
	(148)	(116)
Bachelor's degree or higher	51.5	48.5
	(135)	(127)
Household income		
Less than $50,000	59.1	40.9
	(363)	(251)
$50,000–75,000	51.4	48.6
	(89)	(84)
$75,000–100,000	49.1	50.9
	(52)	(54)
$100,000 and higher	46.5	53.5
	(40)	(46)
Region		
Northeast	46.3	53.7
	(82)	(95)
Midwest	54.3	45.7
	(119)	(100)
South	57.2	42.8
	(206)	(154)
West	61.5	38.5
	(136)	(85)
Age		
18–24	73.3	26.7
	(63)	(23)
25–34	61.6	38.4
	(135)	(84)
35–44	58.0	42.0
	(105)	(76)
45–54	59.2	40.8
	(109)	(75)
55–64	41.7	58.3
	(63)	(88)
65 and higher	43.6	56.4
	(68)	(88)

Note
Cell entries represent the percentage of respondents who fall within each category.
The number of cases is in parentheses.

least one of the three reasons cited in this study. While there are still key demographic, partisan, and ideological differences among respondents, overall support is broader in this analysis. A majority of Republicans oppose an increase no matter what justification is offered, while 57 percent of independents and almost two-thirds of Democrats support an increase. Conservatives remain opposed to the idea and over 60 percent of liberals would favor enlarging the House on at least one question. A deep racial gap persists in the data presented in Table 6.7, although according to this analysis Whites are now split almost equally down the middle in favor of an increase. Altogether what these results signal is that forging a coalition of support among the American public across a broad spectrum of public opinion might be possible if the various dimensions of representation are invoked in these debates. While advocates of House enlargement should not interpret these results as a full-throated endorsement by the American public, they are not a wholesale rejection either.

Conclusion

The absence of available survey data gauging public attitudes toward increasing the size of the U.S. House necessitated gathering a systematic estimate of where Americans stand on this crucial issue. Simply because national lawmakers have taken it off the decision agenda does not mean it is unworthy of attention for survey researchers. The growth of House district constituency size and the tangible consequences for representation that have stemmed from it are deserving of empirical investigation.[50] Serious political observers who have weighed in on this debate have not had the benefit of public opinion data to shape their arguments. Proponents, opponents, and neutral observers now have some empirical data from which to assess public reaction. The evidence supplied in this chapter has gone a long way toward expanding knowledge of public opinion on this subject. The results presented in this chapter reveal a complex picture as it applies to public opinion on this topic. A larger House may be more representative but it does not necessarily represent a policy option the people would be favorably disposed toward. On the other hand, despite the fact that in each instance a majority of respondents opposed an increase, taken together around 56% of the individuals surveyed backed an increase based on one of the justifications provided. If members of Congress were to enact a sizable increase in the size of the U.S. House as advocated, it might not provoke a backlash and further undermine the degree of trust in the institution but it is doubtful it would be warmly received by most Americans either. In their totality the key findings in this chapter suggest that neither opponents nor proponents of House enlargement could confidently enlist American public opinion on behalf of their cause.

When the question was posed providing each side of the legislative tradeoff argument the vast majority of citizens selected the status quo. Less than 20% want an increase even if it would help counter the growth in the average size of congressional districts and improve the quality of representation. The financial costs and possible damage to the legislative operations of the U.S. House of Representatives outweighed the possible benefits that would accrue to representation. The U.S. public sees no pressing need for an expansion of the House beyond the 435 limit. It must also be noted in this discussion that there is no clamor among American citizens for a decrease in the size of the House either. Americans are not reflexively anti-politician, nor do they seek to make radical changes to the institutions of the U.S political system based on their dissatisfaction with the behavior and motivations of members of Congress.

There is no widespread support for an increase to remedy the recurring phenomenon of House seats being transferred from the Midwest and Northeast to the South and West. Most Americans see this outcome as a legitimate result of shifting migration patterns in the country and harbor no desire to reverse it. Even residents in the slowest growing regions of the country or in states that have had their House delegations slashed due to reapportionment are not motivated to support a policy of House enlargement to stem the tide of states losing House seats every ten years. It is a plausible argument that the issue is not particularly salient for most Americans, and that were leaders in these states to mount a concerted campaign to change the existing policy, opinion would shift in favor. That may be a reasonable assumption regarding the citizens of states which lag behind in population growth but not necessarily in the rest of the country. Perhaps advancing an argument that states gaining House seats suffer a loss of representation relative to population growth could generate broader support. However, the more likely outcome is that most citizens will continue voicing opposition on these grounds, if they contemplate the issue at all. Geographic representation in the context of increasing legislative size is poised to galvanize neither wide nor deep support in the U.S. population.

Without question the reason for increasing the size of the House that gathered the highest level of support in this study was the prospect that it would potentially enhance descriptive representation for women and minorities. Though a slim majority was against an increase on these grounds, the results revealed that this argument has resonance for many members of society. This sentiment is especially salient as it applies to women and minorities. Members of these groups feel they are underrepresented in the nation's political institutions and sense that an increase in the size of the U.S. House of Representatives would increase the possibility they would be represented by someone of their own social group and therefore express higher levels of approval toward their member of the House. In a nation as diverse as the US it would be difficult for the national legislature to accurately reflect the demographic makeup of society no matter its size. Still, a larger House would afford those groups of individuals who have been systematically underrepresented in government to have more opportunity to increase their numbers holding elected office. Descriptive representation is a topic that remains controversial in politics and political science but the potential for strengthening a sense of political efficacy toward the

Congress that could be accomplished by House enlargement cannot be discounted even by its most ardent opponents.

Beyond a more ample level of support for the descriptive representation rationale, what distinguished the responses to this question was the polarized reaction it generated. Republicans and conservatives overwhelmingly reject this proposition, while Democrats and liberals openly embrace it. A similar divide makes its presence felt along racial and gender lines as well. Hence, the justification for increasing the size of the House that has the most support also evokes highly partisan reactions. Still, even as conservatives might object to an increase on this basis, conservative elites endorsing an increase on other grounds could lessen some of these partisan divisions if this issue became a serious part of the political dialogue.

In an article previously published on this subject the conclusion I reached was that public sentiment was generally opposed to an increase.[51] However, upon greater reflection the appropriate interpretation requires more nuance. After reanalyzing the data from the original survey by combining supportive responses to each question as laid out in Table 6.7, the results show that a majority coalition in the American electorate behind this idea is possible depending on what representational frames are utilized. Additional justifications not posed in the questions used for this study could generate even further support. There are more important reasons to increase the size of the House than on the basis that it reflects public opinion on the matter. Nevertheless what this chapter illustrates is that the public is potentially receptive to the idea in the right political context.

A final caveat must be offered in assessing the validity of these findings that suggests support for an increase is more robust than was documented in this chapter. This survey was conducted at a time when the popularity of Congress was approaching record lows. For instance, a CBS/*New York Times* survey conducted during a similar interval of time showed approval of Congress stood at a paltry 25%.[52] Given this heightened level of negativity toward the performance of Congress it is not unreasonable to assume that under different circumstances support for an increase on all three questions may have been higher. This assumption is particularly relevant when applied to Democrats and liberals had they not been so disenchanted with Republican control of the U.S. House in the fall of 2006. Of course this speculation would require subsequent polling at a time when the performance of Congress was held in higher esteem in order to be confirmed.

Chapter 7

The Size of the House
Does it Really Matter?

The foregoing chapters amassed a collection of data estimating the impact of retaining the 435-seat limit on the size of the U.S. House of Representatives while the nation's population has soared dramatically over the past century. This study has built on some of the past research on legislative and constituency size by examining the case of the U.S. House in extensive detail. It has added a degree of empirical insight into what has been a largely normative discussion on the optimal size of the U.S. House and the growth of congressional district populations. The results contained this volume illuminate how these developments have impacted electoral competition, perceptions of service responsiveness, and overall job performance and policy representation, in addition to presenting the first original survey data gauging U.S. public opinion on this subject. Generally these findings lend credibility to the case for increasing the size of the House in line with population growth as a means to strengthen representational linkages between citizens and their representatives.

This concluding chapter aims to accomplish three primary objectives. First, it will restate and summarize the findings generated by this study and discuss the implications of the representational tradeoff that has resulted from maintaining the House size status quo over the course of the last century. Second, it will address some of the concerns raised by the critics of House enlargement surrounding the potential drawbacks of adopting this policy. Third, it delves into the future prospects for substantially increasing the size of the U.S. House in the context of the present political environment.

Summary of the Findings

Chapter 2 placed the contemporary debate over the size of the House in historical context. It was once a decennial feature of the American political landscape going back to the deliberations at the Constitutional Convention in 1787. The dispute over the appropriate size of the institution centered on a need to balance the chief requirements of any legislative body, enacting policy in an efficient manner while still providing adequate representation of a diverse population of citizens.[1] The founders were not of one mind on how to achieve this balance but ultimately crafted a policy that would allow the size of the nation's lower house to grow in line with the population every ten years. Though the Anti-Federalists lambasted the original size of the House, the institution experienced an upward adjustment in the number of seats after each census all but one time from the founding until 1920, when the Congress failed to pass a reapportionment bill. Over this period the impetus behind these enlargements shifted from maintaining a small constituency size to preserving representation for the states, as national lawmakers emphasized reducing the costs to representation rather than focusing on worries about the consequences for legislative operations in the House.

In the decade of the 1920s a broad consensus among House members was reached that continuing with further additions of seats would be untenable for the maintenance of an orderly legislative process. Congress failed to enact reapportionment legislation during much of this decade but finally agreed in 1929 to pass a statute that made 435 seats a permanent fixture and provided for the U.S. Commerce Department to automatically apportion seats following every decennial census. The representational imperative was jettisoned in favor of an automatic process of apportioning seats and a fixed numerical composition of members that would not undermine legislative operations in the House. Since this time there has been virtually no interest from members in revisiting whether the current size of the U.S. House should be adjusted to reflect population trends. The inertia of the present policy has not been altered by any internal or external momentum to enact change. There appears to be only minor concern evinced by House members over how representation has been influenced in the aftermath of this decision. Proposals to re-evaluate the size of the House and the average number of citizens per congressional district have received underwhelming support. Chapter 2 concluded with a brief assessment of this decision, arguing that a return to the representational imperative of increasing the size of the House in line with growth in the population is now in order.

The remaining chapters parsed out the extent to which the 435 seat limit has had negative repercussions for representation. Chapter 3 reviewed how the rise in constituency size has influenced the degree of competition in U.S. House elections. The results revealed that as House districts encompass additional citizens, incumbents suffer a decline in the percentage of the vote they receive. Although certainly not as influential as district partisanship or previous margin of victory in determining electoral outcomes, district population does tend to depress the victory margins incumbent representatives are able to achieve. On the other hand, constituency size negatively influences margin of victory, but it does not have a significant impact on the probability that an incumbent will lose.

Although the results in Chapter 3 point to a positive derivative of the 435-seat limitation by stimulating electoral competition, this conclusion does not tell the full story. As Chapter 4 showed, this diminished electoral support for incumbents may be linked to the dissatisfaction of citizens in more populous districts with their members of the House. Supporters of keeping the legislative constituency size as small as possible predict that failing to do so will promote detachment from the constituency on the part of the representative. Indeed, this supposition is corroborated from the data presented throughout Chapter 4. As constituency size increases, citizens are less likely to report having contact with their representative and having met their representative in person. They are also less likely to make an overt attempt to initiate contact as well. Therefore, it seems that serving additional numbers of persons in the district does weaken the citizen-representative connection.

Not only is contact undermined by this phenomenon but so are perceptions of service responsiveness. Citizens in the most heavily populated congressional districts are less likely to believe their representative would be helpful should the need to contact him or her arise. The same holds true when citizens are queried about whether their representative does an adequate job of staying in touch with the people in the district. There is a robust negative relationship between constituency size and perceptions of representatives' ability to remain close to their constituents. As the population level in the district climbs, citizens are less likely to sense that their House member displays the kind of assistance to and contact with the district that they expect. The difficulty of carrying out these duties will only be magnified in future decades as the mean House district constituency size continues on an upward trajectory.

These negative feelings are translated into the overall evaluations people give to their representatives in Washington. Citizens may dislike Congress but tend to like their own member of Congress.[2] However, in the most populous districts the evidence indicates that citizens like their representatives less, all else being equal. As House members' constituency size expands, citizens in their districts feel less warmly toward them. The same holds true for the strength of approval House members receive as well. Serving additional constituents increases the probability they will be disapproved of by the people in their districts. Though most citizens tend to rate their representative highly even when the national political climate is imbued with negative feelings toward politicians, the average House district constituency size could reach a point where it noticeably undermines House incumbents' standing with their constituents. Americans want their representatives to do a better job staying in touch with the people in their districts, and a perceived failure to do so creates greater mistrust of politicians.[3] Future increases in the ratio of citizens per representative seem likely to fuel the discontent citizens feel toward their elected representatives in the U.S. House. Returning to the practice of decennial increases in the size of the House tied to the cube root of the population would serve to strengthen the communication linkages between representatives and the people represented.

A further outgrowth of the skyrocketing House district population average is that it creates more policy divergence between constituents and their representatives than would otherwise be the case. Previous scholarship has shown that as constituencies become larger the probability that a representative will reflect constituency opinion in the district declines.[4] Chapter 5 demonstrated that this representational dynamic is present for the U.S. House as well. This outcome was predicted by opponents of the 435-seat limit at the time it was established. The presence of a considerable number of additional citizens in the district has the effect of pushing representatives further away from the views of their constituents. The result is a voting record that caters to the activist base of party supporters in the district and veers further away from the median voter than would be the case in a smaller constituency. Chapter 5 presented evidence indicating that constituency size is not the primary factor that leads to divergence, so caution should be exhibited in reading too much into these findings. Nevertheless, they do extend support to the theoretical expectations of prior research in this area and lend further credence to the diminished capacity for representation that stems from unchecked constituency population growth.

Chapter 6 aimed to remove this debate from the exclusive domain of academics and political pundits in order to allow the American public to weigh in on the matter. After all, if the implications for representation are to be fully evaluated there must be some accounting of public attitudes on this subject. If it truly is the people's house, then there is great merit in discerning the American people's reaction to a proposed increase in the size of its membership. This chapter presented groundbreaking survey results on this question. Overall, they demonstrated that American citizens evince very little enthusiasm for the idea. Even when the question was prefaced with arguments that failing to increase the size of the House has produced a significant increase in the average population size of congressional districts and reduced the quality of representation, the public was disinclined to accept the tradeoff of greater costs and the possibility the legislative process would become less efficient. The argument for an increase to offset a further loss of seats from states elicited considerable opposition as well. Most citizens are not sympathetic to the plight of states with population growth that is less than the national average and are comfortable with this loss of representation in the House.

The widest degree of support for expanding the size of the House emerged when the public was asked whether this policy should be followed to improve the chances that women and minorities would be elected to serve in the institution. Almost 49% of the respondents agreed that it should. Support for an increase on these grounds exceeded the number of positive responses for the other questions but was still less than a majority. Nevertheless, members of underrepresented groups in Congress were highly supportive of this idea, particularly African-Americans. The results underscored that descriptive representation is of great import for citizens who have not been full participants in the U.S political system.

While much of the evidence in Chapter 6 suggested an increase in the size of the House arouses little enthusiasm among the public, it is not a policy that would be bitterly opposed if the issue was framed in the proper context.

Although in each instance a majority of respondents opposed an increase, taken together about 56% of the individuals surveyed backed an increase based on one of the justifications provided. Hence, the policy of increasing of the size of the House advocated in this book is not out of line with the wishes of the people. A larger House would not only be a more representative institution; it would also represent a policy members of the public could back under the right circumstances.

The totality of the findings in this study paints a clear picture of the representational implications that have emerged from the 435-seat ceiling imposed on the size the U.S. House. The bulk of the evidence suggests that representation is undermined on most of the indicators examined in the previous chapters. These results provide clear empirical validation of the basic contention from normative critics of the present size of House that the institution has become less representative. Increasing the size of the House to conform to the cube root law of national assembly size would improve communication between House members and their constituents. Following this course of action means that following the 2010 census the House should be increased to approximately 675 members, which would be the projected cube root of the population in that year. Permanently linking the size of the House to the cube root of the population would help prevent a further erosion of the representational linkage as the population continues to expand. It would ease the burden of representation in the areas of policy and service responsiveness and bolster citizens' faith in the performance of their House members. Furthermore, an increase opens up new opportunities for women and minorities to serve in the body, which would enhance the sense trust and efficacy these groups feel toward the institution. Even opponents of increasing the size of the House have to acknowledge there are some major representational benefits that would accrue from this change.

Addressing the Arguments of the Critics

Most of the book has concentrated on the detrimental effects that have resulted from placing a numerical ceiling on the size of the House. While increasing the membership of the House may be a boon for representation, the idea still faces a critical audience among many political scientists and other political observers. From their vantage point even if a larger House would be more representative it is not worth the tradeoffs they contend would result if this policy was enacted. This section of the chapter examines some of these critiques in order to evaluate whether any of their concerns present a strong enough justification for not moving toward a larger House.

One of the least persuasive arguments lodged against House enlargement is that it would be too costly.[5] Although the federal budget of the United States government is under severe strain to supply adequate resources for everything from healthcare to national security, this does not mean that there are not sufficient resources to cover the cost of adding over 200 more members to the institution. The annual appropriations for the legislative branch of the federal government constitute a miniscule proportion of the federal budget. Even with the additional funds that would be necessary to provide salaries and benefits for members and their staffers the overall percentage of the budget devoted to funding operations in the House would remain quite small. For instance, the 2009 salary for most House members was $174,000. Multiplying this number by the additional 240 members called for in this book would only cost about $41.8 million. In the 2008 calendar year, according to the Congressional Research Service, each representative was allocated $874,951 for up to 18 permanent employees, which would mean a cost of an extra $210 million in a House with 675 members.[6] Even the most ardent budget hawk would be hard pressed to justify opposition to House enlargement based simply on a lack of budget resources. The wealthiest country in the world can afford to provide its citizens a better quality of representation from the institution in the federal government that is designed to be closest to the people.

Another concern that can be readily dismissed is the available infrastructure in the nation's capital city to accommodate a substantial increase in the size of the House. Anyone who has worked in Congress can tell you that office space and parking places are in short supply. Some critics wonder if it would be possible to house the extra 240 members and the staff they would need in the Capitol and its surrounding buildings. This objection could be dealt with by creative thinking and flexibility from the House membership. First, since they would be representing fewer constituents, members could maintain a smaller average staff size. Second, any new offices that would be constructed for a House of 675 or even 1000 members does not necessarily have to be directly contiguous to the Capitol grounds. Some of them could be dispersed throughout the DC metropolitan area, especially for junior members who have lees influence in the process. As they acquire more seniority House members could increase their chances of landing an office in one of the office buildings adjacent to the Capitol grounds. A lack of available office space is simply not a viable reason to hold down the numerical size of the House to a level that undermines representation.

A third criticism lodged by House enlargement opponents is that it would harm the quality of deliberation in the institution.[7] While this concern is more valid than the ones previously cited, it is less worrisome than many of the opponents would make it seem. As discussed in Chapter 2, the tradeoff inherent in a larger legislative body is that it imposes restrictions on how many representatives can engage in debate and the time allocated for each individual member.[8] Yes, it is true that if the House was constituted of 675 seats a smaller percentage of members would have the opportunity to make their voice heard on certain issues, and when they did get the opportunity to participate in debates they might get less time to speak on the House floor. However, this problem is also true of the House since it has been constituted of 435 members.

Unless the House is dramatically reduced in size, the lengthy speeches that occur on the Senate floor are just not practical in the body as presently constituted.

Furthermore, in some respects the quality of deliberation in the House is currently overrated. Instances where great oratory can convince members to change their votes are extremely rare. Most politicians who get elected to the House have pretty strong belief systems are not going to be persuaded by a speech on the House floor, no matter how well thought or how eloquent it is. Members come to the House floor with prepared remarks at its present size and they would do so in a larger House as well. While some members might lose out on the opportunity to speak, as regular watchers of CSPAN would attest members already speak to a mostly empty chamber and on many issues don't use their alloted time for debate.

Actually allowing the membership of the House to continue to grow might have a positive impact on deliberation. Since it would lead to the election of more women and minorities, these historically underrepresented groups would have more House members articulating their interests during floor debates. Hence, the overall quality of debate in the chamber may improve with additional voices. As Jane Mansbridge points out in her essay on descriptive representation, this outcome is one of the most crucial justifications for a national legislature to reflect the diversity of its people.[9] Therefore, the proposition that House enlargement would harm deliberation in the chamber just does not hold up under closer scrutiny into how the modern House of Representatives truly operates.

Perhaps the most compelling argument advanced by detractors of the idea of increasing the size of the House of Representatives is that it would lead to a legislative process that is more unwieldy and would prevent it from carrying out the basic functions required of it as an institution.[10] Although it might improve dyadic representation, they maintain that legislative efficiency would suffer were the House to be expanded. Accordingly, one skeptic of increasing the size of the House contends, "An enlarged membership would inevitably entail more interested parties, more demands for inclusion, more delay, more compromise, and a greater likelihood that the negotiations would fail to produce the consensus needed for congressional action."[11] This argument cannot be so easily cast aside as were the other objections previously cited. As Chapter 2 of this book highlighted, many members felt compelled to impose a permanent cap on the size of the House for this very reason. Therefore, it requires a serious response from proponents of adjusting the size of the House to conform to the cube root of the population. It must be acknowledged that many conservative supporters of a bigger House do see it as recipe for greater gridlock, an outcome they feel would limit the growth in the size of government.[12] Although this objective might be what some conservative commentators would like to achieve by increasing the institution's membership it is not the goal of most enlargement advocates. While House enlargement opponents have legitimate worries about the ramifications of an increase for the legislative operations in the body, there are sound reasons to believe it likely will not produce the detrimental effects they predict.

First, the rules of the House are already rigidly structured to promote swift passage of most key legislation.[13] If further restrictions are needed to prevent the legislative process from becoming bogged down, then such measures will adopted. Research on the organizational dynamics of legislative bodies has empirically verified a positive relationship between legislative size and the degree of restrictiveness of institutional rules.[14] While there will be some complaints that such rule changes will transfer even more power to the leadership of the House, such a result is already the norm in the contemporary Congress. If House members select leaders who reflect their preferences, then more power in the hands of the leadership should not be as problematic as some predict.

From the standpoint of coalition building in a larger House, it might not be as difficult as anticipated despite the fact that the leadership would have to round up votes from a larger collection of members. As was documented in Chapter 5, since members would represent smaller, less heterogeneous districts they would not feel as conflicted as they do when trying to satisfy competing interests in casting their votes on contentious legislation. This development could offset the more extensive efforts the leadership would have to make in a larger House.

The most significant impact on the operational dynamics in the House seems to be that the influence of individual members would be diluted in the legislative process.[15] Transferring greater power to House leaders to act on their behalf is a necessary tradeoff if the House is to function effectively. As was demonstrated in the debates reviewed in Chapter 2, members themselves would find this development objectionable. In spite of this sentiment, the diminution of each member's role in the process has to be balanced against the reality that individual citizens will have more influence over their representatives. Ultimately, House members are there to serve their constituents and they can do so most effectively if they have to serve fewer of them. Efficient legislative processes in the House are possible as the size of the institution increases in line with the nation's population growth as envisioned by the cube root of national assembly size. Enabling representatives to balance communications with their constituents and their fellow representatives is the logic of this theory. It is up to lawmakers to devise rules that make this outcome possible. As noted by other supporters of enlargement the House clearly possesses the "capacity to produce the administrative procedures necessary to maintain the distinct character of the body as a *representative* institution."[16] If that procedural structure requires less influence for individual members and a more leadership-dominated institution, the gains that would accrue to dyadic representation are certainly worth it.

Outlook for Changes in the Size of the House

This study has gone a long way toward crystallizing how the present policy of automatically reapportioning 435 seats for the House every ten years has detracted from the quality of representation constituents receive from their national legislators. In spite of this evidence the prospects for altering the existing numerical composition of the House seem bleak. The difficulties encountered during the 110th and 111th Congresses in the drive to pass a bill providing for a two-seat increase to grant the residents of Washington, D.C. a seat in the U.S. House would constitute only a minor alteration in the institution's size. Even the chances this legislation will eventually be enacted are highly uncertain at the time of this writing. The absence of widespread congressional support for just a meager increase in the size of the House does not bode well for more ambitious efforts to go beyond the 435-seat threshold. This section of the chapter outlines some of the reasons why the outlook for change is so bleak.

One of the first hurdles is the constitutional design of the U.S. political system. Enacting any change in existing policy is a struggle in a separation of powers system. There is a powerful bias in favor of maintaining the status quo position when the structure of the political system consists of a chief executive elected separately from the legislative branch.[17] In most policy domains there is a stasis that reigns unless a set of developments occurs that undermines support for the existing policy arrangement.[18] In the case of determining the size of the U.S. House very few exogenous or endogenous forces have exerted pressure on lawmakers to depart from the present policy. The need for Congress to pass an apportionment bill every ten years once provided a stimulus forcing the issue to be consistently revisited. However, since the Congress transferred that authority to the executive branch it has been freed from a fundamental re-examination of the institution's size. The entrance of Alaska and Hawaii into the Union created an opportunity to consider a modification of the 435-seat limit, but so few members seemed dissatisfied with it that even a three-seat increase failed to be enacted.

The path for any increase to make it onto the policy agenda and navigate its way through the phalanx of legislative hurdles it would encounter is highly problematic. While it requires only statutory enactment, not amending the Constitution, as would other reforms like term limits, the obstacles in the way of any proposal of this kind are formidable. Even if a majority of members in the House favored an enlargement it would still have to get approval from key committee and House leaders, who would have to deliver a firm commitment to pass it. Next it would have to surpass the pivot point in the Senate, which is typically the 60th vote, to invoke cloture to end debate.[19] Furthermore, the open amendment process in the Senate might unravel any delicate political compromise achieved in the House unless a unanimous consent agreement limiting amendments was reached on the proposed legislation.[20] Then it would have to be signed by the president, who might defer to the legislative branch on this sort of issue, as has been the case in the past. However, if there was public opposition to the plan, the president could veto the proposed law and then the threshold for enactment would be a two-thirds vote in each House. Given the infrequency with which vetoes have been overridden in the past three presidential administrations, the chances of an enlargement coming to fruition under this scenario are quite remote. Hence, for a proposal of this nature to survive the gamut of institutional obstacles present in the legislative process would be an enormous challenge.

Even if the institutional incentives for gridlock could be overcome, there are other factors that would lead House members to want to maintain the 435-seat ceiling. The political effects that would result from a sizable increase also stand as an impediment to the possibility of change. Given the intense partisan divisions in the House over the past few decades, any change of this nature could stoke fears that it would alter the political landscape for one party or the other. There is no compelling political reason for Republicans to reverse the shift of seats from the Northeast and Midwest, where the party's fortunes are declining, to the Sunbelt, where they have steadily acquired more power.[21] Hence, preserving the automatic apportionment of 435 seats has helped Republican electoral fortunes. Furthermore, if their party followers in the electorate are opposed to the idea, why would Republican leaders in Congress endorse any proposal for House enlargement unless there were other compelling incentives to do so?

As mentioned previously, another serious obstacle to a substantial increase in the size of the House is the members themselves. Any additional allocation of seats in the House would diminish the influence of each member.[22] One representative in a 435-member body already needs to exert intense effort to gain power and attention. A further expansion of the institution would only heighten that difficulty. Imagine trying to drum up media coverage to advertise various activities undertaken in office when representing hundreds of extra members, as has been proposed. Since House members already operate in Washington, D.C., with less exposure than do U.S. senators, detracting from the limited state of attention they receive would not go over very well. In addition, it would create more competition for leadership and raise the number of members that would have to be convinced to launch a successful bid for one of the top positions within the caucus. Thus, it makes acquiring more power within the institution a far less taxonomical enterprise. Members would also face the unpleasant choice of either reducing their staffs or raising funds to maintain present staffing levels. They would most likely select the second option, but it would still subject members to being rebuked by their constituents and electoral challengers.[23] The U.S. public already thinks there are too many staff people on Capitol Hill with the House at its present size.[24] It would also have a significant impact on committee membership. Either the number of members on committees would have to be increased or members would have to be limited to fewer committee assignments. Given the efforts of some committee chairs to scale back the size of committees under the present numerical composition and the desire of members to serve on multiple committees to further their electoral and policy goals, neither option appears to be appealing to members of the House.[25] Even if the position outlined in this book is correct—that

members should be willing to make these sacrifices for the good of their constituents—that does not mean they will be made or even seriously considered.

Ultimately, though, it is the impact on the legislative process if the House
were substantially increased that most members probably could not counte-
nance. As was documented by the textual analysis of congressional debates in
Chapter 2, many representatives express the fear that House enlargement
would make the legislative process more unwieldy. Members of the House
spotlighted this concern when they debated stopping decennial increases and
found them so compelling that they have opted to maintain the status quo for
almost a century. These concerns over legislative efficiency existed then and
they continue to provide a driving incentive to keep the House frozen at 435
members in present times. From my perspective this fear has been exaggerated.
Nevertheless, until and unless House members can be convinced that a substantial increase would not make the legislative process less manageable it is
unlikely this idea would ever be seriously entertained on Capitol Hill.

Are there any conditions that could help bring about an increase in the size
of the House? If the ratio of citizens per congressional district reaches the point
where members of the House recognize it has become overly burdensome, this
development might create an impetus for change. A heavier workload or the
declining approval rate that comes from a larger constituency may be catalysts
for re-examination of the issue. At this point, however, very few members of
the House publicly articulate this concern. Though the representation of more
populated constituencies is a greater burden, most individual members of the
House still enjoy favorable evaluations from voters in their districts.[26] However,
that does not mean that as the ratio of citizens per district continues its upward
drift and begins to pose a threat to their electoral security, members might be
prompted to start re-evaluating the status quo. A sense of electoral jeopardy
serves as a powerful motivator for a great deal of legislative behavior,[27] and
the possibility that constituency size undermines their chances of keeping their
job could force lawmakers to take a second look at maintaining the present
policy.

If organized groups representing the interests of women and minorities
made a priority of increasing the size of the House it might garner sympathy
from some Democratic members who could champion the cause. It certainly
receives broad support among women, African-Americans, and Hispanics in
the general population. At this point, beyond some interest by a limited number
of members of the Congressional Black Caucus, most of these groups have had
little to say about this policy option as a vehicle to improve descriptive representation. Even if this cause did garner the backing of civil rights and feminist
groups, it would still face stiff resistance from Republicans in the U.S. Congress.

In the final analysis, a United States House of Representatives consisting
of close to 435 members seems likely to remain a permanent fixture of the
political system for years to come. Increasing the size of the House may carry
tangible benefits for representation, but the odds that it will ever occur in the

foreseeable future are significantly lower than for other ideas to reform the way the institution operates. Enlarging the House would not be a panacea for curing all the ills that plague the institution; other reforms beyond the scope of this book would be essential as well. Nevertheless, for the US House to truly live up to its ideal status as the people's House, it ultimately must be a larger House and continue to grow as the nation's population grows. To do otherwise would be counter to the representative character this institution is supposed to embody. Even though the prospects for an increase seem grim at this juncture, that does not mean it should be discounted as a policy option that is on the table for serious consideration from policymakers. The fact that a policy option is not likely to gain any traction does not make it any less worthy of being adopted. Increasing the size of the House falls into the same category.

This study has illuminated some of the consequences for representation if this policy remains in effect, but it should not be viewed as the last word on the subject. Legislative and constituency size still remain areas in need of further empirical exploration. More work can be done concerning the ramifications of the size of the U.S. House that and the surge in the average number of constituents each member represents.[28] There are other areas of representation related to the size of the House ought to be scrutinized in order to fully appreciate how the present policy has influenced the linkages between citizens and their representatives. While this study has provided an extensive accounting of these issues, future research must continue to enhance scholarly understanding in this area of legislative politics.

Appendix: Chapter 6
Survey Questions

Q1 When the U.S. House of Representatives was first constituted it consisted of 65 members with each congressional district having approximately 30,000 people. As you may know, the House of Representatives has grown to 435 members with each member representing approximately 640,000 people. Some have argued that the number of representatives should be increased so that each member would represent fewer people, would be closer to the people and provide better representation. Others have argued that a House of Representatives with greater than 435 members would be more costly and make the legislative process less efficient. In your opinion, should the size of the House be:

1   Increased?
2   Kept at its current size?
3   Decreased?

Q2 After the U.S. census is taken every ten years some states lose seats in the U.S. House of Representatives because their population growth is slower than the national rate. Would you support increasing the size of the House to prevent states from losing any seats?

1   Yes.
2   No.

Q3 Some argue that increasing the numerical size of the U.S. House of Representatives would create more opportunities for members of underrepresented groups such as women and racial minorities to get elected. Would you be very supportive, somewhat supportive, somewhat opposed, or very opposed to increasing the size of the House for this purpose?

1   Very supportive.
2   Somewhat supportive.
3   Somewhat opposed.
4   Very opposed.

List of Variables

African American: Dummy variable coded 1 for African American respondents and 0 otherwise.

Hispanic: Dummy variable coded 1 for Hispanic respondents and 0 otherwise.

Female: Dummy variable coded 1 for female respondents and 0 otherwise.

Age: Actual age in years.

Education: Highest degree received coded: 1 = Less than High School (HS); 2 = Some HS, no diploma; 3 = Graduated from HS—Diploma or equivalent (GED); 4 = Some college, no degree; 5 = Associate degree (AA, AS); 6 = Bachelor's degree; 7 = Master's degree; 8 = Professional degree (MD, DDS, LLB, JD); 9 = Doctorate degree.

Income: Household income coded: 1 = Less than $5,000; 2 = $5,000 to $7,499; 3 = $7,500 to $9,999; 4 = $10,000 to $12,499; 5 = $12,500 to $14,999; 6 = $15,000 to $19,999; 7 = $20,000 to $24,999; 8 = $25,000 to $29,999; 9 = $30,000 to $34,999; 10 = $35,000 to $39,999; 11 = $40,000 to $49,999; 12 = $50,000 to $59,999; 13 = $60,000 to $74,999; 14 = $75,000 to $84,999; 15 = $85,000 to $99,999; 16 = $100,000 to $124,999; 17 = $125,000 to $149,999; 18 = $150,000 to $174,999; 19 = $175,000 or more.

Marital Status: Dummy variable coded 1 for married respondents and 0 otherwise.

Political Interest: In general, how interested are you in politics and public affairs? 4 = Very Interested; Somewhat Interested = 3; Slightly Interested = 2; Not At All Interested = 1.

State Lost a Seat in the Last Census: Coded 1 for respondents in Connecticut, New York, Pennsylvania, Ohio, Illinois, Indiana, Michigan, Mississippi, Oklahoma, or Wisconsin and 0 otherwise.

Republican: Dummy variable coded 1 for respondents identifying as Republican and 0 otherwise.

Independent: Dummy variable coded 1 for those respondents not identifying as either Republicans or Democrats.

Personally Acquainted with a Politician: Are you personally acquainted with any of the following people? 1 = A current member of the U.S. Congress or Senate; A current member of your state legislature; A local government official; 0 = None of these.

Gay/Lesbian/Bisexual: Dummy variable coded 1 for gay, lesbian, or bisexual respondents and 0 otherwise.

Ideology: In general, do you think of yourself as: 1 = Extremely Liberal; 2 = Liberal; Slightly Liberal; 3 = Slightly Liberal; 4 = Moderate or Middle of the Road; 5 = Slightly Conservative; Conservative; 7 = Extremely Conservative.

Northeast: Dummy variable coded 1 if respondent resides in Maine, New Hampshire, Vermont, Massachusetts, Rhode Island, Connecticut, New York, New Jersey, or Pennsylvania and 0 otherwise.

Midwest: Dummy variable coded 1 if respondent resides in Ohio, Indiana, Illinois, Michigan, Wisconsin, Minnesota, North Dakota, South Dakota, Nebraska, Kansas, Iowa, or Missouri and 0 otherwise.

West: Dummy variable coded 1 if respondent resides in Montana, Idaho, Wyoming, Colorado, New Mexico, Arizona, Utah, Nevada, Washington, Oregon, California, Hawaii, or Alaska and 0 otherwise.

Notes

1 Why Study the Size of the House?

1 Robert A. Dahl and Edward R. Tufte, *Size and Democracy* (Stanford, CA: Stanford University Press, 1973).
2 U.S. Census Bureau, *Interim Projections of the Total Population for the United States and States: April 1, 2000 to July 1, 2030* (Washington, DC: GPO, 2005), Table A-1.
3 Charles A. Kromkowski and John A. Kromkowski, "Why 435? A Question of Political Arithmetic," *Polity* 24 (1991): 129–145. Charles A. Kromkowski and John A. Kromkowski, "Beyond Administrative Apportionment: Rediscovering the Constitutional Calculus of Representative Government," *Polity* 24 (1992): 495–497; L. Marvin Overby, "Apportionment, Politics and Political Science: A Response to Kromkowski and Kromkowski," *Polity* 24 (1992): 483–494; Christopher St. John Yates, "A House of Our Own or a House We've Outgrown? An Argument for Increasing the Size of the House of Representatives," *Columbia Journal of Law and Social Problems* 25 (1992): 157–196; Jonathan I. Lieb and Gerald R. Webster, "On Enlarging the U.S. House of Representatives," *Political Geography* 17 (1997): 319–329; Lawrence C. Evans and Walter J. Oleszek, "If It Ain't Broke Don't Fix It a Lot," in *The U.S. House of Representatives: Reform or Rebuild*, eds. Joseph Zimmerman and Wilma Rule (Westport, CT: Praeger Publishing, 2000), 187–194; Arend Lijphart, "Reforming the House: Three Moderately Radical Proposals," in *The U.S. House of Representatives: Reform or Rebuild*, eds. Joseph Zimmerman and Wilma Rule (Westport, CT: Praeger Publishing 2000), 135–140; DeWayne L. Lucas and Michael D. McDonald, "Is It Time to Increase the Size of the House of Representatives?" *American Review of Politics* 21 (2000): 367–381; Joseph Zimmerman, "Eliminating Disproportionate Representation in the House," in *The U.S. House of Representatives: Reform or Rebuild*, eds. Joseph Zimmerman and Wilma Rule (Westport, CT: Praeger Publishing, 2000), 163–186; Jeffrey W. Ladewig and Mathew P. Jasinski, "On the Causes and Consequences of and Remedies for Interstate Malapportionment of the U.S. House of Representatives," *Perspectives on Politics* 6 (2008):89–107.
4 Rosemarie Zagarri, *The Politics of Size: Representation in the United States, 1776–1850* (Ithaca, NY: Cornell University Press, 1987).
5 Johanna Nicol Shields, "Whigs Reform the 'Bear Garden': Representation and the Apportionment Act of 1942," *Journal of the Early Republic* 5 (1985): 355–82.
6 Charles W. Eagles, *Democracy Delayed: Congressional Reapportionment and Urban-Rural Conflict in the 1920s* (Athens, GA: University of Georgia Press, 1990). For another discussion of the failure to reapportion in the 1920s, see Margo J. Anderson, *The American Census: A Social History* (New Haven, CT: Yale University Press, 1988), Chapter 6.

7 Laurence F. Schmeckebrier, *Congressional Apportionment* (Westport, CT: Glenwood Press, 1976); Kromkowski and Kromkowski, "Why 435," 134–135.

8 Kromkowski and Kromkowski, "Why 435"; Yates, "A House of Our Own or a House We've Outgrown"; Lucas and McDonald, "Is It Time to Increase the Size of the House of Representatives?"

9 Lucas and McDonald, "Is It Time to Increase the Size of the House of Representatives," 374.

10 Rein Taagepera and Mathew Soberg Shugart, *Seats and Votes: The Effects and Determinants of Electoral Systems* (New Haven CT: Yale University Press, 1989), Lijphart, "Reforming the House"; Lucas and McDonald "Is It Time to Increase the Size of the House of Representatives"; Leib and Weber, "On Enlarging the House of Representatives," 326; Margo Anderson, "Growth of US Population Calls for Larger House of Representatives," *Population Today* 28 (2000): 1–4; Ladewig and Jasinski, "On the Causes and Consequences of and Remedies for Interstate Malapportionment of the U.S. House of Representatives," 89–107.

11 J. Dennis Derbyshire and Ian Derbyshire, *Encyclopedia of World Political Systems*, vol. 1 (Armonk, NY: M.E. Sharpe, 2000), 79.

12 Lijphart, "Reforming the House," 135–140.

13 Charles Kromkowski, "Framers Would Approve of a Larger House," *New York Times*, January 31, 1991, A22; Kromkowski and Kromkowski, "Why 435," 134; Kromkowski and Kromkowski, "Beyond Administrative Apportionment"; Yates, "A House of Our Own or a House We've Outgrown,"159–160; Lucas and McDonald, "Is It Time to Increase the Size of the House of Representatives," 371–334; Brickner, *Article the First of the Bill of Rights* (United States: Lulu.com, 2006*).*

14 Phil Duncan, "Enlarging the Congress: Boon for Democracy," *CQ Weekly Report*, October 28 1989, 2914; Matthew Cossolotto, "Enlarge the House," *Christian Science Monitor*, December 22, 1989, 19; James Glassman, "Let's Build a Bigger House: Why Shouldn't the Number of Congressmen Grow with the Population," *Washington Post*, June 17, 1990, D2; Michael Merrill and Sean Wilentz, "The Big House: An Alternative to Term Limits," *New Republic*, November 16, 1992, 16–18; Matthew Cossolotto, "America Has Outgrown the House of Representatives," *The Hill*, November 21, 2001; Jeff Jacoby, "A Bigger More Democratic Congress," *Boston Globe*, January 13, 2005.

15 Robert Novak, *Completing the Revolution: A Vision for Victory in 2000* (New York: The Free Press 2000), 187–188; George Will, "Congress Just Isn't Big Enough," *Washington Post*, January 14, 2001, B7.

16 Kromkowski and Kromkowski, "Why 435," 138, Table IV. Calculations through 2000 were updated by the author.

17 Stephen Ohlemacher, "Growing Population Shifts Political Power," *Associated Press*, December 22, 2005; Vincent B. Thompson, "Projecting Reapportionment," *Indiana Business Review* 40 (2005): 4–6.

18 Kromkowski and Kromkowski, "Why 435," 137–144; Yates, "a House of Our Own or a House We've Outgrown," 169; Brickner, *Article the First of the Bill of Rights*.

19 Kromkowski and Kromkowski, "Why 435"; Wilma Rule, "Expanded Congress Would Help Women," *New York Times*, February 24, 1991, E16; Yates, "A House of Our Own or a House We've Outgrown," 193; Ladewig and Jasinski, "On the Causes and Consequences of and Remedies for Interstate Malapportionment of the U.S. House of Representatives," 103.

20 For the most comprehensive listing of all of the reasons for increasing the size of the House, see Kromkowski and Kromkowski, "Why 435," 144–145.

21 Overby, "Apportionment, Politics and Political Science," 483.

22 One exception is Michael G. Neubauer and Joel Zeitlin, "Outcomes of Presidential Elections and the House Size," *PS: Political Science and Politics* 36 (2003): 721–725.

This article looks at how variation in the size of the U.S. House would have brought about alternative outcomes in the Electoral College for the closely contested 2000 U.S. presidential election.

23 Ladewig and Jasinski, "On the Causes and Consequences of and Remedies for Interstate Malapportionment of the U.S. House of Representatives," 89–107.

24 Lucas and McDonald, "Is It Time to Increase the Size of the House of Representatives," 367–381.

25 Morris Silverman, "Better Yet, Reduce the Size of the House," *New York Times*, January 14, 1991, A17.

26 William Proxmire, "A House Divided in Half; Wanna Save Money? Fire Every Other Person on Capitol Hill," *Washington Post*, February 5, 1989, D5.

27 Zimmerman, "Eliminating Disproportionate Representation in the House," 178; Evans and Oleszek, "If It Ain't Broke Don't Fix It a Lot," 189–190.

28 Evans and Oleszek, "If It Ain't Broke Don't Fix It a Lot," 190.

29 William F. Willoughby, *Principles of Legislative Organization and Administration* (Washington, DC: The Brookings Institution, 1934), 263; Silverman, "Better Yet, Reduce the Size of the House," A17; Evans and Oleszek, "If it Ain't Broke Don't Fix it a Lot," 190.

30 Nelson W. Polsby, "The Institutionalization of the House of Representatives," *American Political Science Review* 62 (1968): 144–168; Kenneth A. Shepsle, "Representation and Governance: The Great Legislative Trade-off," *Political Science Quarterly* 103 (1988): 461–484.

31 Peverill Squire and Keith E. Hamm, *101 Chambers: Congress, State Legislatures and the Future of Legislative Studies* (Columbus, OH: The Ohio State University Press: 2005), 55–58.

32 George. J. Stigler, "The Sizes of Legislatures," *Journal of Legal Studies* 5 (1976): 17–34; W. Mark Crain and Robert D. Tollison, "Legislative Size and Voting Rules," *Journal of Legal Studies* 6 (1977): 235–241; W. Mark Crain, "Cost and Output in the Legislative Firm," *Journal of Legal Studies* 8 (1979): 607–621; Barry R. Weingast, Kenneth Shepsle, and Christopher Johnson, "The Political Economy of Benefits and Costs: A Neoclassical Approach to Distributive Politics," *Journal of Political Economy* 93 (1981): 642–664; Robert E. McCormick and Robert D. Tollison, *Politicians, Legislation and the Economy: An Inquiry into the Interest-Group Theory of Government* (Boston, MA: Martinus Nijhoff Publishing, 1981); William F. Shugart and Robert D. Tollison, "On the Growth of Government and the Political Economy," *Research in Law and Economics* 9 (1986): 111–127; Thomas W. Gilligan and John G. Matsusaka, "Deviations from Constituents' Interest: The Role of Legislative Structures and Political Parties in the States," *Economic Inquiry* 33 (1995): 383–401; Thomas W. Gilligan and John G. Matsusaka, "Fiscal Policy, Legislature Size, and Political Parties: Evidence from State and Local Governments in the First Half of the 20th Century," *National Tax Journal* 54 (2001): 57–82; John Charles Bradbury and W. Mark Crain, "Legislative Organization and Government Spending: Cross-Country Evidence," *Journal of Public Economics* 82 (2001): 309–325; Reza Baqir, "Districting and Overspending," *Journal of Political Economy* 110 (2002): 1318–1354; Jowei Chen and Neil Malhota, "The Law of k/n: The Effect of Chamber Size on Government Spending in Bicameral Legislatures," *American Political Science Review* 4 (2007): 657–676.

33 Stigler, "The Sizes of Legislatures"; Rein Taagepera, "The Size of National Assemblies," *Social Science Research* 1 (1972): 385–401; Dahl and Tufte, *Size and Democracy*; Taagepera and Shugart, *Seats and Votes*; Rein Taagepera and Steven Recchia, "The Size of Second Chambers and European Assemblies," *European*

Journal of Political Research 41 (2002) 165–185; Squire and Hamm, *101 Chambers*, 48; Ladewig and Jasinski, "On the Causes and Consequences of and Remedies for Interstate Malapportionment of the U.S. House of Representatives," 89–107.

34 Lucas and McDonald, "Is It Time to Increase the Size of the House of Representatives," 374.

35 Crain and Tollison, "Legislative Size and Voting Rules," 238.

36 Andrew Taylor, "Size, Power and Electoral Systems: Exogenous Determinants of Legislative Procedural Choice," *Legislative Studies Quarterly* 31 (2006): 323–345.

37 Squire and Hamm, 101 *Chambers*, 55–56.

38 John R. Hibbing and John R. Alford, "Constituency Population and Representation in the U.S. Senate," *Legislative Studies Quarterly* 15 (1990): 581–598.

39 Hibbing and Alford, "Constituency Population and Representation in the U.S. Senate," 581–598; Jonathan Krasno, *Challengers, Competition and Reelection: Comparing Senate and House Elections* (New Haven, CT: Yale University Press, 1994). Bruce I. Oppenheimer, "The Effect of State Population on Senator-Constituency Linkages," *American Journal of Political Science* 40 (1996): 1280–1299; Sarah Binder, Forrest Maltzman, and Lee Siegelman, "Accounting for Senators' Home State Reputations: Why Do Constituents Love a Bill Cohen So Much More than an Al D'Amato," *Legislative Studies Quarterly* 23 (1998): 545–560; Frances Lee and Bruce I. Oppenheimer, *Sizing Up the Senate: The Unequal Consequences of Equal Representation* (Chicago: University of Chicago Press), 64; Jeffrey E. Cohen and James D. King, "Relative Unemployment and Gubernatorial Popularity," *Journal of Politics* 66 (2004): 1267–1282; James D. King and Jeffrey E. Cohen, "What Determines a Governor's Popularity," *State Politics and Policy Quarterly* 5 (2005): 225–247.

40 Peverill Squire, "Professionalization and Public Opinion of State Legislatures," *Journal of Politics* 55 (1993): 479–491.

41 John R. Hibbing and Sarah Brandes, "State Population and the Electoral Success of U.S. Senators," *American Journal of Political Science* 27 (1983): 808–819; Alan I. Abramowitz, "Explaining Senate Outcomes," *American Political Science Review* 82 (1988): 385–403; Alan I. Abramowitz and Jeffrey Segal, *Senate Elections* (Ann Arbor, MI: University of Michigan Press, 1992); Frances Lee and Bruce I. Oppenheimer, "Senate Apportionment: Competitiveness and Partisan Advantage," *Legislative Studies Quarterly* 22 (1997): 3–24; Frances Lee and Bruce I. Oppenheimer, *Sizing Up the Senate: The Unequal Consequences of Equal Representation*, (Chicago: University of Chicago Press, 1999), 93–95.

42 Krasno, *Challengers, Competition and Reelection.*

43 Mark Thornton and Marc Ulrich, "Constituency Size and Government Spending," *Public Finance Review* 27 (1999): 588–599.

44 Squire and Hamm, *101 Chambers*, 54–55.

45 For one representation of this view, see Federal Framer, "Letter VII December 31, 1787," in *The Essential Antifederalist*, 2nd ed., eds. W. B. Allen and Gordon Lloyd (Lanham, MD: Rowan and Littlefield, 2002), 289.

46 Squire and Hamm, *101 Chambers.*

47 Heinz Eulau and Paul D. Karps, "The Puzzle of Representation: Specifying Components of Responsiveness," *Legislative Studies Quarterly* 2 (1977): 233–255; Robert Weissberg, "Collective Versus Dyadic Representation in Congress," *American Political Science Review* 72 (1978), 535–547; Janet Box-Steffensmeier, David C. Kimball, Scott R. Meinke, and Katherine Tate, "The Effects of Political Representation of the Electoral Advantages of House Incumbents," *Political Research Quarterly* 56 (2003): 259–270.

2 Debating the Size of the House

1 Johanna Nicol Shields, "Whigs Reform the 'Bear Garden': Representation and the Apportionment Act of 1942," *Journal of the Early Republic* 5 (1985): 355–382; Eugene W. Hickock, "The Framers' Understanding of Constituional Deliberation in Congress," Georgia Law Review 21 (1986): 217–272; Rosemarie Zagarri, *The Politics of Size: Representation in the United States, 1776–1850* (Ithaca, NY: Cornell University Press, 1987); Charles W. Eagles, *Democracy Delayed: Congressional Reapportionment and Urban-Rural Conflict in the 1920s* (Athens, GA: University of Georgia Press, 1990); Charles A. Kromkowski and John A. Kromkowski "Why 435? A Question of Political Arithmetic," *Polity* 24 (1991): 129–145; Christopher St. John Yates, "A House of Our Own or a House We've Outgrown? An Argument for Increasing the Size of the House of Representatives," *Columbia Journal of Law and Social Problems* 25 (1992): 157–196; DeWayne L. Lucas and Michael D. McDonald, "Is It Time to Increase the Size of the House of Representatives," *American Review of Politics* 21 (2000): 367–381; Bryan W. Brickner, *Article the First of the Bill of Rights* (United States: Lulu.com, 2006); Jeffrey W. Ladewig and Mathew P. Jasinski, "On the Causes and Consequences of and Remedies for Interstate Malapportionment of the U.S. House of Representatives," *Perspectives on Politics* 6 (2008):89–107.
2 Nelson W. Polsby, "The Institutionalization of the House of Representatives," *American Political Science Review* 62 (1968): 144–168; Kenneth A. Shepsle, "Representation and Governance: The Great Legislative Trade-off," *Political Science Quarterly* 103 (1988): 461–484.
3 William F. Willoughby, *Principles of Legislative Organization and Administration* (Washington, DC: The Brookings Institution, 1934), 263.
4 Polsby, "The Institutionalization of the House of Representatives," 144; Shepsle, "Representation and Governance," 482.
5 Lucas and McDonald, "Is It Time to Increase the Size of the House of Representatives," 368; Peverill Squire and Keith E. Hamm, *101 Chambers: Congress, State Legislatures, and the Future of Legislative Studies* (Columbus, OH: The Ohio University Press, 2005).
6 Robert Weissberg, "Collective Versus Dyadic Representation in Congress," *American Political Science Review* 72 (1978): 535–547.
7 Willoughby, *Principles of Legislative Organization and Administration*, 258.
8 Shepsle, "Representation and Governance," 482.
9 Robert A. Dahl and Edward R. Tufte, *Size and Democracy* (Stanford, CA: Stanford University Press, 1973), 80–81.
10 W. Mark Crain and Robert D. Tollison, "Legislative Size and Voting Rules," *Journal of Legal Studies* 6 (1977): 235–241; Andrew J. Taylor, "Size Power and Electoral Systems: Exogenous Determinants of Legislative Procedural Choice," *Legislative Studies Quarterly* 31 (2006): 323–345.
11 Bertrand De Jouvenal, "The Chairman's Problem," *American Political Science Review* 55 (1961): 368–372; Dahl and Tufte, *Size and Democracy*, 80–81; Lucas and McDonald, "Is It Time to Increase the Size of the House of Representatives," 370.
12 Rein Taagepera and Mathew Soberg Shugart, *Seats and Votes: The Effects and Determinants of Electoral Systems* (New Haven, CT: Yale University Press, 1989).
13 Willoughby, *Principles of Legislative Organization and Administration*, 258.
14 Rein Taagepera, "The Size of National Assemblies," *Social Science Research* 1 (1972): 385–401; Taagepera and Shugart, *Seats and Votes*.
15 Taagepera and Shugart, *Seats and Votes*, 179.
16 Dahl and Tufte, *Size and Democracy*, 80.
17 For further evidence, see Taagepera and Shugart, *Seats and Votes*, 175; Lucas and McDonald, "Is It Time to Increase the Size of the House of Representatives," 372;

Anderson, "Growth of U.S. Population Calls for Larger House of Representatives," *Population Today* 28(2000): 2; Ladewig and Jasiniski, "On the Causes and Consequences of and Remedies for Interstate Malapportionment of the U.S. House of Representatives," 100.

18 Max Farrand, ed., *Records of the Federal Convention*, vol. 1 (New Haven, CT: Yale University Press 1966), 351.

19 Ibid., 354.

20 Laurence F. Schmeckebier, *Congressional Apportionment* (Westport, CT: Glenwood Press, 1976); Hickock, "The Framers' Understanding of Constitutional Deliberation in Congress," 230.

21 William H. Riker, "Why Negative Campaigning Is Rational: The Rhetoric of the Ratification Campaign of 1787–1788," *Studies in American Political Development* 5 (1991): 224–283.

22 Hickock, "The Framers' Understanding of Constitutional Deliberation in Congress," 237.

23 Farrand, *Records of the Federal Convention*, vol. 1, 526.

24 Ibid., 533.

25 Ibid., vol. 2, 553–554. Alexander Hamilton voiced his concern over the apportionment ratio, complaining "it was essential that the popular branch should be on a solid foundation. He was seriously of the opinion that the House of Representatives was so narrow a scale to be really dangerous, and to warrant a jealousy in the people for their liberties."

26 Ibid., 221. Roger Sherman of Connecticut made the motion in concert with Madison.

27 Ibid., 643–644.

28 Ibid., 644.

29 Ibid. Washington's action was likely in anticipation of the forthcoming attacks from the Anti-Federalists over this issue.

30 Ibid., vol. 1, 578.

31 Ibid.

32 Ibid., 577.

33 Ibid., 590.

34 Ibid., 358.

35 Hickock, "The Framers' Understanding of Constitutional Deliberation in Congress," 236.

36 Polsby, "The Institutionalization of the House of Representatives," 144; Sheplsle, "Representation and Governance," 482.

37 Farrand, *Records of the Federal Convention*, vol. 1, 557.

38 Ibid., 563.

39 Ibid., 568.

40 Ibid., 569.

41 Ibid., 569.

42 Ibid., 570.

43 Ibid.

44 Richard Henry Lee, "Objections, October 16, 1787," in *The Essential Antifederalist*, 2nd ed., eds. W. B. Allen and Gordon Lloyd (Lanham, MD: Rowan and Littlefield, 2002), 23. Lee was but one of the Anti-Federalists to denounce the small size of the House and urge an increase in its membership.

45 Zagarri, *The Politics of Size*, 89.

46 Hannah Fenichel Pitkin, *The Concept of Representation* (Berkeley, CA: University of California Press, 1967).

47 Federal Farmer, "Letter II, October 9, 1787," in *The Essential Antifederalist*, 149–150.

48 Zagarri, *The Politics of Size*, 90.
49 Brutus, "Essay III, November 15, 1787," in *The Essential Antifederalist*, 254.
50 Federal Farmer, "Letter VII, December 31, 1787," in *The Essential Antifederalist*, 279.
51 Brutus, "Essay III, November 15, 1787," in *The Essential Antifederalist*, 254.
52 Patrick Henry, "Virginia Ratifying Convention, June 4 and 5, 1788," in *The Essential Antifederalist*, 132. Henry openly wondered why provisions of the Constitution pertaining to the ratio of population per representative were so vague. He suggested this lack of clarity would severely undermine representation.
53 Federal Farmer, "Letter III, October 10, 1787," in *The Essential Antifederalist*, 159.
54 Federal Farmer, "Letter VII, December 31 1787," in *The Essential Antifederalist*, 280.
55 Brutus, "Essay III, November 15, 1787," in *The Essential Antifederalist*, 256.
56 Federal Farmer, "Letter III, October 10, 1787," in *The Essential Antifederalist*, 154.
57 Alexander Hamilton, James Madison, and John Jay, *The Federalist*, ed. Terrence Ball (Cambridge, U.K.: Cambridge University Press, 2003), 269.
58 Ibid., 270.
59 Ibid.
60 Ibid., 271.
61 Ibid., 274.
62 Ibid., 275.
63 Ibid., 276–277.
64 Ibid., 278.
65 Zagarri, *The Politics of Size*, 100.
66 Hamilton, Madison, and Jay, *The Federalist*, 159.
67 Ibid., 281.
68 Ibid., 282–283.
69 Kromkowski and Kromkowski, "Why 435," 131–132; Yates, "A House of Our Own or a House We've Outgrown," 178; Brickner, *Article the First of the Bill of Rights*.
70 Michael Balinski and H. Peyton Young, *Fair Representation: Meeting the Ideal of One Man One Vote* (Washington, DC: Brookings Institution Press, 2001), 10–11.
71 Ibid., 13.
72 Zagarri, *The Politics of Size*, 136.
73 Ibid., 135–136.
74 Balinski and Young, *Fair Representation*, 13.
75 Margo J. Anderson, *The American Census: A Social History* (New Haven, CT: Yale University Press, 1988), 15.
76 Zagarri, *The Politics of Size*, 136–137.
77 Balinski and Young, *Fair Representation*, 19–20.
78 John C. Fitzpatrick, ed., *The Writings of George Washington* (Washington, DC: U.S. Government Printing Office, 1931–1944), 16–17.
79 Balinski and Young, *Fair Representation*, 21.
80 Kromkowski and Kromkowski, "Why 435," 132; Brickner, *Article the First of the Bill of Rights*, 64.
81 Zagarri, *The Politics of Size*, 139.
82 Balinski and Young, *Fair Representation*, 23.
83 Shields, "Whigs Reform the 'Bear Garden,'" 363.
84 *Congressional Globe*, 27th Congress, Second Session, April 21, 1842, 436.
85 Ibid, June 21, Appendix, 884.
86 Ibid., April 21, 1842, 437.
87 Shields, "Whigs Reform the 'Bear Garden,'" 372–373.
88 *Congressional Globe*, 27th Congress, Second Session, April 21, 1842, 436.
89 Shields, "Whigs Reform the 'Bear Garden,'" 380.
90 5 Stat. 491.

91 Lucas and McDonald, "Is It Time to Increase the Size of the House," 369–370.
92 Kromkowski and Kromkowski, "Why 435," 133.
93 Willoughby, *Principles of Legislative Organization and Administration*, 263.
94 37 Stat. 13.
95 Eagles, *Democracy Delayed*, 32–33.
96 "Congress Must Fix House Membership," *New York Times*, October 9, 1920, 7.
97 Ibid. Clark became House Minority Leader in the 66th Congress when the Democrats lost control of the House in the 1918 midterm elections.
98 Eagles, *Democracy Delayed*, 36.
99 Ibid., 40.
100 *Congressional Record*, 66th Congress, 3rd Session, January 18, 1921, 1632.
101 Ibid., 1626.
102 Ibid., 1635.
103 Eagles, *Democracy Delayed*, 42.
104 *Congressional Record*, 66th Congress, 3rd Session, January 18, 1921, 1642.
105 Joseph Cooper and David Brady, "Institutional Context and Leadership Style: The House from Cannon to Rayburn," *American Political Science Review* 75 (1981): 411–425; Eric Schickler, *Disjointed Pluralism: Institutional Innovation and the Development of the U.S. Congress* (Princeton, NJ: Princeton University Press, 2001).
106 Ideology is measured using the first and second dimensions of Poole and Rosenthal's DW-NOMINATE scores. These scores are routinely used as an estimate of the ideological position of members of Congress. Members' ideal points are derived by utilizing a dynamic, weighted, nominal three-step estimation procedure based on all nonunanimous roll-call votes taken in each Congress. For more details on this measure, see Keith Poole and Howard Rosenthal, *Congress: A Political-Economic History of Roll Call Voting* (Oxford: Oxford University Press, 1997). Data collected from: http://voteview.com/dwnomin.htm.
107 Predicted probabilities calculated using CLARIFY. See Gary King, Michael Tomz, and Jason Wittenberg, "Making the Most of Statistical Analyses: Improving Interpretation and Presentation," *American Journal of Political Science* 44 (2000): 347–361.
108 Willoughby, *Principles of Legislative Organization and Administration*, 263.
109 Anderson, *The American Census*, 140.
110 Kromkowski and Kromkowski, "Why 435," 132–133; Eagles, *Democracy Delayed*, Chapter 3.
111 Eagles, *Democracy Delayed*, 51.
112 Kromkowski and Kromkowski, "Why 435," 134.
113 Eagles, *Democracy Delayed*, 64–67.
114 Orville Sweeting, "John Q. Tilson: The Reapportionment Act of 1929," *Western Political Quarterly* 9 (1956): 442.
115 Eagles, *Democracy Delayed*, 69.
116 Ibid., 78–81.
117 Ibid., 82.
118 46 Stat. 26.
119 Polsby, "The Institutionalization of the House of Representatives," 145.
120 Nelson W. Polsby, *How Congress Evolves: Social Bases of Institutional Change* (Oxford: Oxford University Press, 2004), 152.
121 Willoughby, *Principles of Legislative Organization and Administration*, 263.
122 Kromkowski and Kromkowski, "Why 435," 135.
123 Yates, "A House of Our Own or a House We've Outgrown," 186.
124 Section 9 of PL 85–508 and Section 8 of PL 86–3 authorizing the admittance of Alaska and Hawaii mandated a return to the 435 membership level if no legislative action was taken to make the temporary increase permanent.

125 *CQ Almanac*, vol. 18 (Washington, DC: Congressional Quarterly Press, 1962), 395.

126 U.S. House, Subcommittee No. 3 of the House Committee on the Judiciary, *Increasing the Membership of the House of Representatives and Redistricting Congressional Districts: Hearings on H.R. 841, 1178, 1183, 1998, 2531, 2704, 2718, 2739, 2768, 2770, 2783, 3012, 3176, 3414, 3725, 3804, 3890, 4068, 4609, 6431, 7355, 8075, 8468, 8616 and HJ Res. 419* Before Subcommittee No. 3 of the House Committee on the Judiciary, 87th Congress, 1st Session, 44, August 24 and 30, 1961 (Washington, DC: GPO, 1964), 34.

127 Ibid., 87–88.

128 Ibid., 33.

129 *CQ Almanac*, vol. 18, 395.

130 Ibid.

131 Ibid., 396.

132 *Congressional Record*, 87th Congress, 2nd Session, March 15, 1962, 3736.

133 Ibid., 3735.

134 *CQ Almanac*, vol. 18, 396. The Pennsylvania delegation was instrumental in killing the amended version of HR 10264 because it was perceived that the amendment would force at-large elections in the state.

135 Ibid., 395.

136 For background on the proposal, see Spencer Hu, "House Bill Would Give District the Vote," *Washington Post*, June 23, 2004, B1. Bills introduced in the 108th through the 110th Congresses include: HR 4640, District of Columbia Fairness in Representation Act, 108th Congress; HR 2043, District of Columbia Fairness in Representation Act, 109th Congress; HR 1905, District of Columbia House Voting Rights Act.

137 U.S. House, Government Reform Committee, *Hearing on Common Sense Justice for the Nation's Capital: An Examination of Proposals to Give D.C. Residents Direct Representation*, 108th Congress, 2nd Session, June 23, 2004, http://reform.house. gov/GovReform/Hearings/EventSingle.aspx?EventID=15697. See opening statement of Chairman Tom Davis.

138 Lori Montgomery and Elissa Silverman, "Plan to Give D.C. a Vote in Congress Advances," *Washington Post*, May 11, 2006, A01.

139 Mary Beth Sheridan, "Senators Block D.C. Vote Bill, Delivering Possibly Fatal Blow," *Washington Post*, September 19, 2007, A01.

140 Mary Beth Sheridan and Hamil R. Harris, "D.C. Voting Measure Clears the Senate," *Washington Post*, February 27, 2009, A01.

141 HR 415, Congress 2006 Commission Act, 108th Congress; HR 1989, Congress 2008 Commission Act, 109th Congress.

142 *Congressional Record*, 108th Congress, 1st Session, January 28, 2003, E81.

143 Margo Anderson, "Growth of US Population Calls for Larger House of Representatives," 1–4. Though some African-American members of the House favor reforms like cumulative voting or multimember districts that may be coupled with a proposal to expand the size of the House of Representatives, the Congressional Black Caucus has taken no official position on an increase. The highest ranking African-American member in the U.S. House, Jim Clyburn of South Carolina, has expressed support for an enlargement of the body to reduce constituency size.

144 Lucas and McDonald, "Is It Time to Increase the Size of the House," 369–370; Ladewig and Jasiniski, "On the Causes and Consequences of and Remedies for Interstate Malapportionment of the U.S. House of Representatives," 100.

3 The Growth of House District Populations and Electoral Competition

1 Morris P. Fiorina, Samuel J. Abrams, and Jeremy C. Pope, *Culture War? The Myth of a Polarized America* (New York: Pearson-Longman, 2005).
2 Gary C. Jacobson, *The Politics of Congressional Elections*, 6th ed. (New York: Pearson, 2004).
3 David R. Mayhew, "Congressional Elections: The Case of the Vanishing Marginals," *Polity* 6 (1974): 295–317.
4 Gary C. Jacobson, "The Marginals Never Vanished: Incumbency and Competition to the U.S. House of Representatives 1952–82," *American Journal of Political Science* 31 (1987): 126–141; Jeffrey M. Stonecash, *Reassessing the Incumbency Effect* (Cambridge: Cambridge University Press, 2008).
5 Gary W. Cox and Jonathan N. Katz, *Elbridge Gerry's Salamander: The Electoral Consequences of the Reapportionment Revolution* (Cambridge: Cambridge University Press, 2002).
6 Edward R. Tufte, "The Relationship Between Seats and Votes in Two-Party Systems," *American Political Science Review* 67 (1973): 540–554; Cox and Katz, *Elbridge Gerry's Salamander*.
7 Michael P. McDonald, "Drawing the Line on Competition," *PS: Political Science and Politics* 34 (2006): 91–95.
8 John A. Ferejohn, "On the Decline of Competition in Congressional Elections," *American Political Science Review* 71 (1977): 166–176.
9 Bruce Oppenheimer, "Deep Red and Blue Congressional Districts: The Causes and Consequences of Declining Party Competitiveness," in *Congress Reconsidered*, 8th ed., eds. Lawrence C. Dodd and Bruce Oppenheimer (Washington, DC: CQ Press, 2005), 135–159; Alan Abramowitz, Brad Alexander, and Matthew Gunning, "Incumbency, Redistricting, and the Decline of Competition in U.S. House Elections," *Journal of Politics* 68 (2006): 75–88; Alan Abramowitz, Brad Alexander, and Matthew Gunning, "Don't Blame Redistricting for Uncompetitive Elections," *PS: Political Science and Politics* 29 (2006): 87–90.
10 Ferejohn, "On the Decline of Competition in Congressional Elections"; Water D. Burnham, "Insulation and Responsiveness in Congressional Elections," *Political Science Quarterly* 90 (1975): 411–435.
11 Larry M. Bartels, "Partisanship and Voting Behavior, 1952-1996," *American Journal of Political Science* 44 (2000): 35–50; Jeffrey M. Stonecash, *Political Parties Matter: Realignment and the Return of Partisan Voting* (Boulder, CO: Lynne Rienner Publishers, 2006).
12 David Mayhew, *Congress: The Electoral Connection* (New Haven, CT: Yale University Press, 1974).
13 Ferejohn, "On the Decline of Competition in Congressional Elections," 174.
14 Morris P. Fiorina, "The Case of the Vanishing Marginals: The Bureaucracy Did It," *American Political Science Review* 71 (1977): 177–181.
15 Glenn R. Parker and Suzanne L. Parker, "The Correlates and Effects of Attention to District by House Members," *Legislative Studies Quarterly* 10 (1985): 223–242.
16 John R. Johannes and John C. McAdams, "The Congressional Incumbency Effect: Is It Casework Policy Compatibility or Something Else? An Examination of the 1978 Election," *American Journal of Political Science* 25 (1981): 513–542.
17 George Serra and Albert Cover, "The Electoral Consequences of Perquisite Use: The Casework Case," *Legislative Studies Quarterly* 17(1992): 233–246; David W. Romero, "The Case of Missing Reciprocal Influence: Incumbent Reputation and the Vote," *Journal of Politics* 58 (1996): 1198–1207.

18 R. Michael Alvarez and Jason L. Saving, "Deficits, Democrats, and Distributive Benefits: Congressional Elections and the Pork Barrel in the 1980s," *Political Research Quarterly* 50 (1997): 809–831.

19 Paul G. Feldman and James Jundrow, "Congressional Elections and Local Federal Spending," *American Journal of Political Science* 28 (1984): 147–163; Janet Box-Stefensmeier, David C. Kimball, Scott Meinke, and Katherine Tate, "The Effects of Political Representation of the Electoral Advantages of House Incumbents," *Political Research Quarterly* 56 (2003): 259–270.

20 Alan I. Abramowitz, "Incumbency, Campaign Spending, and the Decline of Competition in U.S. House Elections," *Journal of Politics* 53 (1991): 34–56.

21 Oppenheimer, "Deep Red and Blue Congressional Districts," 140.

22 Peverill Squire and Keith E. Hamm, *101 Chambers: Congress, State Legislature and the Future of Legislative Studies* (Columbus, OH: The Ohio State University Press, 2005).

23 Lex Renda, "The End of Midterm Decline? Congressional Elections in Historical Perspective," *Social Science History* 27 (2003): 139–164.

24 Jacobson, *Politics of Congressional Elections*, 24–25.

25 John R. Hibbing and Sarah Brandes, "State Population and the Electoral Success of U.S. Senators," *American Journal of Political Science* 27 (1983): 808–819; Alan I. Abramowitz, "Explaining Senate Outcomes," *American Political Science Review* 82 (1988): 385–403; Alan I. Abramowitz and Jeffrey Segal, *Senate Elections* (Ann Arbor, MI: University of Michigan Press, 1992); Frances Lee and Bruce I. Oppenheimer, "Senate Apportionment: Competitiveness and Partisan Advantage," *Legislative Studies Quarterly* 22 (1997): 3–24; Frances Lee and Bruce I. Oppenheimer, *Sizing Up the Senate: The Unequal Consequences of Equal Representation* (Chicago, IL: University of Chicago Press, 1999), 93–95.

26 Hibbing and Brandes, "State Population and the Electoral Success of U.S. Senators," 808–819.

27 Abramowitz and Segal, *Senate Elections*, 110–111.

28 Lee and Oppenheimer, *Sizing Up the Senate*, 93–95.

29 Jonathan Krasno, *Challengers, Competition and Reelection: Comparing Senate and House Elections* (New Haven, CT: Yale University Press, 1994), 39–46; Mark C. Westlye, *Senate Elections and Campaign Intensity* (Baltimore, MD: Johns Hopkins University Press, 1991), 153–157.

30 John Carey, Richard Niemi, and Lynda Powell, "Incumbency and the Probability of Reelection in State Legislative Elections," *Journal of Politics* 62 (2000): 671–700.

31 Robert E. Hogan, "Challenger Emergence, Incumbent Success and Electoral Accountability in State Legislative Elections," *Journal of Politics* 66 (2004): 1283–1303.

32 Gordon S. Black, "Conflict in the Community: A Theory of the Effects of Community Size," *American Political Science Review* 68 (1974): 1245–1261; Timothy Bledsoe, *Careers in City Politics: The Case for Urban Democracy* (Pittsburgh, PA: University of Pittsburgh Press, 1993).

33 Edward L. Lascher, "Constituency Size and Incumbent Safety: A Reexamination," *Political Research Quarterly* 58 (2005): 269–278.

34 Brian Nutting and H. Amy Stern, eds., *CQ's Politics in America 2002, the 107th Congress* (Washington, DC: Congressional Quarterly Inc., 2001).

35 John R. Alford and David W. Brady, "Personal and Partisan Advantage in U.S. Congressional Elections, 1846–1990," in *Congress Reconsidered*, 5th ed., eds. Lawrence C. Dodd and Bruce Oppenheimer (Washington, DC: Congressional Quarterly Press, 1993), 146–147.

36 Abramowitz, "Incumbency, Campaign Spending, and the Decline of Competition in U.S. House Elections"; Abramowitz, Alexander, and Gunning, "Incumbency Redistricting, and the Decline of Competition in U.S. House Elections";

Abramowitz, Alexander and Gunning, "Don't Blame Redistricting for Uncompetitive Elections."

37 Oppenheimer, "Deep Red and Blue Congressional Districts," 140.

38 Robert S. Erikson and Gerald C. Wright, "Voters, Candidates, and Issues in Congressional Elections," in *Congress Reconsidered*, 8th ed., eds. Lawrence C. Dodd and Bruce I. Oppenheimer (Washington, DC: CQ Press, 2005), 87.

39 Abramowitz, "Incumbency, Campaign Spending, and the Decline of Competition in U.S. House Elections."

40 Bandice Canes-Wrone, David W. Brady, and John F. Cogan, "Out of Step, Out of Office: Electoral Accountability and House Members' Voting," *American Political Science Review* 96 (2002): 127–140.

41 Keith T. Poole and Howard Rosenthal, *Congress: A Political-Economic History of Roll Call Voting* (Oxford: Oxford University Press, 1997). Data downloaded from: http://voteview.com/dwnomin.htm.

42 John R. Hibbing, *Congressional Careers: Contours of Life in the Modern U.S. House of Representatives* (Chapel Hill, NC: University of North Carolina Press, 1991).

43 Albert D. Cover and David Mayhew, "Congressional Dynamics and the Decline of Competitive Congressional Elections," in *Congress Reconsidered*, 2nd ed., eds. Lawrence Dodd and Bruce I. Oppenheimer (Washington, DC: Congressional Quarterly Press, 1981), 70.

44 Edward R. Tufte, "Determinants of Midterm Elections," *American Political Science Review* 69 (1975): 812–826.

45 James E. Campbell, "The Revised Theory of Surge and Decline," *American Journal of Political Science* 31 (1987): 956–978.

46 Gary C. Jacobson, *Money in Congressional Elections* (New Haven, CT: Yale University Press, 1980); Gary C. Jacobson, "Strategic Politicians and the Dynamics of U.S. House Elections, 1946–1986," *American Political Science Review* 83 (1989): 773–793; Abramowitz, "Incumbency, Campaign Spending, and the Decline of Competition in U.S. House Elections"; Emily Van Dunk, "Challenger Quality in State Legislative Elections" *Political Research Quarterly* 50 (1997): 793–807; Jamie Carson, Erik J. Engstrom, and Jason M. Roberts, "Candidate Quality, the Personal Vote and the Incumbency Advantage in Congress," *American Political Science Review* 101 (2007): 289–303.

47 For a more detailed discussion of challenger quality, see Peverill Squire and Eric R. A. N. Smith, "A Further Examination of Challengers' Quality in Senate Elections," *Legislative Studies Quarterly* 21 (1996): 235–248.

48 The data on challenger quality was generously shared with the author by Gary Jacobson.

49 Gary C. Jacobson, *The Politics of Congressional Elections*, 6th ed. (New York: Pearson, 2004).

50 Gary C. Jacobson, *Money in Congressional Elections* (New Haven, CT: Yale University Press, 1980); Gary C. Jacobson, "The Effects of Campaign Spending in Congressional Elections: New Evidence for Old Arguments," *American Journal of Political Science* 34 (1990): 334–362.

51 Donald P. Green and Jonathan Krasno, "Salvation for the Spendthrift Incumbent: Reestimating the Effects of Campaign Spending in House Elections," *American Journal of Political Science* 32 (1988): 884–907; Donald P. Green and Jonathan Krasno, "Rebuttal to Jacobson's New Evidence for Old Arguments," *American Journal of Political Science* 34 (1990): 363–372.

52 This approach provided a better empirical fit than alternative transformations.

53 In most cases the typical course of action would be to employ logistic regression when there is a binary dependent variable. However, in the present analysis, because

an incumbent being defeated is such an infrequent event (approximately 5 percent in this sample), a rare events logit model is utilized for this analysis. As prior research has documented, traditional logit models may be subject to bias and can underpredict rare events. See Michael Tomz, Gary King, and Lanche Zeng, "Relogit: Rare Events Logistic Regression," *Journal of Statistical Software* 8 (2003): 138–163. Traditional logit analysis yielded substantively similar results.

54 Hibbing and Brandes, "State Population and the Electoral Success of U.S. Senators"; Abramowitz, "Explaining Senate Outcomes"; Abramowitz and Segal, *Senate Elections*; Lee and Oppenheimer, "Senate Apportionment"; Lee and Oppenheimer, *Sizing Up the Senate*, 93–95; Carey, Niemi, and Powell, "Incumbency and the Probability of Reelection in State Legislative Elections"; Hogan, "Challenger Emergence, Incumbent Success and Electoral Accountability in State Legislative Elections."

55 Krasno, *Challengers, Competition and Reelection*, 39–46; Westlye, *Senate Elections and Campaign Intensity*, 153–157.

56 Warren E. Miller and Donald E. Stokes, "Constituency Influence in Congress," *American Political Science Review* 57 (1963): 45–56, although a number of studies raise serious questions about whether competitive elections actually lead legislators to be more responsive to the median voter. See, Morris P. Fiorina, *Representatives, Roll Call and Constituencies* (Lexington, MA: D.C. Heath, 1974); James H. Kuklinski, "District Competitiveness and Legislative Roll-Call Behavior: A Reassessment of the Marginality Hypothesis," *American Journal of Political Science* 21 (1977): 627–638; Girish Gulatti, "Revisiting the Link Between Electoral Competition and Policy Extremism in the U.S. Congress," *American Politics Research* 32 (2004): 495–530.

57 Thomas Brunell, *Redistricting and Representation: Why Competitive Elections are Bad for America* (New York: Routledge, 2008).

4 Constituents: How Many is Too Many?

1 One observer complained after the 1990 census that "a member cannot be close to, much less adequately represent, 572,000 people." See Christopher St. John Yates, "A House of Our Own or a House We've Outgrown? An Argument for Increasing the Size of the House of Representatives," *Columbia Journal of Law and Social Problems* 25 (1992): 179.

2 Testimony of Rep. Frank Chelf: U.S. House, Subcommittee No. 3 of the House Committee on the Judiciary, *Increasing the Membership of the House of Representatives and Redistricting Congressional Districts: Hearings on H.R. 841, 1178, 1183, 1998, 2531, 2704, 2718, 2739, 2768, 2770, 2783, 3012, 3176, 3414, 3725, 3804, 3890, 4068, 4609, 6431, 7355, 8075, 8468, 8616 and HJ Res. 419 Before Subcommittee No. 3 of the House Committee on the Judiciary, 87th Congress, 1st Session 44*, August 24 and 30, 1964 (Washington, DC: GPO, 1964), 34.

3 Rein Taagepera and Mathew Soberg Shugart, *Seats and Votes: The Effects and Determinants of Electoral Systems* (New Haven, CT: Yale University Press, 1989).

4 Arend Lijphart, "Reforming the House: Three Moderately Radical Proposals," in *The US House of Representatives: Reform or Rebuild*, eds. Joseph Zimmerman and Wilma Rule (Westport, CT: Praeger Publishing 2000): 135–140.

5 Peverill Squire and Keith Hamm, *101 Chambers: Congress, State Legislatures and the Future of Legislative Studies* (Columbus, OH: The Ohio University Press, 2005): 55–58.

6 For a summary of the findings in this chapter, see Brian Frederick, "Constituency Population and Representation in the U.S. House." *American Politics Research* 36 (2008): 358–338.

7 John R. Hibbing and John R. Alford, "Constituency Population and Representation in the U.S. Senate," *Legislative Studies Quarterly* 15 (1990): 581–598; Jonathan Krasno, *Challengers, Competition and Reelection: Comparing Senate and House Elections* (New Haven, CT: Yale University Press, 1994); Frances Lee and Bruce I. Oppenheimer, *Sizing Up the Senate: The Unequal Consequences of Equal Representation* (Chicago, IL: University of Chicago Press, 1999).

8 Lee and Oppenheimer, *Sizing Up the Senate*, 64–65.

9 Hibbing and Alford, "Constituency Population and Representation in the U.S. Senate," 585; Krasno, *Challengers, Competition and Reelection*, 50–51.

10 Peverill Squire, "Professionalization and Public Opinion of State Legislatures," *Journal of Politics* 55 (1993): 479–491.

11 John M. Carey, Richard Niemi, and Lynda Powell, *Term Limits in the State Legislatures* (Ann Arbor, MI: University of Michigan Press, 2000), 53.

12 John M. Carey, Richard Niemi, Lynda Powell, and Gary F. Moncrief, "The Effects of Term Limits on State Legislatures: A New Survey of the 50 States," *Legislative Studies Quarterly* 31 (2006): 105–134.

13 Gary C. Jacobson, *The Politics of Congressional Elections*, 6th ed. (New York: Pearson, 2004).

14 Hibbing and Alford, "Constituency Population and Representation in the U.S. Senate"; Krasno, *Challengers, Competition and Reelection*.

15 Lee and Oppenheimer, *Sizing Up the Senate*, 64; Bruce I. Oppenheimer, "The Effect of State Population on Senator-Constituency Linkages," *American Journal of Political Science* 40 (1996): 1280–1299.

16 Sarah Binder, Forrest Maltzman, and Lee Siegelman, "Accounting for Senators' Home-State Reputations: Why Do Constituents Love a Bill Cohen So Much More Than an Al D'Amato," *Legislative Studies Quarterly* 23 (1998): 545–560.

17 Squire, "Professionalization and Public Opinion of State Legislatures."

18 Jeffrey E. Cohen and James D. King, "Relative Unemployment and Gubernatorial Popularity," *Journal of Politics* 66 (2004): 1267–1282; James D. King and Jeffrey E. Cohen, "What Determines a Governor's Popularity," *State Politics and Policy Quarterly* 5 (2005): 225–247.

19 Squire and Hamm, *101 Chambers*, 55–58.

20 Angus Campbell, Phillip W. Converse, Warren E. Miller, and Donald E. Stokes, *The American Voter* (New York: John Wiley and Sons, 1960); Donald Green, Bradley Palmquist, and Eric Schickler, *Partisan Hearts and Minds: Political Parties and the Social Identities of Voters* (New Haven, CT: Yale University Press, 2002).

21 Jane Mansbridge, "Should Blacks Represent Blacks and Women Represent Women? A Contingent Yes," *Journal of Politics* 61 (1999): 628–657.

22 Claudine Gay, "Spirals of Trust? The Effect of Descriptive Representation on the Relationship Between Citizens and Their Government," *American Journal of Political Science* 46 (2002): 717–732; Janet M. Box-Steffensmeier, David C. Kimball, Scott R. Meinke, and Katherine Tate, "The Effects of Political Representation on the Electoral Advantages of House Incumbents," *Political Research Quarterly* 56 (2003): 259–270; Katherine Tate, *Black Faces in the Mirror: African Americans and Their Representatives in the U.S. Congress* (Princeton, NJ: Princeton University Press, 2003); John D. Griffin and Patrick Flavin, "Racial Differences in Information, Expectations and Accountability," *Journal of Politics* 69 (2007): 220–236.

23 This relationship may be particularly strong for African-American citizens represented by an African-American member of Congress. Hence, the models also include an interaction term controlling for this relationship.

24 Robert Darcy, Susan Welch, and Janet Clark, *Women, Elections, and Representation*, 2nd ed. (Lincoln, NE: University of Nebraska Press, 1994): 84–85.

25 Box-Steffensmeier, Kimball, Meinke, and Tate, "The Effects of Political Representation on the Electoral Advantages of House Incumbents"; Jennifer L. Lawless, "Politics of Presence? Congresswomen and Symbolic Representation," *Political Research Quarterly* 57 (2004): 81–99.

26 Richard Fenno, *Home Style: House Members in Their Districts* (Boston, MA: Little Brown, 1978).

27 John R. Hibbing, *Congressional Careers: Contours of Life in the U.S. House of Representatives* (Chapel Hill, NC: University of North Carolina Press), Chapter 5.

28 Sidney Verba, Kay Lehman Schlozman, and Henry E. Brady, *Voice and Equality: Civic Voluntarism in American Politics* (Cambridge, MA: Harvard University Press, 1995).

29 Box- Steffensmeier, Kimball, Meinke, and Tate, "The Effects of Political Representation on the Electoral Advantages of House Incumbents," 263.

30 Bruce Cain, John Ferejohn, and Morris Fiorina, *The Personal Vote* (Cambridge, MA: Harvard University Press, 1997); Richard Born, "The Shared Fortune of Congress and Congressmen, " *Journal of Politics* 52 (1990): 1223–1241; John R. Hibbing and Elizabeth Theiss-Morse, *Congress as Public Enemy* (New York: Cambridge University Press, 1995); Robert H. Durr, John Gilmour, and Christina Wolbrecht, "Explaining Congressional Approval," *American Journal of Political Science* 41 (1997): 175–207.

31 The statistics on district level area size were collected from data posted by Professor Scott Adler, http://socsci.colorado.edu/~esadler/districtdatawebsite/Congressional DsitrictDatasetwebpage.htm.

32 Since the number of respondents in this sample varies from 1 per district all the way up to 70 respondents per district the reliability of the point approximation for each dependent variable will be stronger for some incumbents than others. To address this disparity, the models tested in this study the data were weighted for the number of respondents in each district. Finally, because the key independent variable, con- stituency population, is identical for each respondent in the district the models are estimated with robust standard errors clustered on the congressional district.

33 All of the models tested in this study were estimated using a battery of year dummy variables. The results of the models were not substantively different than what is presented in this article's results. These models are not presented here in order to facilitate the calculation of predicted probabilities based on changes in level of dis- trict population.

34 This approach was utilized for all of the predicted probabilities cited in this study. Probabilities were calculated using CLARIFY. See Gary King, Michael Tomz, and Jason Wittenberg, "Making the Most of Statistical Analyses: Improving Interpretation and Presentation," *American Journal of Political Science* 44 (2000): 347–361.

35 Robert A. Dahl and Edward R. Tufte, *Size and Democracy* (Stanford, CA: Stanford University Press, 1973), 87.

36 Hibbing and Alford, "Constituency Population and Representation in the U.S. Senate"; Krasno, *Challengers, Competition and Reelection*; Oppenheimer, "The Effect of State Population on Senator-Constituency Linkages"; Lee and Oppenheimer, *Sizing Up the Senate.*

37 Hibbing and Theiss-Morse, *Congress as Public Enemy*, 64–66.

38 Ordered probit is the estimation technique for this analysis because the dependent variable is measured on an ordinal scale ranging from poor, coded 1, to very good, coded 4.

39 Heinz Eulau and Paul D. Karps, "The Puzzle of Representation: Specifying Components of Responsiveness," *Legislative Studies Quarterly* 2 (1977): 233–255.

40 For a more detailed explanation of this survey, see Daniel Romar, Kate Kenski, Paul Waldman, Christopher Adasiewicz, and Kathleen Hall Jamieson, *Capturing*

Campaign Dynamics: The National Annenberg Election Survey (New York: Oxford University Press, 2004).

41 A similar minimum threshold of cases is used for aggregation in other studies using the 2000 NAES data. See Joshua D. Clinton "Representation in Congress: Constituents and Roll Calls in the 106th House," *Journal of Politics* 68 (2006): 397–410. Clinton also uses survey data from Knowledge Networks in this study.

42 An errors-in-variables regression model was run in STATA 9 using the eivreg command and it produced substantively similar results.

43 Lee and Oppenheimer, *Sizing Up the Senate*, 64–65; Oppenheimer, "The Effect of State Population on Senator-Constituency Linkages"; Binder, Maltzman, and Siegelman, "Accounting for Senators' Home-State Reputations," 554.

44 For evidence of this trend, see Norman Ornstein, Thomas E. Mann, and Michael Malbin, *Vital Statistics on Congress, 2001–2002* (Washington, DC: American Enterprise Institute, 2002), Table 5–2.

45 David R. Mayhew, *Congress: The Electoral Connection* (New Haven, CT: Yale University Press, 1974); Morris P. Fiorina, *Congress: Keystone of the Washington Establishment* (New Haven, CT: Yale University Press, 1989).

46 For evidence of this phenomenon, see E. Scott Adler, Chariti E. Gent, and Cary B. Overmeyer, "The Home Style Homepage: Legislator Use of the World Wide Web for Constituency Contact," *Legislative Studies Quarterly* 23 (1998): 585–595; Jim VandeHei and Charles Babington, "Technology Sharpens the Incumbent's Edge: Redistricting also Complicates Democrats' Effort to Take Control of the House," *Washington Post*, June 7, 2006, A1.

47 Jacobson, *Politics of Congressional Elections*, 139.

48 Hibbing and Theiss-Morse, *Congress as Public Enemy*, 64.

49 Timothy Cook, "Legislature vs. Legislator: A Note on the Paradox of Congressional Support," *Legislative Studies Quarterly* 4 (1979): 43–52; Glenn R. Parker and Roger H. Davidson, "Why Do Americans Love Their Congressman So Much More Than Their Congress," *Legislative Studies Quarterly* 4 (1979): 53–61.

50 *Congressional Record*, 108th Congress, 1st Session, January 28, 2003, E81.

5 House Constituency Size and Voting Patterns

1 Heinz Eulau and Paul Karps, "The Puzzle of Representation: Specifying Components of Responsiveness," *Legislative Studies Quarterly* 2 (1977): 233–255.

2 V. O. Key, *Public Opinion and Democracy* (New York: Knopf, 1961).

3 David W. Rohde, *Parties and Leaders in the Postreform House* (Chicago: University of Chicago Press, 1991); Keith Poole and Howard Rosenthal, *Congress: A Political-Economic History of Roll Call Voting* (Oxford: Oxford University Press, 1997); Nolan M. McCarty, Keith T. Poole, and Howard Rosenthal, *Income Redistribution and the Realignment of American Politics* (Washington, DC: AEI Press, 1997); Tim Groseclose, Steven D. Levitt, and James M. Snyder, "Comparing Interest Group Scores across Time and Chamber: Adjusted ADA Scores for the U.S. Congress," *American Political Science Review* 93 (1999): 33–50; Keith T. Poole and Howard Rosenthal, "D-Nominate after 10 Years: A Comparative Update to *Congress: A Political-Economic History of Roll Call Voting*," *Legislative Studies Quarterly* 26 (2001): 5–29; Gary C. Jacobson, "Partisan Polarization in Presidential Support: The Electoral Connection," *Congress and the Presidency* 30 (2003): 1–36; Richard Fleischer and John R. Bond, "The Shrinking Middle in Congress," *British Journal of Political Science* 34 (2004): 429–451; Eric Schickler and Kathryn Pearson, "The House Leadership in an Era of Partisan Warfare," in *Congress Reconsidered*, 8th ed., eds. Lawrence C. Dodd and Bruce I. Oppenheimer (Washington, DC: CQ Press, 2005): 207–226; Nolan M. McCarthy, Keith T. Poole, and Howard Rosenthal, *Polarized America: The Dance of*

Ideology and Unequal Riches (Boston, MA: MIT Press, 2006); Barbara Sinclair, *Party Wars: Polarization and the Politics of National Policy Making* (Norman, OK: University of Oklahoma Press, 2006); Keith T. Poole and Howard Rosenthal, *Ideology and Congress* (Piscataway, NJ: Transaction Publishers, 2007).

4 Morris Fiorina, Samuel J. Abrams, and Jeremy C. Pope, *Culture War? The Myth of a Polarized America* (New York: Pearson-Longman, 2005); Juliet Eilperin, *Fight Club Politics, How Partisanship Is Poisoning the U.S. House of Representatives* (Washington, DC: Rowan and Littlefield, 2006).

5 For a thorough review of literature on the connection between public opinion and policy outcomes, see Paul Burstein, "The Impact of Public Opinion on Public Policy: A Review and an Agenda," *Political Research Quarterly* 56 (2003): 29–40.

6 Lawrence R. Jacobs and Robert Y. Shapiro, *Politicians Don't Pander: Political Manipulation and the Loss of Democratic Control* (Chicago, IL: University of Chicago Press, 2000); Jacob S. Hacker and Paul Pierson, *Off Center: The Republican Revolution and the Erosion of American Democracy* (New Haven, CT: Yale University Press, 2005).

7 James A. Stimson, Michael MacKuen, and Robert S. Erikson, "Dynamic Representation," *American Political Science Review* 89 (1995): 543–565; Robert S. Erikson, Michael B. MacKuen, and James A. Stimson, *The Macro Polity* (Cambridge: Cambridge University Press, 2002).

8 Larry M. Bartels, "Constituency Opinion and Congressional Policy Making: The Reagan Defense Build Up," *American Political Science Review* 85 (1991): 457–474; Cheryl Lyn Herrera, Richard Herrera, and Eric R. A. N. Smith, "Public Opinion and Congressional Representation," *Public Opinion Quarterly* 56 (1992): 185–205; Robert S. Erikson and Gerald C. Wright, "Voters, Candidates, and Issues in Congressional Elections," in *Congress Reconsidered*, 8th ed., eds. Lawrence C. Dodd and Bruce I. Oppenheimer (Washington, DC: CQ Press, 2005), 100.

9 Alan I. Abramowitz, "Incumbency, Campaign Spending, and the Decline of Competition in U.S. House Elections," *Journal of Politics* 53 (1991): 34–56; Alan I. Abramowitz and Jeffrey Segal, *Senate Elections* (Ann Arbor, MI: University of Michigan Press, 1992; Stephen Ansolabehere, James Snyder, and Charles Stewart, "Candidate Positioning in U.S. House Elections," *American Journal of Political Science* 45 (2001): 17–34; Brandice Canes-Wrones, David W. Brady, and John F. Cogan, "Out of Step, Out of Office: Electoral Accountability and House Members' Voting," *American Political Science Review* 96 (2002): 127–140; Erikson and Wright, "Voters, Candidates, and Issues in Congressional Elections."

10 Ansolabehere, Snyder, and Stewart, "Candidate Positioning in U.S. House Elections."

11 Fiorina, Abrams, and Pope, *Culture War?*

12 For documentation of this trend, see Gary C. Jacobson, *The Politics of Congressional Elections*, 6th ed. (New York: Pearson, 2004), 139.

13 Federal Farmer, "Letter VII December 31, 1787," in *The Essential Antifederalist*, 2nd ed., eds. W. B. Allen and Gordon Lloyd (Lanham, MD: Rowan and Littlefield, 2002), 289.

14 See the remarks of Rep. Stan Tupper, *Congressional Record*, 87th Congress, 2nd Session, March 15, 1962, 3736.

15 William F. Willoughby, *Principles of Legislative Organization and Administration* (Washington, DC: The Brookings Institution, 1934): 261–262.

16 Robert A. Dahl and Edward R. Tufte, *Size and Democracy* (Stanford, CA: Stanford University Press, 1973), 84–85.

17 Rein Taagepera and Mathew Soberg Shugart, *Seats and Votes* (New Haven, CT: Yale University Press, 1989), 179.

18 John M. Carey, Richard G. Niemi, and Linda W. Powell, *Term Limits in the State Legislatures* (Ann Arbor, MI: University of Michigan Press, 2000), 60.

19 John R. Hibbing, "Ambition in the House: Behavioral Consequences of Higher Office Goals Among U.S. Representatives," *American Journal of Political Science* 30 (1986): 651–665.

20 David Mayhew, *Congress: The Electoral Connection* (New Haven, CT: Yale University, 1974).

21 Anthony Downs, *An Economic Theory of Democracy* (New York: Harper Brothers, 1957); Gerald C. Wright, "Policy Voting in the U.S. Senate: Who is Represented," *Legislative Studies Quarterly* 14 (1989): 465–486.

22 Morris P. Fiorina, *Representatives, Roll Call and Constituencies* (Lexington, MA: D. C. Heath, 1974); Elizabeth R. Gerber and Jeffrey B. Lewis, "Beyond the Median: Voter Preferences, District Heterogeneity and Political Representation," *Journal of Political Economy* 112 (2004): 1364–1383.

23 Joshua D. Clinton, "Representation in Congress: Constituents and Roll Calls in the 106th House," *Journal of Politics* 68 (2006): 397–410.

24 John R. Hibbing and Sarah Brandes, "State Population and the Electoral Success of U.S. Senators," *American Journal of Political Science* 27 (1983): 808–819; Alan I. Abramowitz, "Explaining Senate Outcomes," *American Political Science Review* 82 (1988): 385–403; Abramowitz and Segal, *Senate Elections*; Frances Lee and Bruce I. Oppenheimer, "Senate Apportionment: Competitiveness and Partisan Advantage," *Legislative Studies Quarterly* 22 (1997): 3–24; Frances Lee and Bruce I. Oppenheimer, *Sizing Up the Senate: The Unequal Consequences of Equal Representation* (Chicago: University of Chicago Press, 1999): 93–95.

25 Dahl and Tufte, *Size and Democracy*, 85.

26 Fiorina, *Representatives, Roll Call and Constituencies*; Elizabeth R. Gerber and Jeffrey B. Lewis, "Beyond the Median."

27 The corresponding years for each Congress are 92nd Congress (1971–1972), 97th Congress (1981–1982), 102nd Congress (1991–1992), 103rd Congress (2001–2002).

28 Erikson and Wright, "Voters, Candidates, and Issues in Congressional Elections," 100; Phillip J. Arodin and James C. Garrand, "Measuring Constituency Ideology in U.S. House Districts: A Top-Down Simulation Approach," *Journal of Politics* 65 (2003): 1165–1189.

29 Gerber and Lewis, "Beyond the Median," 1375–1376.

30 Christopher Achen, "Measuring Representation," *American Journal of Political Science* 22 (1978): 475–510; Robert S. Erikson, "Constituency Opinion and Congressional Behavior: A Reexamination of the Miller-Stokes Representation Data," *American Journal of Political Science* 22 (1978): 511–535.

31 Warren E. Miller and Donald E. Stokes, "Constituency Influence in Congress," *American Political Science Review* 57 (1963): 45–56.

32 Clinton, "Representation in Congress," 397–410.

33 Arodin and Garrand, "Measuring Constituency Ideology in U.S. House Districts," 1165–1189; Erikson, "Constituency Opinion and Congressional Behavior," 511–535.

34 Clinton, "Representation in Congress," 399; Kim Quaile Hill and Patricia A. Hurley, "Dyadic Representation Reappraised," *American Journal of Political Science* 43 (1999): 109–137.

35 Ansolabehere, Snyder, and Stewart, "Candidate Positioning in U.S. House Elections," 17–34; Canes-Wrones, Brady, and Cogan, "Out of Step, Out of Office: Electoral Accountability and House Members' Voting," 127–140; Erikson and Wright, "Voters, Candidates, and Issues in Congressional Elections."

36 Matthew S. Levendusky, Jeremy C. Pope, and Simon Jackman, "Measuring District Level Preferences with Implications for the Analysis of U.S. Elections," Working Paper, http:// jackman.stanford.edu/ papers/download.php?i=8.

37 Poole and Rosenthal, *Congress: A Political-Economic History of Roll Call Voting*. DW-NOMINATE scores downloaded from: http://voteview.com/dwnomin.htm.

38 However, there are periods in U.S. history when divisions within the party coalitions create a second dimension, like the issue of race in the middle of the twentieth century.

39 Fiorina, *Representatives, Roll Call and Constituencies*; James H. Kuklinski, "District Competitiveness and Legislative Roll-Call Behavior: A Reassessment of the Marginality Hypothesis," *American Journal of Political Science* 21 (1977): 627–638; Ansolabehere, Snyder, and Stewart, "Candidate Positioning in U.S. House Elections"; Girish Gulatti, "Revisiting the Link Between Electoral Competition and Policy Extremism in the U.S. Congress," *American Politics Research* 32 (2004): 495–530. For contrary evidence on the marginality hypothesis, see John D. Griffin, "Electoral Competition and Democratic Responsiveness: A Defense of the Marginality Hypothesis," *Journal of Politics* 68 (2006): 911–921.

40 Rebekah Herrick, Michael K. Moore, and John R. Hibbing, "Unfastening the Electoral Connection: The Behavior of U.S. Representatives when Reelection is No Longer a Factor," *Journal of Politics* 56 (1994): 214–227. However, the connection between retirement status and shifts in roll-call voting behavior is quite marginal. See Lawrence S. Rothenberg and Mitchell S. Sanders, "Severing the Electoral Connection: Shirking in the Contemporary Congress," *American Journal of Political Science* 44 (2000): 316–325.

41 Hibbing, "Ambition in the House," 651–665.

42 Rohde, *Parties and Leaders in the Postreform House*.

43 McCarthy, Poole, and Rosenthal, *Polarized America*.

44 Southern states include Alabama, Arkansas, Florida, Georgia, Kentucky, Louisiana, Mississippi, North Carolina, Oklahoma, South Carolina, Tennessee, Texas, and Virginia.

45 David Lublin, *The Paradox of Representation: Racial Gerrymandering and Minority Interest in Congress* (Princeton, NJ: Princeton University Press, 1997), 69.

46 Katherine Tate, *Black Faces in the Mirror: African Americans and Their Representatives in the U.S. Congress* (Princeton, NJ: Princeton University Press, 2003).

47 Barbara C. Burrell, *A Woman's Place Is in the House: Campaigning for Congress in the Feminist Era* (Ann Arbor, MI: University of Michigan Press, 1994); Arturo Vega and Juanita M. Firestone, "The Effects of Gender on Congressional Behavior and the Substantive Representation of Women," *Legislative Studies Quarterly* 20 (1995): 213–222; Janet Clark, "Women at the National Level: An Update on Roll Call Voting Behavior," in *Women and Elective Office: Past Present and Future*, eds. Sue Thomas and Clyde Wilcox (New York: Oxford University Press, 1998), 118–129; Michele L. Swers, "Are Women More Likely to Vote for Women's Issues Bills than Their Male Colleagues," *Legislative Studies Quarterly* (1998): 435–448.

48 McCarty, Poole, and Rosenthal, *Income Redistribution and the Realignment of American Politics*, 26–27; Leslie A. Schwindt-Bayer and Renato Corbetta, "Gender Turnover and Roll-Call Voting in the U.S. House of Representatives," *Legislative Studies Quarterly* 25 (2004): 215–229.

49 Gary W. Cox and Matthew D. McCubbins, *Setting the Agenda: Responsible Party Government in the U.S. House of Representatives* (Cambridge: Cambridge University Press, 2005).

50 In recent Congresses the median of the majority party has been further toward the extreme than the minority party median. See Rohde, *Parties and Leaders in the Postreform House*; John H. Aldrich and David W. Rohde, "The Consequences of Party Organization in the House: The Role of Majority and Minority Parties in Conditional Party Government," in *Polarized Politics: Congress and the President in a Partisan Era*, eds. John R. Bond and Richard Fleisher, (Washington, DC: CQ Press, 2000), 64.

51 Hacker and Pierson, *Off Center*.
52 Rohde, *Parties and Leaders in the Postreform House*; Aldrich and Rhode, "The Consequences of Party Organization in the House," 64; Bernard Groffman, William Koetze, and Anthony J. McGann, "Congressional Leadership 1965–1996: A New Look at the Extremism Versus Centrality Debate," *Legislative Studies Quarterly* 27 (2002): 87–105; Eric Heberlig, Marc Hetherington, and Bruce Larson, "The Price of Leadership: Campaign Money and the Polarization of Congressional Parties," *Journal of Politics* 68 (2006): 992–1005.
53 John H. Aldrich and David W. Rohde, "Congressional Committees in a Partisan Era," in *Congress Reconsidered*, 8th ed., eds. Lawrence C. Dodd and Bruce I. Oppenheimer (Washington, DC: CQ Press, 2005), 249–270.
54 John R. Hibbing, *Congressional Careers: Contours of Life in the Modern U.S. House of Representatives* (Chapel Hill, NC: University of North Carolina Press, 1991).
55 The results for the individual Congresses reveal that district population achieves statistical significance in the 97th, 102nd, and 107th at least the .05 level. However, in the 92nd Congress there appears to be no significant relationship between these variables.
56 Models estimated for each individual Congress reveal that the coefficient for district population is in the expected negative direction for each Congress, but only achieves statistical significance in the 97th and 102nd at least at the .05 level. For the 92nd and 107th Congresses there is no significant relationship between these variables.
57 Gary C. Jacobson, "Party Polarization in National Politics: The Electoral Connection," in *Polarized Politics: Congress and the President in a Partisan Era*, eds. Jon R. Bond and Richard Fleischer (Washington, DC: CQ Press, 2000), 9–30; Kyle L. Saunders and Alan I. Abramowitz, "Ideological Realignment and Active Partisans in the Electorate," *American Politics Research* 32 (2004): 285–309.
58 Jacobs and Shapiro, *Politicians Don't Pander*; Ansolabehere, Snyder, and Stewart, "Candidate Positioning in U.S. House Elections."
59 Fleischer and Bond, "The Shrinking Middle in Congress," 446–450; Fiorina, Abrams, and Pope, *Culture War*, Chapter 8.
60 Dahl and Tufte, *Size and Democracy*, 84–85.

6 Public Opinion on the Size of the House

1 Brian Frederick. "The People's Perspective on the Size of the People's House," *PS: Political Science and Politics* 41 (2008): 329–335.
2 John R. Hibbing and Elizabeth Theiss-Morse, *Congress as Public Enemy: Public Attitudes Toward American Political Institutions* (New York: Cambridge University, 1995); John R. Hibbing, "Images of Congress," in *Institutions of American Democracy: The Legislative Branch*, eds. Paul J. Quirk and Sarah A. Binder (Oxford: Oxford University Press, 2005), 461–490; John R. Hibbing and Christopher W. Larimer, "What the American Public Wants Congress to Be," in *Congress Reconsidered*, 8th ed., eds. Lawrence Dodd and Bruce Oppenheimer (Washington, DC: CQ Press, 2005), 55–77.
3 Samuel C. Patterson and Gregory A. Caldiera, "Standing Up for Congress: Variations in Public Esteem Since the 1960s," *Legislative Studies Quarterly* 15 (1990): 25–47; Robert H. Durr, John Gilmour, and Christina Wolbrecht, "Explaining Congressional Approval," *American Journal of Political Science* 41 (1997): 175–207; Hibbing and Larimer, "What the American Public Wants Congress to Be," 57.
4 Glenn R. Parker and Roger H. Davidson, "Why Do Americans Love Their Congressmen So Much More Than Their Congress," *Legislative Studies Quarterly* 4 (1979): 52–61; Timothy Cook, "Legislature vs. Legislator: A Note on the Paradox of Congressional Support," *Legislative Studies Quarterly* 4 (1979): 43–52.

5 Richard Fenno, *Home Style: House Members in Their Districts* (Boston, MA: Little Brown, 1978). For evidence that this tactic is not as widespread as previously thought, see Daniel Lipinski, *Congressional Communication: Content and Consequences* (Ann Arbor, MI: University of Michigan Press, 2004).

6 John R. Hibbing and Elizabeth Theiss-Morse, *Stealth Democracy: Americans' Beliefs About How Government Should Work* (New York: Cambridge University Press, 2002); John R. Hibbing and James T. Smith, "Is It the Middle That Is Frustrated? Americans' Ideological Positions and Government Trust," *American Politics Research* 32 (2004): 652–678.

7 Hibbing and Theiss-Morse, *Congress as Public Enemy*; David C. Kimball and Samuel C. Patterson, "Living Up to Expectations: Public Attitudes Toward Congress," *Journal of Politics* 59 (1997): 701–728.

8 Marc J. Hetherington, *Why Political Trust Matters and the Demise of American Liberalism* (Princeton, NJ: Princeton University Press, 2005).

9 Hibbing and Theiss-Morse, *Stealth Democracy*; Hibbing and Larimer, "What the American Public Wants Congress to Be," 55–77.

10 Michael Merrill and Sean Wilentz, "The Big House: An Alternative to Term Limits," *New Republic* November 16, 1992, 16.

11 Alan Ehrenhalt, "Rightsizing the Legislature," *Governing*, July 2001, 6–8.

12 Hibbing and Theiss-Morse, *Congress as Public Enemy*; Kimball and Patterson, "Living Up to Expectations," 701–728.

13 Hibbing and Theiss-Morse, *Congress as Public Enemy*.

14 For a more thorough review of the average citizen's lack of political knowledge, see Michael X. Deli Carpini and Scott Keeter, *What Americans Know About Politics and Why It Matters* (New Haven, CT: Yale University Press, 1996).

15 Hibbing and Theiss-Morse, *Stealth Democracy*; John R. Hibbing, "How to Make Congress Popular," *Legislative Studies Quarterly* 27 (2002): 219–244.

16 Hibbing and Theiss-Moore, *Congress as Public Enemy*, 25.

17 Jon A. Krosnik and Lin Chait Chang, "A Comparison of the Random Digit Dialing Telephone Survey Methodology with Internet Survey Methodology as Implemented by Knowledge Networks and Harris Interactive," Stanford University, http://www.knowledgenetworks.com/ganp/docs/OSUpaper.pdf.

18 Recent studies using Knowledge Networks data include Jennifer L. Lawless, "Women, War and Winning Elections: Gender Stereotyping in the Post-September 11th Era," *Political Research Quarterly* 57 (2004): 479–490; D. Sunshine Hillygus and Todd Shields, "Moral Issues and Voter Decision Making in the 2004 Presidential Election," *PS: Political Science and Politics* 33 (2005): 201–209; Joshua D. Clinton, "Representation in Congress: Constituents and Roll Calls in the 106th House," *Journal of Politics* 68 (2006): 397–410.

19 Poststratification weighting was employed to control for minor variations in the sample compared to the general population.

20 William F. Willoughby, *Principles of Legislative Organization and Administration* (Washington, DC: The Brookings Institution, 1934).

21 Nelson W. Polsby, "The Institutionalization of the House of Representatives," *American Political Science Review* 62 (1968): 144–168; Kenneth A. Shepsle, "Representation and Governance: The Great Legislative Trade-off," *Political Science Quarterly* 103 (1988): 461–484.

22 William Proxmire, "A House Divided in Half; Wanna Save Money? Fire Every Other Person on Capitol Hill," *Washington Post*, February 5, 1989, D5; Morris Silverman, "Better Yet, Reduce the Size of the House," *New York Times*, January 14, 1991, A17.

23 Charles A. Kromkowski and John A. Kromkowski, "Why 435? A Question of Political Arithmetic," *Polity* 24 (1991): 137; Christopher St. John Yates, "A House

of Our Own or a House We've Outgrown? An Argument for Increasing the Size of the House of Representatives," *Columbia Journal of Law and Social Problems* 25 (1992): 161.

24 James Glassman, "Let's Build a Bigger House; Why Shouldn't the Number of Congressmen Grow with the Population," *Washington Post*, June 17, 1990, D2; Kromkowski and Kromkowski, "Why 435," 141; Wilma Rule, "Expanded Congress Would Help Women," *New York Times*, February 24, 1991, E16; Yates, "A House of Our Own or a House We've Outgrown," 193.

25 Ronald Keith Gaddie and Charles S. Bullock, *Elections to Open Seats in the U.S. House: Where the Action Is* (Lanham, MD: Rowan & Littlefield Publishers, 2000).

26 Barbara C. Burrell, "Women Candidates in Open Seat Primaries for the U.S. House: 1968–1990," *Legislative Studies Quarterly* 17 (1992): 493–508.

27 Barbara C. Burrell, *A Woman's Place Is in the House: Campaigning for Congress in the Feminist Era* (Ann Arbor, MI: University of Michigan Press, 1994); Barbara Palmer and Dennis Simon, *Breaking the Political Glass Ceiling: Women and Congressional Elections* (New York: Routledge, 2006).

28 Glassman, "Let's Build a Bigger House," D2; Kromkowski and Kromkowski, "Why 435," 141. For a contrary assessment disputing the potential benefits to minorities, see L. Marvin Overby, "Apportionment, Politics and Political Science: A Response to Kromkowski and Kromkowski," *Polity* 24 (1992): 483–494; Mark E. Rush, "Making the House More Representative: Hidden Costs and Unintended Consequences," in *The U.S. House of Representatives: Reform or Rebuild*, eds. Joseph F. Zimmerman and Wilma Rule (Westport, CT: Praeger, 2000), 53–54.

29 Rosemarie Zagarri, *The Politics of Size: Representation in the United States, 1776–1850* (Ithaca, NY: Cornell University Press, 1987), 49.

30 Jane Mansbridge, "Should Blacks Represent Blacks and Women Represent Women? A Contingent 'Yes,'" *Journal of Politics* 61 (1999): 628–657.

31 Claudine Gay, "Spirals of Trust? The Effect of Descriptive Representation on the Relationship between Citizens and Their Government," *American Journal of Political Science* 46 (2002): 717–732; Katherine Tate, *Black Faces in the Mirror: African Americans and Their Representatives in the U.S. Congress* (Princeton, NJ: Princeton University Press, 2003); John D. Griffin and Patrick Flavin, "Racial Differences in Information, Expectations and Accountability," *Journal of Politics* 69 (2007): 220–236.

32 Jennifer L. Lawless, "Politics or Presence? Congresswomen and Symbolic Representation," *Political Research Quarterly* 57 (2004): 81–99.

33 Of course these results could simply be a reflection of the reality that increasing the size of the House is of little salience to most Americans. On this issue, many individuals respond even if the question asks for what is for them a non-attitude.

34 Hibbing and Theiss-Morse, *Congress as Public Enemy*.

35 Multinomial probit was employed instead of multinomial logit because, since it allows errors to be correlated across choices, a multinomial probit model eliminates the independence of irrelevant alternatives (IIA) assumption. See J. Scott Long, *Regression Models for Categorical and Limited Dependent Variables* (Thousand Oaks, CA: Sage, 1997), 184.

36 This lack of support among conservatives runs counter to the views of a number of conservative opinion writers who have come out in favor of increasing the U.S. House in recent years. See Robert Novak, *Completing the Revolution: A Vision for Victory in 2000* (New York: The Free Press, 2000), 187–188; George Will, "Congress Just Isn't Big Enough," *Washington Post*, January 14, 2001, B7; Jeff Jacoby, "A Bigger More Democratic Congress," *Boston Globe*, January 13, 2005.

37 Hibbing and Theiss-Morse, *Congress as Public Enemy*, 120.

38 Steven E. Finkel, Thomas M. Guterbock, and Marian J. Borg, "Race-of-Interviewer-Effects in Preelection Polls: Virginia 1989," *Public Opinion Quarterly* 55 (1991): 313–330; Emily W. Kane and Laura J. Macaulay, "Interviewer Gender and Gender Attitudes," *Public Opinion Quarterly* 57 (1993): 1–28; Adam J. Berinsky, "The Two Faces of Public Opinion," *American Journal of Political Science* 43 (1999): 1209–1230.

39 For evidence that increased levels of privacy in the administration of surveys reduces the likelihood that White respondents will give socially desirable answers, see Maria Krysan, "Privacy and the Expression of White Racial Attitudes: A Comparison Across Three Contexts," *Public Opinion Quarterly* 62 (1998): 506–544.

40 Alan I. Abramowitz and Kyle L. Saunders, "Ideological Realignment in the US Electorate," *Journal of Politics* 60 (1998): 634–652.

41 Edward G. Carmines and James A. Stimson, *Issue Evolution: Race and the Transformation of American Politics* (Princeton, NJ: Princeton University Press, 1989).

42 Alan I. Abramowitz, "Issue Evolution Reconsidered: Racial Attitudes and Partisanship in the U.S. Electorate," *American Journal of Political Science* 38 (1994): 1–24.

43 Virginia Sapiro, "It's the Context, Situation and Opinion, Stupid: The Gender Basis of Public Opinion," in *Understanding Public Opinion*, eds. Barbra Norrander and Clyde Wilcox (Washington, DC: CQ Press, 2002), 21–42.

44 It is possible that the racial divisions on a question like this one could have been diminished following the election of President Barack Obama.

45 Donald R. Kinder and Lynn M. Sanders, *Divided by Color: Racial Politics and Democratic Ideals* (Chicago: Chicago University Press, 1996).

46 Fifty-six percent of the African American respondents in this sample resided in the South.

47 Jeffrey M. Stonecash, *Class and Party in American Politics* (Boulder, CO: Westview Press, 2000); Nolan M. McCarty, Keith T. Poole, and Howard Rosenthal, *Polarized America: The Dance of Ideology and Unequal Riches* (Boston, MA: MIT Press, 2006); Jeffrey M. Stonecash, *Political Parties Matter: Realignment and the Return of Partisan Voting* (Boulder, CO: Lynne Rienner Publishers, 2006).

48 African-American Republicans were not included in this analysis due to their limited presence in this sample.

49 Gay, "Spirals of Trust"; Tate, *Black Faces in the Mirror*; Lawless, "Politics or Presence?"

50 Peverill Squire and Keith E. Hamm, *101 Chambers: Congress, State Legislatures and the Future of Legislative Studies* (Columbus, OH: The Ohio State University Press, 2005), 55–58.

51 Frederick, "The People's Perspective on the Size of the People's House," 347.

52 Adam Nagourney and Janet Elder, "Only 25% in Poll Approve of the Congress," *New York Times*, September 21, 2006, A1.The survey was conducted September 15–19, 2006.

7 The Size of the House: Does it Really Matter?

1 Nelson W. Polsby, "The Institutionalization of the House of Representatives," *American Political Science Review* 62 (1968): 144–168; Kenneth A. Shepsle, "Representation and Governance: The Great Legislative Trade-off," *Political Science Quarterly* 103 (1988): 461–484.

2 Glenn R. Parker and Roger H. Davidson, "Why Do Americans Love Their Congressmen So Much More Than Their Congress," *Legislative Studies Quarterly* 4

(1979); 52–61; Timothy Cook, "Legislature vs. legislator: A Note on the Paradox of Congressional Support," *Legislative Studies Quarterly* 4 (1979): 43–52.

3 John R. Hibbing and Elizabeth Theiss-Morse, *Congress as Public Enemy: Public Attitudes Toward American Political Institutions* (New York: Cambridge University, 1995); David C. Kimball and Samuel C. Patterson, "Living Up to Expectations: Public Attitudes toward Congress," *Journal of Politics* 59 (1997): 701–728.

4 Robert A. Dahl and Edward R. Tufte, *Size and Democracy* (Stanford, CA: Stanford University Press, 1973), 84–85.

5 Morris Silverman, "Better Yet, Reduce the Size of the House," *New York Times*, January 14, 1991, A17.

6 See Congressional Research Service at http://www.loc.gov/crsinfo/.

7 William F. Willoughby, *Principles of Legislative Organization and Administration* (Washington, DC: Brookings Institution, 1934).

8 Bertrand De Jouvenal, "The Chairman's Problem," *American Political Science Review* 55 (1961): 368–372.

9 Jane Mansbridge, "Should Blacks Represent Blacks and Women Represent Women? A Contingent 'Yes,'" *Journal of Politics* 61 (1999): 628–657.

10 Lawrence C. Evans and Walter J. Oleszek, "If It Ain't Broke Don't Fix It a Lot," in *The U.S. House of Representatives: Reform or Rebuild*, eds. Joseph Zimmerman and Wilma Rule (Westport, CT: Praeger Publishing, 2000), 189–190.

11 L. Marvin Overby, "Apportionment, Politics and Political Science: A Response to Kromkowski and Kromkowski," *Polity* 24 (1992): 489.

12 Robert Novak, *Completing the Revolution: A Vision for Victory in 2000* (New York: The Free Press 2000), 187–188; George Will, "Congress Just Isn't Big Enough," *Washington Post*, January 14, 2001, B7; Jeff Jacoby, "A Bigger More Democratic Congress." *Boston Globe*, January 13, 2005.

13 Barbara Sinclair. 2007. *Unorthodox Lawmaking: New Legislative Processes in the U.S. Congress, 3rd ed.* (Washington, DC: CQ Press, 2007).

14 Overby, "Apportionment, Politics and Political Science," 489.

15 William Proxmire, "A House Divided in Half; Wanna Save Money? Fire Every Other Person on Capitol Hill," *Washington Post*, February 5, 1989, D5; Jeffrey W. Ladewig and Mathew P. Jasinski, "On the Causes and Consequences of and Remedies for Interstate Malapportionment of the U.S. House of Representatives," *Perspectives on Politics* 6 (2008): 89–107.

16 Charles A. Kromkowski and John A. Kromkowski, "Beyond Administrative Apportionment: Rediscovering the Constitutional Calculus of Representative Government," *Polity*, 24 (1992): 497.

17 Terry Moe, "Political Institutions: The Neglected Side of the Story," *Journal of Law, Economics and Organization* 6 (1990): 213–254.

18 Frank R. Baumgartner and Bryan D. Jones, *Agendas and Instability in American Politics* (Chicago: University of Chicago Press, 1993).

19 Keith Krehbiel, *Pivotal Politics: A Theory of U.S. Lawmaking* (Chicago: University of Chicago Press, 1998).

20 Barbara Sinclair, "The New World of U.S. Senators," in *Congress Reconsidered*, 8th ed., eds. Lawrence Dodd and Bruce Oppenheimer (Washington, DC: CQ Press, 2005), 1–22.

21 Stephen Ohlemacher, "Growing Population Shifts Political Power," *Associated Press*, December 22, 2005; Vincent B. Thompson, "Projecting Reapportionment," *Indiana Business Review* 40 (2005): 4–6.

22 Proxmire, "A House Divided in Half," D5; Ladewig and Jasinski, "On the Causes and Consequences of and Remedies for Interstate Malapportionment of the U.S. House of Representatives," 89–107.

23 Overby, "Apportionment, Politics and Political Science," 490.
24 Hibbing and Theiss-Morse, *Congress as Public Enemy*, 67.
25 Evans and Oleszek, "If It Ain't Broke Don't Fix It a Lot," 189–190.
26 Gary C Jacobson, *The Politics of Congressional Elections*, 6th ed. (New York: Pearson, 2004), 137–138.
27 David Mayhew, *Congress: The Electoral Connection* (New Haven, CT: Yale University Press, 1974).
28 Peverill Squire and Keith E. Hamm, *101 Chambers: Congress, State Legislatures and the Future of Legislative Studies* (Columbus, OH: The Ohio State University Press: 2005).

References

Abramowitz, Alan I. "Explaining Senate Outcomes." *American Political Science Review* 82 (1988): 385–403.

Abramowitz, Alan I. "Incumbency, Campaign Spending, and the Decline of Competition in U.S. House Elections." *Journal of Politics* 53 (1991): 34–56.

Abramowitz, Alan I. "Issue Evolution Reconsidered: Racial Attitudes and Partisanship in the US Electorate." *American Journal of Political Science* 38 (1994): 1–24.

Abramowitz, Alan I., and Kyle L. Saunders. "Ideological Realignment in the US Electorate." *Journal of Politics* 60 (1998): 634–652.

Abramowitz, Alan I., and Jeffrey Segal. *Senate Elections*. Ann Arbor: University of Michigan Press, 1992.

Abramowitz, Alan I., Brad Alexander, and Matthew Gunning. "Don't Blame Redistricting for Uncompetitive Elections." *PS: Political Science and Politics* 29 (2006): 87–90.

Abramowitz, Alan I., Brad Alexander, and Matthew Gunning. "Incumbency, Redistricting, and the Decline of Competition in U.S. House Elections." *Journal of Politics* 68 (2006): 75–88.

Achen, Christopher. "Measuring Representation." *American Journal of Political Science* 22 (1978): 475–510.

Adler, E. Scott, Chariti E. Gent, and Cary B. Overmeyer. "The Home Style Homepage: Legislator Use of the World Wide Web for Constituency Contact." *Legislative Studies Quarterly* 23 (1998): 585–595.

Aldrich, John H., and David W. Rohde. "The Consequences of Party Organization in the House: The Role of Majority and Minority Parties in Conditional Party Government." In *Polarized Politics: Congress and the President in a Partisan Era*. Edited by John R. Bond and Richard Fleisher, 249–270. Washington, DC: CQ Press, 2000.

Aldrich John H., and David W. Rohde. "Congressional Committees in a Partisan Era." In *Congress Reconsidered*, 8th ed. Edited by Lawrence C. Dodd and Bruce I. Oppenheimer, 249–270. Washington, DC: CQ Press, 2005.

Alford, John R., and David W. Brady. "Personal and Partisan Advantage in U.S. Congressional Elections, 1846–1990." In *Congress Reconsidered*, 5th ed., Edited by Lawrence C. Dodd and Bruce Oppenheimer, 146–147. Washington, DC: Congressional Quarterly Press, 1993.

Allen, W.B,. and Gordon Lloyd, eds. *The Essential Antifederalist*, 2nd ed. Lanham, MD: Rowan and Littlefield, 2002.

Alvarez, R. Michael, and Jason L. Saving. "Deficits, Democrats, and Distributive Benefits: Congressional Elections and the Pork Barrel in the 1980s." *Political Research Quarterly* 50 (1997): 809–831.

Anderson, Margo J. *The American Census: A Social History.* New Haven, CT: Yale University Press, 1988.

Anderson, Margo. "Growth of US Population Calls for Larger House of Representatives." *Population Today* 28 (2000): 1–4.

Ansolabehere, Stephen, James Snyder, and Charles Stewart. "Candidate Positioning in U.S. House Elections." *American Journal of Political Science* 45 (2001): 17–34.

Arodin, Phillip J., and James C. Garrand. "Measuring Constituency Ideology in U.S. House Districts: A Top-Down Simulation Approach." *Journal of Politics* 65 (2003): 1165–1189.

Balinski, Michael, and H. Peyton Young. *Fair Representation: Meeting the Ideal of One Man One Vote.* Washington, DC: Brookings Institution Press, 2001.

Baqir, Reza. "Districting and Overspending." *Journal of Political Economy* 110 (2002): 1318–1354.

Bartels, Larry M. "Constituency Opinion and Congressional Policy Making: The Reagan Defense Build Up." *American Political Science Review* 85 (1991): 457–474.

Bartels, Larry M. "Partisanship and Voting Behavior, 1952–1996." *American Journal of Political Science* 44 (2000): 35–50.

Baumgartner, Frank R., and Bryan D. Jones. *Agendas and Instability in American Politics.* Chicago: University of Chicago Press, 1993.

Berinsky, Adam J. "The Two Faces of Public Opinion." *American Journal of Political Science* 43 (1999): 1209–1230.

Binder, Sarah, Forrest Maltzman, and Lee Siegelman. "Accounting for Senators' Home-State Reputations: Why Do Constituents Love a Bill Cohen So Much More Than an Al D'Amato?" *Legislative Studies Quarterly* 23 (1998): 545–560.

Black, Gordon S. "Conflict in the Community: A Theory of the Effects of Community Size." *American Political Science Review* 68 (1974): 1245–1261.

Bledsoe, Timothy. *Careers in City Politics: The Case for Urban Democracy.* Pittsburgh, PA: University of Pittsburgh Press, 1993.

Born, Richard. "The Shared Fortune of Congress and Congressmen." *Journal of Politics* 52 (1990): 1223–1241.

Box-Steffensmeier, Janet, David C. Kimball, Scott R. Meinke, and Katherine Tate. "The Effects of Political Representation on the Electoral Advantages of House Incumbents." *Political Research Quarterly* 56 (2003): 259–270.

Bradbury, John Charles, and W. Mark Crain. "Legislative Organization and Government Spending: Cross-Country Evidence." *Journal of Public Economics* 82 (2001): 309–325.

Brickner, Bryan W. *Article the First of the Bill of Rights.* United States: Lulu.com, 2006.

Brunell, Thomas. *Redistricting and Representation: Why Competitive Elections Are Bad for America.* New York: Routledge, 2008.

Burnham, Water D. "Insulation and Responsiveness in Congressional Elections." *Political Science Quarterly* 90 (1975): 411–435.

Burrell, Barbara C. "Women Candidates in Open Seat Primaries for the U.S. House: 1968–1990." *Legislative Studies Quarterly* 17 (1992): 493–508.

Burrell, Barbara C. *A Woman's Place Is in the House: Campaigning for Congress in the Feminist Era.* Ann Arbor: University of Michigan Press: 1994.

Burstein, Paul. "The Impact of Public Opinion on Public Policy: A Review and an Agenda." *Political Research Quarterly* 56 (2003): 29–40.

Cain, Bruce, John Ferejohn, and Morris Fiorina. *The Personal Vote.* Cambridge, MA: Harvard University Press, 1987.

Campbell, Angus, Phillip W. Converse, Warren E. Miller, and Donald E. Stokes. *The American Voter.* New York: John Wiley and Sons, 1960.

Campbell, James E. "The Revised Theory of Surge and Decline." *American Journal of Political Science* 31 (1987): 956–978.

Canes-Wrone, Brandice, David W. Brady, and John F. Cogan. "Out of Step, Out of Office: Electoral Accountability and House Members' Voting." *American Political Science Review* 96 (2002): 127–140.

Carey, John M., Richard G. Niemi, and Lynda W. Powell. *Term Limits in the State Legislatures.* Ann Arbor: University of Michigan Press, 2000.

Carey, John M., Richard G. Niemi, and Lynda W. Powell. "Incumbency and the Probability of Reelection in State Legislative Elections." *Journal of Politics* 62 (2000): 671–700.

Carey, John M., Richard Niemi, Lynda Powell, and Gary F. Moncrief. "The Effects of Term Limits on State Legislatures: A New Survey of the 50 States." *Legislative Studies Quarterly* 31 (2006): 105–134.

Carmines, Edward G., and James A. Stimson. *Issue Evolution: Race and the Transformation of American Politics.* Princeton: Princeton University Press, 1989.

Carson, Jamie, Erik J. Engstrom, and Jason M. Roberts. "Candidate Quality, the Personal Vote and the Incumbency Advantage in Congress." *American Political Science Review* 101 (2007): 289–303.

Chen, Jowei, and Neil Malhotra. "The Law of k/n: The Effect of Chamber Size on Government Spending in Bicameral Legislatures." *American Political Science Review* 101 (2007): 657–676.

Clark, Janet. "Women at the National Level: An Update on Roll Call Voting Behavior." In *Women and Elective Office: Past Present and Future.* Edited by Sue Thomas and Clyde Wilcox, 118–129. New York: Oxford University Press, 1998.

Clinton, Joshua D. "Representation in Congress: Constituents and Roll Calls in the 106th House." *Journal of Politics* 68 (2006): 397–410.

Cohen, Jeffrey E., and James D. King. "Relative Unemployment and Gubernatorial Popularity." *Journal of Politics* 66 (2004): 1267–1282.

"Congress Must Fix House Membership." *New York Times.* October 9, 1920, 7.

Cook, Timothy. "Legislature vs. Legislator: A Note on the Paradox of Congressional Support." *Legislative Studies Quarterly* 4 (1979): 43–52.

Cooper, Joseph, and David Brady. "Institutional Context and Leadership Style: The House from Cannon to Rayburn." *American Political Science Review* 75 (1981): 411–425.

Cossolotto, Matthew. "Enlarge the House." *Christian Science Monitor*, December 22, 1989, 19.

Cossolotto, Matthew. "America has Outgrown the House of Representatives." *The Hill*, November 21, 2001.

Cover, Albert D., and David Mayhew. "Congressional Dynamics and the Decline of Competitive Congressional Elections." In *Congress Reconsidered*, 2nd ed. Edited by Lawrence Dodd and Bruce I. Oppenheimer, 62–82. Washington, DC: Congressional Quarterly Press, 1981.

Cox, Gary W., and Jonathan N. Katz. *Elbridge Gerry's Salamander: The Electoral Consequences of the Reapportionment Revolution.* Cambridge: Cambridge University Press, 2002.

Cox, Gary W. and Matthew D. McCubbins. *Setting the Agenda: Responsible Party Government in the U.S. House of Representatives.* Cambridge, U.K.: Cambridge University Press, 2005.

Crain, W. Mark. "Cost and Output in the Legislative Firm." *Journal of Legal Studies* 8 (1979): 607–621.

Crain, W. Mark, and Robert D. Tollison. "Legislative Size and Voting Rules." *Journal of Legal Studies* 6 (1977): 235–241.

CQ Almanac, Vol. 18. Washington, DC: Congressional Quarterly Press, 1962.

Dahl, Robert A., and Edward R. Tufte. *Size and Democracy.* Stanford, CA: Stanford University Press, 1973.

Darcy, Robert, Susan Welch, and Janet Clark. *Women, Elections, and Representation,* 2nd ed. Lincoln, NE: University of Nebraska Press, 1994.

De Jouvenal, Bertrand. "The Chairman's Problem." *American Political Science Review* 55 (1961): 368–372.

Deli Carpini, Michael X., and Scott Keeter. *What Americans Know About Politics and Why It Matters.* New Haven, CT: Yale University Press, 1996.

Derbyshire, J. Dennis, and Ian Derbyshire. *Encyclopedia of World Political Systems,* Vol. 18. Armonk, NY: M. E. Sharpe, 2000.

Downs, Anthony. *An Economic Theory of Democracy.* New York: Harper Brothers, 1957.

Duncan, Phil. "Enlarging the Congress: Boon for Democracy?" *CQ Weekly Report,* October 28, 1989, 2914.

Durr, Robert H., John Gilmour, and Christina Wolbrecht. "Explaining Congressional Approval." *American Journal of Political Science* 41 (1997): 175–207.

Eagles, Charles W. *Democracy Delayed: Congressional Reapportionment and Urban-Rural Conflict in the 1920s.* Athens, GA: University of Georgia Press, 1990.

Ehrenhalt, Alan. "Rightsizing the Legislature." *Governing,* July 2001, 6–8.

Eilperin, Juliet. *Fight Club Politics, How Partisanship Is Poisoning the U.S. House of Representatives.* Washington, DC: Rowan and Littlefield, 2006.

Erikson, Robert S. "Constituency Opinion and Congressional Behavior: A Reexamination of the Miller-Stokes Representation Data." *American Journal of Political Science* 22 (1978): 511–535.

Erikson, Robert S., and Gerald C. Wright. "Voters, Candidates, and Issues in Congressional Elections." In *Congress Reconsidered,* 8th ed. Edited by Lawrence C. Dodd and Bruce I. Oppenheimer, 77–106. Washington, DC: CQ Press, 2005.

Erikson, Robert S., Michael B. MacKuen, and James A. Stimson. *The Macro Polity.* Cambridge: Cambridge University Press, 2002.

Eulau, Heinz, and Paul D. Karps. "The Puzzle of Representation: Specifying Components of Responsiveness." *Legislative Studies Quarterly* 2 (1977): 233–255.

Evans, Lawrence C., and Walter J. Oleszek. "If It Ain't Broke Don't Fix It a Lot." In *The US House of Representatives: Reform or Rebuild.* Edited by Joseph Zimmerman and Wilma Rule, 187–193. Westport, CT: Praeger Publishing, 2000.

Farrand, Max, ed. *The Records of the Federal Convention of 1787,* Vols. 1–2. New Haven, CT: Yale University Press, 1966.

Feldman, Paul G., and James Jundrow. "Congressional Elections and Local Federal Spending." *American Journal of Political Science* 28 (1984): 147–163.

Fenno, Richard. *Home Style: House Members in Their Districts*. Boston, MA: Little Brown, 1978.

Ferejohn, John A. "On the Decline of Competition in Congressional Elections." *American Political Science Review* 71 (1977): 166–176.

Finkel, Steven E., Thomas M. Guterbock, and Marian J. Borg. "Race-of-Interviewer Effects in Preelection Polls: Virginia 1989." *Public Opinion Quarterly* 55 (1991): 313–330.

Fiorina, Morris P. *Representatives, Roll Call and Constituencies*. Lexington, MA: D.C. Heath, 1974.

Fiorina, Morris P. "The Case of the Vanishing Marginals: The Bureaucracy Did It." *American Political Science Review* 71 (1977): 177–181.

Fiorina, Morris P. *Congress: Keystone of the Washington Establishment*. New Haven, CT: Yale University Press, 1989.

Fiorina, Morris P., Samuel J. Abrams, and Jeremy C. Pope. *Culture War? The Myth of a Polarized America*. New York: Pearson-Longman, 2005.

Fitzpatrick, John C., ed. *The Writings of George Washington*. Washington, DC: U.S. Government Printing Office, 1931–1944.

Fleischer, Richard, and John R. Bond. "The Shrinking Middle in Congress." *British Journal of Political Science* 34 (2004): 429–451.

Frederick, Brian. "Constituency Population and Representation in the U.S. House." *American Politics Research* 36 (2008): 358–381.

Frederick, Brian. "The People's Perspective on the Size of the People's House." *PS: Political Science and Politics* 41 (2008): 329–335.

Gaddie, Ronald Keith, and Charles S. Bullock. *Elections to Open Seats in the U.S. House: Where the Action Is*. Lanham, MD: Rowan & Littlefield, 2000.

Gay, Claudine. "Spirals of Trust? The Effect of Descriptive Representation on the Relationship Between Citizens and Their Government." *American Journal of Political Science* 46 (2002): 717–732.

Gerber, Elizabeth R., and Jeffrey B. Lewis. "Beyond the Median: Voter Preferences, District Heterogeneity and Political Representation." *Journal of Political Economy* 112 (2004): 1364–1383.

Gilligan, Thomas W., and John G. Matsusaka. "Deviations from Constituents' Interest: The Role of Legislative Structures and Political Parties in the States." *Economic Inquiry* 33 (1995): 383–401.

Gilligan, Thomas W., and John G. Matsusaka. "Fiscal Policy, Legislature Size, and Political Parties: Evidence from State and Local Governments in the First Half of the 20th Century." *National Tax Journal* 54 (2001): 57–82.

Glassman, James. "Let's Build a Bigger House; Why Shouldn't the Number of Congressmen Grow with the Population?" *Washington Post*, June 17, 1990, D2.

Green, Donald P., and Jonathan Krasno. "Salvation for the Spendthrift Incumbent: Reestimating the Effects of Campaign Spending in House Elections." *American Journal of Political Science* 32 (1988): 884–907.

Green, Donald P., and Jonathan Krasno. "Rebuttal to Jacobson's New Evidence for Old Arguments." *American Journal of Political Science* 34 (1990): 363–372.

Green, Donald P., Bradley Palmquist, and Eric Schickler. *Partisan Hearts and Minds: Political Parties and the Social Identities of Voters*. New Haven, CT: Yale University Press, 2002.

Griffin, John D. "Electoral Competition and Democratic Responsiveness: A Defense of the Marginality Hypothesis." *Journal of Politics* 68 (2006): 911–921.

Griffin, John D., and Patrick Flavin. "Racial Differences in Information, Expectations and Accountability." *Journal of Politics* 69 (2007): 220–236.

Groffman, Bernard, William Koetze, and Anthony J. McGann. "Congressional Leadership 1965–1996: A New Look at the Extremism Versus Centrality Debate." *Legislative Studies Quarterly* 27 (2002): 87–105.

Groseclose, Tim, Steven D. Levitt, and James M. Snyder. "Comparing Interest Group Scores Across Time and Chamber: Adjusted ADA Scores for the U.S. Congress." *American Political Science Review* 93 (1999): 33–50.

Gulatti, Girish. "Revisiting the Link Between Electoral Competition and Policy Extremism in the U.S. Congress." *American Politics Research* 32 (2004): 495–530.

Hacker, Jacob S., and Paul Pierson. *Off Center: The Republican Revolution and the Erosion of American Democracy*. New Haven, CT: Yale University Press, 2005.

Hamilton, Alexander, James Madison, and John Jay. *The Federalist*. Edited by Terrence Ball. Cambridge, U.K.: Cambridge University Press, 2003.

Heberlig, Eric, Marc Hetherington, and Bruce Larson. "The Price of Leadership: Campaign Money and the Polarization of Congressional Parties." *Journal of Politics* 68 (2006): 992–1005.

Herrera, Cheryl Lyn, Richard Herrera, and Eric R. A. N. Smith. "Public Opinion and Congressional Representation." *Public Opinion Quarterly* 56 (1992): 185–205.

Herrick, Rebekah, Michael K. Moore, and John R. Hibbing. "Unfastening the Electoral Connection: The Behavior of U.S. Representatives When Reelection Is No Longer a Factor." *Journal of Politics* 56 (1994): 214–227.

Hetherington, Marc J. *Why Political Trust Matters and the Demise of American Liberalism*. Princeton: Princeton University Press, 2005.

Hibbing, John R. "Ambition in the House: Behavioral Consequences of Higher Office Goals Among U.S. Representatives." *American Journal of Political Science* 30 (1986): 651–665.

Hibbing, John R. *Congressional Careers: Contours of Life in the Modern U.S. House of Representatives*. Chapel Hill, NC: University of North Carolina Press, 1991.

Hibbing, John R. "How to Make Congress Popular." *Legislative Studies Quarterly* 27 (2002): 219–244.

Hibbing, John R. "Images of Congress." In *Institutions of American Democracy: The Legislative Branch*. Edited by Paul J. Quirk and Sarah A. Binder, 461–489. Oxford: Oxford University Press, 2005.

Hibbing, John R., and John R. Alford. "Constituency Population and Representation in the U.S. Senate." *Legislative Studies Quarterly* 15 (1990): 581–598.

Hibbing, John R., and Sarah Brandes. "State Population and the Electoral Success of U.S. Senators." *American Journal of Political Science* 27 (1983): 808–819.

Hibbing, John R., and Christopher W. Larimer. "What the American Public Wants Congress to Be." In *Congress Reconsidered*, 8th ed. Edited by Lawrence Dodd and Bruce Oppenheimer, 55–76. Washington, DC: CQ Press, 2005.

Hibbing, John R., and James T. Smith. "Is It the Middle That Is Frustrated? Americans' Ideological Positions and Government Trust." *American Politics Research* 32 (2004): 652–678.

Hibbing, John R., and Elizabeth Theiss-Morse. *Congress as Public Enemy: Public Attitudes Toward American Political Institutions*. New York: Cambridge University Press, 1995.

Hibbing, John R., and Elizabeth Theiss-Morse. *Stealth Democracy: Americans' Beliefs About How Government Should Work*. New York: Cambridge University Press, 2002.

Hickock, Eugene W. "The Framers' Understanding of Constituional Deliberation in Congress." *Georgia Law Review* 21 (1986): 217–272.

Hill, Kim Quaile, and Patricia A. Hurley. "Dyadic Representation Reappraised." *American Journal of Political Science* 43 (1999): 109–137.

Hillygus, D. Sunshine, and Todd Shields. "Moral Issues and Voter Decision Making in the 2004 Presidential Election." *PS: Political Science and Politics* 33 (2005): 201–209.

Hogan, Robert E. "Challenger Emergence, Incumbent Success and Electoral Accountability in State Legislative Elections." *Journal of Politics* 66 (2004): 1283–1303.

Hu, Spencer. "House Bill Would Give District the Vote." *Washington Post*, June 23, 2004, B1.

Jacobs, Lawrence R., and Robert Y. Shapiro. *Politicians Don't Pander: Political Manipulation and the Loss of Democratic Control.* Chicago: University of Chicago Press, 2000.

Jacobson, Gary C. *Money in Congressional Elections.* New Haven, CT: Yale University Press, 1980.

Jacobson, Gary C. "The Marginals Never Vanished: Incumbency and Competition to the US House of Representatives 1952–82." *American Journal of Political Science* 31 (1987): 126–141.

Jacobson, Gary C. "Strategic Politicians and the Dynamics of U.S. House Elections, 1946–1986." *American Political Science Review* 83 (1989): 773–793.

Jacobson, Gary C. "The Effects of Campaign Spending in Congressional Elections: New Evidence for Old Arguments." *American Journal of Political Science* 34 (1990): 334–362.

Jacobson, Gary C. "Party Polarization in National Politics: The Electoral Connection." In *Polarized Politics: Congress and the President in a Partisan Era.* Edited by Jon R. Bond and Richard Fleischer, 9–30. Washington, DC: CQ Press, 2000.

Jacobson, Gary C. "Partisan Polarization in Presidential Support: The Electoral Connection." *Congress and the Presidency* 30 (2003): 1–36.

Jacobson, Gary C. *The Politics of Congressional Elections,* 6th ed. New York: Pearson, 2004.

Jacoby, Jeff. "A Bigger More Democratic Congress." *Boston Globe*, January 13, 2005.

Johannes, John R., and John C. McAdams. "The Congressional Incumbency Effect: Is It Casework Policy Compatibility or Something Else? An Examination of the 1978 Election." *American Journal of Political Science* 25 (1981): 513–542.

Kane, Emily W., and Laura J. Macaulay. "Interviewer Gender and Gender Attitudes." *Public Opinion Quarterly* 57 (1993): 1–28.

Key, V. O. *Public Opinion and Democracy.* New York: Knopf, 1961.

Kimball, David C., and Samuel C. Patterson. "Living Up to Expectations: Public Attitudes Toward Congress." *Journal of Politics* 59 (1997): 701–728.

Kinder, Donald R., and Lynn M. Sanders. *Divided by Color: Racial Politics and Democratic Ideals.* Chicago: Chicago University Press, 1996.

King, Gary, Michael Tomz, and Jason Wittenberg. "Making the Most of Statistical Analyses: Improving Interpretation and Presentation." *American Journal of Political Science* 44 (2000): 347–361.

King, James D., and Jeffrey E. Cohen. "What Determines a Governor's Popularity?" *State Politics and Policy Quarterly* 5 (2005): 225–247.

Krasno, Jonathan. *Challengers, Competition and Reelection: Comparing Senate and House Elections.* New Haven, CT: Yale University Press, 1994.

Krehbiel, Keith. *Pivotal Politics: A Theory of U.S. Lawmaking.* Chicago: University of Chicago Press, 1998.

Kromkowski, Charles. "Framers Would Approve of a Larger House." *New York Times*, January 31, 1991, A22.

Kromkowski, Charles A., and John A. Kromkowski. "Why 435? A Question of Political Arithmetic." *Polity* 24 (1991): 129–145.

Kromkowski, Charles A., and John A. Kromkowski. "Beyond Administrative Apportionment: Rediscovering the Constitutional Calculus of Representative Government." *Polity* 24 (1992): 495–497.

Krosnik, Jon A., and Lin Chait Chang. "A Comparison of the Random Digit Dialing Telephone Survey Methodology with Internet Survey Methodology as Implemented by Knowledge Networks and Harris Interactive." http://www.knowledgenetworks.com/ganp/docs/OSUpaper.pdf.

Krysan, Maria. "Privacy and the Expression of White Racial Attitudes: A Comparison Across Three Contexts." *Public Opinion Quarterly* 62 (1998): 506–544.

Kuklinski, James H. "District Competitiveness and Legislative Roll-Call Behavior: A Reassessment of the Marginality Hypothesis." *American Journal of Political Science* 21 (1977): 627–638.

Lascher, Edward L. "Constituency Size and Incumbent Safety: A Reexamination." *Political Research Quarterly* 58 (2005): 269–278.

Lawless, Jennifer L. "Politics of Presence? Congresswomen and Symbolic Representation." *Political Research Quarterly* 57 (2004): 81–99.

Lawless, Jennifer L. "Women, War and Winning Elections: Gender Stereotyping in the Post-September 11th Era." *Political Research Quarterly* 57 (2004): 479–490.

Lee, Frances, and Bruce I. Oppenheimer. "Senate Apportionment: Competitiveness and Partisan Advantage." *Legislative Studies Quarterly* 22 (1997): 3–24.

Lee, Frances, and Bruce I. Oppenheimer. *Sizing Up the Senate: The Unequal Consequences of Equal Representation.* Chicago: University of Chicago Press, 1999.

Levendusky, Matthew S., Jeremy C. Pope, and Simon Jackman. "Measuring District Level Preferences with Implications for the Analysis of U.S. Elections." Working Paper. http://jackman.stanford.edu/papers/download.php?i=8.

Lijphart, Arend. "Reforming the House: Three Moderately Radical Proposals." In *The US House of Representatives: Reform or Rebuild.* Edited by Joseph Zimmerman and Wilma Rule, 135–140. Westport, CT: Praeger Publishing, 2000.

Lipinski, Daniel. *Congressional Communication: Content and Consequences.* Ann Arbor: University of Michigan Press, 2004.

Long, J. Scott. *Regression Models for Categorical and Limited Dependent Variables.* Thousand Oaks, CA: Sage, 1997.

Lublin, David. *The Paradox of Representation: Racial Gerrymandering and Minority Interest in Congress.* Princeton: Princeton University Press, 1997.

Lucas, DeWayne L., and Michael D. McDonald. "Is It Time to Increase the Size of the House of Representatives?" *American Review of Politics* 21 (2000): 367–381.

McCarty, Nolan M., Keith T. Poole, and Howard Rosenthal. *Income Redistribution and the Realignment of American Politics.* Washington, DC: AEI Press, 1997.

McCarty, Nolan M., Keith T. Poole, and Howard Rosenthal. *Polarized America: The Dance of Ideology and Unequal Riches.* Boston, MA: MIT Press 2006.

McCormick, Robert E., and Robert D. Tollison. *Politicians, Legislation and the Economy: An Inquiry into the Interest-Group Theory of Government.* Boston, MA: Martinus, Nijhoff Publishing, 1981.

McDonald, Michael P. "Drawing the Line on Competition." *PS: Political Science and Politics* 34 (2006): 91–95.

Mansbridge, Jane. "Should Blacks Represent Blacks and Women Represent Women? A Contingent 'Yes.'" *Journal of Politics* 61 (1999): 628–657.

Mayhew, David R. *Congress: The Electoral Connection*. New Haven, CT: Yale University Press, 1974.

Mayhew, David R. "Congressional Elections: The Case of the Vanishing Marginals." *Polity* 6 (1974): 295–317.

Merrill, Michael, and Sean Wilentz. "The Big House: An Alternative to Term Limits." *New Republic*, November 16, 1992, 16–17.

Miller, Warren E., and Donald E. Stokes. "Constituency Influence in Congress." *American Political Science Review* 57 (1963): 45–56.

Moe, Terry. "Political Institutions: The Neglected Side of the Story." *Journal of Law, Economics and Organization* 6 (1990): 213–254.

Montgomery, Lori, and Elissa Silverman. "Plan to Give D.C. a Vote in Congress Advances." *Washington Post*, May 11, 2006, A01.

Nagourney, Adam, and Janet Elder. "Only 25% in Poll Approve of the Congress." *New York Times*, September 21, 2006, A1.

Neubauer, Michael G., and Joel Zeitlin. "Outcomes of Presidential Elections and the House Size." *PS: Political Science and Politics* 36 (2003): 721–725.

Novak, Robert. *Completing the Revolution: A Vision for Victory in 2000*. New York: The Free Press, 2000.

Nutting, Brian, and H. Amy Stern, eds. *CQ's Politics in America 2002, the 107th Congress*. Washington, DC: Congressional Quarterly Inc., 2001.

Ohlemacher, Stephen. "Growing Population Shifts Political Power." *Associated Press*, December 22, 2005. http://news.yahoo.com/s/ap/20051222/ap_on_re/population.htm.

Oppenheimer, Bruce I. "The Effect of State Population on Senator-Constituency Linkages." *American Journal of Political Science*, 40 (1996): 1280–1299.

Oppenheimer, Bruce. "Deep Red and Blue Congressional Districts: The Causes and Consequences of Declining Party Competitiveness." In *Congress Reconsidered*, 8th ed. Edited by Lawrence C. Dodd and Bruce Oppenheimer, 135–158. Washington, DC: CQ Press, 2005.

Ornstein, Norman, Thomas E. Mann, and Michael Malbin. *Vital Statistics on Congress, 2001–2002*. Washington, DC: American Enterprise Institute, 2002.

Overby, L. Marvin. "Apportionment, Politics and Political Science: A Response to Kromkowski and Kromkowski." *Polity* 24 (1992): 483–494.

Palmer, Barbara, and Dennis Simon. *Breaking the Political Glass Ceiling: Women and Congressional Elections*. New York: Routledge, 2006.

Parker, Glenn R., and Roger H. Davidson. "Why Do Americans Love Their Congressmen So Much More Than Their Congress." *Legislative Studies Quarterly* 4 (1979): 53–61.

Parker, Glenn R., and Suzanne L. Parker. "The Correlates and Effects of Attention to District by House Members." *Legislative Studies Quarterly* 10 (1985): 223–242.

Patterson, Samuel C., and Gregory A. Caldiera. "Standing Up for Congress: Variations in Public Esteem Since the 1960s." *Legislative Studies Quarterly* 15 (1990): 25–47.

Pitkin, Hannah Fenichel. *The Concept of Representation*. Berkeley, CA: University of California Press, 1967.

Polsby, Nelson W. "The Institutionalization of the House of Representatives." *American Political Science Review* 62 (1968): 144–168.

Polsby, Nelson W. *How Congress Evolves: Social Bases of Institutional Change.* Oxford: Oxford University Press, 2004.

Poole, Keith T. "DW-NOMINATE Page." http://voteview.com/dwnomin.htm, accessed June 1, 2009.

Poole, Keith T., and Howard Rosenthal. *Congress: A Political-Economic History of Roll Call Voting.* Oxford: Oxford University Press, 1997.

Poole, Keith T., and Howard Rosenthal. "D-Nominate after 10 Years: A Comparative Update to *Congress: A Political-Economic History of Roll Call Voting.*" *Legislative Studies Quarterly* 26 (2001): 5–29.

Poole, Keith T., and Howard Rosenthal. *Ideology and Congress.* Piscataway, NJ: Transaction Publishers, 2007.

Proxmire, William. "A House Divided in Half; Wanna Save Money? Fire Every Other Person on Capitol Hill." *Washington Post,* February 5, 1989, D5.

Renda, Lex. "The End of Midterm Decline? Congressional Elections in Historical Perspective." *Social Science History* 27 (2003): 139–164.

Riker, William H. "Why Negative Campaigning Is Rational: The Rhetoric of the Ratification Campaign of 1787–1788." *Studies in American Political Development* 5 (1991): 224–283.

Rohde, David W. *Parties and Leaders in the Postreform House.* Chicago: University of Chicago Press, 1991.

Romar, Daniel, Kate Kenski, Paul Waldman, Christopher Adasiewicz, and Kathleen Hall Jamieson. *Capturing Campaign Dynamics: The National Annenberg Election Survey.* New York: Oxford University Press, 2004.

Romero, David W. "The Case of Missing Reciprocal Influence: Incumbent Reputation and the Vote." *Journal of Politics* 58 (1996): 1198–1207.

Rothenberg, Lawrence S., and Mitchell S. Sanders. "Severing the Electoral Connection: Shirking in the Contemporary Congress." *American Journal of Political Science* 44 (2000): 316–325.

Rule, Wilma. "Expanded Congress Would Help Women." *New York Times,* February 24, 1991, E16.

Rush, Mark E. "Making the House More Representative: Hidden Costs and Unintended Consequences." In *The US House of Representatives: Reform or Rebuild.* Edited by Joseph F. Zimmerman and Wilma Rule, 51–58. Westport, CT: Praeger Publishing, 2000.

Sapiro, Virginia. "It's the Context, Situation and Opinion, Stupid: The Gender Basis of Public Opinion." In *Understanding Public Opinion.* Edited by Barbra Norrander and Clyde Wilcox, 21–42. Washington DC: CQ Press, 2002.

Saunders, Kyle L., and Alan I. Abramowitz. "Ideological Realignment and Active Partisans in the Electorate." *American Politics Research* 32 (2004): 285–309.

Schickler, Eric. *Disjointed Pluralism: Institutional Innovation and the Development of the U.S. Congress.* Princeton: Princeton University Press, 2001.

Schickler, Eric, and Kathryn Pearson. "The House Leadership in an Era of Partisan Warfare." In *Congress Reconsidered,* 8th Ed. Edited by Lawrence C. Dodd and Bruce I. Oppenheimer, 207–226. Washington, DC: CQ Press, 2005.

Schmeckebier, Laurence F. *Congressional Apportionment.* Westport, CT: Greenwood Press Publishers, 1976.

Schwindt-Bayer, Leslie A., and Renato Corbetta. "Gender Turnover and Roll-Call Voting in the U.S. House of Representatives." *Legislative Studies Quarterly* 25 (2004): 215–229.

Serra, George, and Albert Cover. "The Electoral Consequences of Perquisite Use: The Casework Case." *Legislative Studies Quarterly* 17 (1992): 233–246.

Shepsle, Kenneth A. "Representation and Governance: The Great Legislative Trade-off." *Political Science Quarterly* 103 (1988): 461–484.

Sheridan, Mary Beth. "Senators Block D.C. Vote Bill, Delivering Possibly Fatal Blow." *Washington Post*, September 19, 2007, A01.

Sheridan, Mary Beth, and Hamil R. Harris. "D.C. Voting Measure Clears the Senate." *Washington Post*, February 27, 2009, A01.

Shields, Johanna Nicol. "Whigs Reform the 'Bear Garden': Representation and the Apportionment Act of 1942." *Journal of the Early Republic* 5 (1985): 355–382.

Shugart, William F., and Robert D. Tollison. "On the Growth of Government and the Political Economy." *Research in Law and Economics* 9 (1986): 111–127.

Silverman, Morris. "Better Yet, Reduce the Size of the House." *New York Times*, January 14, 1991, A17.

Sinclair, Barbara. "The New World of US Senators." In *Congress Reconsidered*, 8th ed. Edited by Lawrence Dodd and Bruce Oppenheimer, 1–22. Washington, DC: CQ Press, 2005.

Sinclair, Barbara. *Party Wars: Polarization and the Politics of National Policy Making.* Norman, OK: University of Oklahoma Press, 2006.

Sinclair, Barbara. *Unorthodox Lawmaking: New Legislative Processes in the U.S. Congress,* 3rd ed. Washington, DC: CQ Press, 2007.

Squire, Peverill. "Professionalization and Public Opinion of State Legislatures." *Journal of Politics* 55 (1993): 479–491.

Squire, Peverill, and Keith E. Hamm. *101 Chambers: Congress, State Legislatures and the Future of Legislative Studies.* Columbus: The Ohio State University Press, 2005.

Squire, Peverill, and Eric R. A. N. Smith. "A Further Examination of Challengers Quality in Senate Elections." *Legislative Studies Quarterly* 21 (1996): 235–248.

Stigler, George J. "The Sizes of Legislatures." *Journal of Legal Studies* 5 (1976): 17–34.

Stimson, James A., Michael MacKuen, and Robert S. Erikson. "Dynamic Representation." *American Political Science Review* 89 (1995): 543–565.

Stonecash, Jeffrey M. *Class and Party in American Politics.* Boulder CO: Westview Press, 2000.

Stonecash, Jeffrey M. *Political Parties Matter: Realignment and the Return of Partisan Voting.* Boulder, CO: Lynne Rienner Publishers, 2006.

Stonecash, Jeffrey M. *Reassessing the Incumbency Effect.* Cambridge, U.K.: Cambridge University Press, 2008.

Sweeting, Orville. "John Q. Tilson: The Reapportionment Act of 1929." *Western Political Quarterly* 9 (1956): 434–453.

Swers, Michele L. "Are Women More Likely to Vote for Women's Issues Bills than Their Male Colleagues?" *Legislative Studies Quarterly* (1998): 435–448.

Taagepera, Rein. "The Size of National Assemblies." *Social Science Research* 1 (1972): 385–401.

Taagepera, Rein, and Steven Recchia. "The Size of Second Chambers and European Assemblies." *European Journal of Political Research* 41 (2002): 165–185.

Taagepera, Rein, and Mathew Soberg Shugart. *Seats and Votes: The Effects and Determinants of Electoral Systems*. New Haven, CT: Yale University Press, 1989.

Tate, Katherine. *Black Faces in the Mirror: African Americans and Their Representatives in the U.S. Congress*. Princeton: Princeton University Press, 2003.

Taylor, Andrew. "Size, Power and Electoral Systems: Exogenous Determinants of Legislative Procedural Choice." *Legislative Studies Quarterly* 31 (2006): 323–345.

Thompson, Vincent B. "Projecting Reapportionment." *Indiana Business Review* 40 (2005): 4–6.

Thornton, Mark, and Marc Ulrich. "Constituency Size and Government Spending." *Public Finance Review* 27 (1999): 588–598.

Tomz, Michael, Gary King, and Lanche Zeng. "Relogit: Rare Events Logistic Regression." *Journal of Statistical Software* 8 (2003): 138–163.

Tufte, Edward R. "The Relationship Between Seats and Votes in Two-Party Systems." *American Political Science Review* 67 (1973): 540–554.

Tufte, Edward R. "Determinants of Midterm Elections." *American Political Science Review* 69 (1975): 812–826.

United States Census Bureau. *Interim Projections of the Total Population for the United States and States: April 1, 2000 to July 1, 2030*. Washington, DC: GPO, 2005. http://www.un.org/esa/population/publications/wpp2002/WPP2002_VOL_pdf.

U.S. House. *Congressional Globe*. Washington, DC: U.S. Government Printing Office.

U.S. House. *Congressional Record*. Washington, DC: U.S. Government Printing Office.

U.S. House. Government Reform Committee. *Hearing on Common Sense Justice for the Nation's Capital: An Examination of Proposals to Give D.C. Residents Direct Representation*, 108th Congress, 2nd Session, June 23, 2004. http://reform.house.gov/GovReform/Hearings/EventSingle.aspx?EventID=5697.

U.S. House. Subcommittee No. 3 of the House Committee on the Judiciary. *Increasing the Membership of the House of Representatives and Redistricting Congressional Districts: Hearings on H.R. 841, 1178, 1183, 1998, 2531, 2704, 2718, 2739, 2768, 2770, 2783, 3012, 3176, 3414, 3725, 3804, 3890, 4068, 4609, 6431, 7355, 8075, 8468, 8616 and HJ Res. 419 Before Subcommittee No. 3 of the House Committee on the Judiciary*, 87th Congress, 1st Session 44, August 24 and 30, 1961. Washington, D.C.: GPO, 1964.

Van Dunk, Emily. "Challenger Quality in State Legislative Elections." *Political Research Quarterly* 50 (1997): 793–807.

VandeHei, Jim, and Charles Babington. "Technology Sharpens the Incumbents' Edge: Redistricting Also Complicates Democrats' Effort to Take Control of the House." *Washington Post*, June 7, 2006, A1.

Vega, Arturo, and Juanita M. Firestone. "The Effects of Gender on Congressional Behavior and the Substantive Representation of Women." *Legislative Studies Quarterly* 20 (1995): 213–222.

Verba, Sidney, Kay Lehman Schlozman, and Henry E. Brady. *Voice and Equality: Civic Voluntarism in American Politics*. Cambridge, MA: Harvard University Press, 1995.

Weingast, Barry R., Kenneth Shepsle, and Christopher Johnson. "The Political Economy of Benefits and Costs: A Neoclassical Approach to Distributive Politics." *Journal of Political Economy* 93 (1981): 642–664.

Weissberg, Robert. "Collective Versus Dyadic Representation in Congress." *American Political Science Review* 72 (1978): 535–547.

Westlye, Mark C. *Senate Elections and Campaign Intensity*. Baltimore, MD: Johns Hopkins University Press, 1991.

Will, George. "Congress Just Isn't Big Enough." *Washington Post*, January 14, 2001, B7.

Willoughby, William F. *Principles of Legislative Organization and Administration*. Washington, DC: Brookings Institution, 1934.

Wright, Gerald C. "Policy Voting in the U.S. Senate: Who Is Represented?" *Legislative Studies Quarterly* 14 (1989): 465–486.

Yates, Christopher St. John. "A House of Our Own or a House We've Outgrown? An Argument for Increasing the Size of the House of Representatives." *Columbia Journal of Law and Social Problems* 25 (1992): 157–196.

Zagarri, Rosemarie. *The Politics of Size: Representation in the United States, 1776–1850*. Ithaca, NY: Cornell University Press, 1987.

Zimmerman, Joseph. "Eliminating Disproportionate Representation in the House." In *The US House of Representatives: Reform or Rebuild*. Edited by Joseph Zimmerman and Wilma Rule, 163–186. Westport, CT: Praeger Publishing, 2000.

Index

Entries in **bold** refer to Tables

eBooks – at www.eBookstore.tandf.co.uk

A library at your fingertips!

eBooks are electronic versions of printed books. You can store them on your PC/laptop or browse them online.

They have advantages for anyone needing rapid access to a wide variety of published, copyright information.

eBooks can help your research by enabling you to bookmark chapters, annotate text and use instant searches to find specific words or phrases. Several eBook files would fit on even a small laptop or PDA.

NEW: Save money by eSubscribing: cheap, online access to any eBook for as long as you need it.

Annual subscription packages

We now offer special low-cost bulk subscriptions to packages of eBooks in certain subject areas. These are available to libraries or to individuals.

For more information please contact webmaster.ebooks@tandf.co.uk

We're continually developing the eBook concept, so keep up to date by visiting the website.

www.eBookstore.tandf.co.uk